On Children and Death

Elisabeth Kübler-Ross, M.D.

Collier Books
Macmillan Publishing Company
New York

Maxwell Macmillan Canada
Toronto

Maxwell Macmillan International
New York Oxford Singapore Sydney

Collier Books
Macmillan Publishing Company
866 Third Avenue
New York, NY 10022

Maxwell Macmillan Canada, Inc.
1200 Eglinton Avenue East
Suite 200
Don Mills, Ontario M3C 3N1

Macmillan Publishing Company is part of the Maxwell Communication Group of Companies.

Library of Congress Cataloging-in-Publication Data
Kübler-Ross, Elisabeth.
On children and death / Elisabeth Kübler-Ross.
p. cm.
Includes bibliographical references.
ISBN 0-02-089144-X
1. Children and death. 2.Terminally ill children—Psychology.
3. Children—Death—Psychological aspects. 4. Parent and child.
I. Title.
BF723.D3K82   1993   93-9170   CIP
155.9 ' 37 ' 083—dc20

Macmillan books are available at special discounts for bulk purchases for sales promotions, premiums, fund-raising, or educational use. For details, contact: Special Sales Director, Macmillan Publishing Company, 866 Third Avenue, New York, NY 10022.

First Collier Books Trade Edition 1993

First Collier Books Edition 1985

10 9 8 7 6 5 4 3 2 1

Printed in the United States of America

To Kenneth, Manny, and Barbara,
who taught me how to be a mom.

* * *

I also dedicate this book to the parents and children who so generously shared their love and pain, their hopes and despair with me.

This is a heartfelt thank-you to them, the thousands of mothers, fathers, grandparents, and siblings who have shared their feelings with me—at the time of a terminal illness of a child, after a suicide, or after the discovery of the body of their murdered child.

They have all carried their burden and pain in their own personal way, and yet they share the sadness of the loss of a child, and they have emerged with compassion, understanding, and an increased capacity to love.

Let us hope that this book will help others to live more fully and with more appreciation for life—while we can share it together.

A human being is a part of the whole, called by us "universe," a part limited in time and space. He experiences himself, his thoughts and feelings, as something separate from the rest—a kind of optical delusion of his consciousness. This delusion is a kind of prison for us, restricting us to our personal decisions and to affection for a few persons nearest to us. Our task must be to free ourselves from this prison by widening our circle of compassion to embrace all living creatures and the whole nature in its beauty.

—ALBERT EINSTEIN

Contents

Acknowledgments

I want to thank Tom for endless hours of typing besides an already overloaded work schedule; Mary Lou and Alexandra for many hours of putting the final manuscript together until the early morning hours; Donna for her review; Charlotte for her untiring assistance; Tara, Ira, and Stephen for their unconditional love and support; and last but not least, my family and my own two children, who gave me the life experiences necessary to grow in understanding and compassion.

E.K.-R.

Introduction
Reflections

I AM SITTING IN MY LIVING ROOM after a long week in New York running a workshop with eighty-five people, many of whom had a terminal illness or were contemplating the misery and senselessness of life or suicide. Many others had lost a child or a spouse, and a few came to grow, to appreciate life more fully, or simply to "recharge their battery," to enable them to work better with those in need.

And while sitting here at my typewriter, I am looking out through the huge windowpane, watching the bluebirds and hummingbirds, a baby rabbit who crosses the porch, a salamander who looks into my house, and then suddenly I see an eagle high above the trees behind my vegetable garden. It seems to me that this is what paradise must be like: the trees and flowers, the hills and mountains behind, the blue sky, the peace and quiet of a place to which one can retreat.

My thoughts drift, and I see the Indians roaming this land, building the mounds for their dead. I hear their prayers to the wind and their mourning of the passing of one of their children.

Then, as if I were watching a movie of the old days, I see the settlers coming, the young men during the gold rush, their dreams of the "Great West," where they would find a piece of land to plant, a place to raise a family, and a fortune. I see their wagons struggling through toward the West; I see their women sitting bent, hot, and tired; I see them cooking a meal in a kettle and taking shelter in a storm. I see these women getting pregnant and dreading the journey; I hear the cry of a newborn baby, and see the pride and the sweat on the father's face as he views his firstborn child. I see them dig a grave somewhere on the path to the West, and I see the young couple struggling on to survive, to start anew, again and again and again. Nothing has changed much in the last few thousand years, I think. Human beings have always struggled, hoped, waited, dreamed, made it, lost it, and started again.

Just then, a visitor drops by to deliver some items, and before she leaves she takes one look at my typing and says in a curious way, "How can you write seven books about dying and death?" And without waiting for an answer, she is off.

Isn't that a strange question, I contemplate. How many books have been written, how many medical libraries are filled with hundreds of books about pregnancy, delivery, home births, stillborns, Cesarean deliveries, nutrition for pregnant women, breast-feeding versus bottle-feeding of newborns, and every conceivable aspect of issues revolving around conception, development of the future human being in the uterus, and finally the birth of yet another human being into this world?

And all human beings are different, even before they are here. They have been conceived under different circumstances, have shared different lives and experiences within their mothers, have been loved or resented, have been threatened with abortion or other traumas, have been prayed over or lovingly touched, have been listened to and patted, or have been cursed before they were even born.

And then they are here to share this world with us, and all human beings have different lives, different experiences, numerous people to face and to learn to get along with; and every encounter in their lives plants the seeds of their tomorrows. Has anybody ever thought about the trillions of possibilities that life offers each one of us?

And so it is with death—the culmination of life, the graduation, the good-bye before another hello, the end before another beginning. Death is the great transition.

To see and to study, to learn and to comprehend the ways, the thousands of ways this transition is made by people of all ages and all cultures, of all times and places, is a miracle just as great as birth is. It is greater, I would say, since it is the door of understanding into the human nature, the human struggle and survival, and ultimately, the human spiritual evolution. It gives us the only cues we have so far about the WHYS and WHERES and the ultimate purpose of life with all its pain and all its beauty.

Yes, I have written seven books, but the more I study human beings in the face of death, the more I learn about life and its ultimate mysteries. Maybe that is a knowledge all thinkers of days gone by had when they expressed their thoughts in paintings, in poetry and sculpture, in words, and in whatever form they were able to express their sense of awe, of mystery, and of enigma about our daily companion that we call so unlovingly DEATH.

Those who learned to KNOW death, rather than to fear and fight it, become our teachers about LIFE. There are thousands of children who know death far beyond the knowledge adults have. Adults may listen to these children and shrug it off; they may think that children do not comprehend death; they may reject their ideas. But one day they may remember these teachings, even if it is only decades later when they face "the ultimate enemy" themselves. Then they will discover that those little children were the wisest of teachers, and they, the novice pupils.

*   *   *

I have been asked many times to formulate my ideas about Children and Death, since most of my published material has concerned itself with adults. So this book deals with the questions: How are children different from adults when faced with terminal illness? Do little ones also go through the five stages of dying? Are they aware of their impending death, even if parents or hospital staff do not mention the seriousness of the terminal illness? What is their concept of death at different ages, the nature of their unfinished business? How can we best help them and their parents, grandparents, and siblings during this time of parting? And last but not least, can we—in any way—reduce the ever-increasing rate of childhood suicide, one of the most painful separations?

The material in this book stems from a decade of working with dying children of all ages. It comes from the vast knowledge of parents who have gone through this ordeal, of mothers and fathers who have lost one, two—yes, even three—children. It comes from families who have discovered a child missing only to discover that their child was murdered, that there was no way they could protect their little one, that he or she is gone without a good-bye.

I want to use this opportunity to thank all those who have contributed to my knowledge, who have been willing to share their grief and pain, their growth, and their evolving wisdom and knowledge with me through discussion and letters.

I want to share with you, the reader, the inner knowledge of these dying children so that you can also grow and learn to understand the importance of the inner voice, to which we need to listen. It is my conviction that it is the intuitive, spiritual aspect of us humans—the inner voice—that gives us the "knowing," the peace, and the direction to go through the windstorms of life, not shattered but whole, joining in love and understanding.

Remember also not to block and shield your surviving children from those pains of death but let them share in the care of their sick sibling to the extent they can. One of my favorite sayings is:

> Should you shield the canyons from the windstorms,
> You would never see the beauty of their carvings.

Thank you for allowing me to share what we have learned from our children.

Chapter 1
Letter to Bereaved Parents

MY DEAR FRIENDS,

This is a letter to you who are in the process of losing a child. We have accompanied and followed so many moms and dads on this difficult journey, and this book is about the concerns they expressed and the lessons we learned.

As your child gets weaker and closer to death, you will wonder how much a child should know about the possible terminal outcome of the illness. I say "possible" because I have witnessed many miracles.

All children know (not consciously, but intuitively) about the outcome of their illness. All little ones are aware (not on an intellectual, but on a spiritual level) if they are close to death. They will ask occasionally, "Mom, am I going to die?" Or if they sense that you are unable to talk or even think about it, older children will write a poem or a page in their diary about it. They may confide in a friend or a special person who is not necessarily a member of the family, and thus more able to hear their often symbolic language. If they have a roommate in the hospital or a playmate in the hospital playroom, they may share their knowledge with another sick child. Few grownups ever know how many secrets are shared in such a way.

Every person, big or small, needs one person in which to confide. Children often choose the least expected person: a nurse's aide, a cleaning woman, or at times a handicapped child who comes to visit them in a wheelchair. They have brief but deep talks together that adults would marvel at, and since they have gone through the windstorms of life at an early age, they know things that others of their age would not comprehend. Thus God who creates us all compensates the little ones as they fail physically. They become stronger in inner wisdom and intuitive knowledge.

They are aware of your pains and worries, your sleepless nights and concerns, and you should not hide them. Don't go into their room with a false "cheerful" smile. Children cannot be fooled. Don't lie to them that you just chopped some onions. How many onions are you going to cut? Tell them you are sad and sometimes feel so useless that you cannot help more. They will hold you in their little arms and feel good that they can help you by sharing comfort. Shared sorrow is much easier to bear than leaving them with feelings of guilt and fear that they are the cause of all your anxiety.

Should the siblings be involved and informed? Yes, every brother and sister of a critically ill child should become part of the care in one way or another. If the patient is at home, the brothers and sisters should be given specific tasks in the care of the sick one. They may be responsible for bringing the favorite dog in for regular visits after school. They may help to make yarn handicrafts (like "Eyes of God," a favorite pastime for children six years and up) when the patient's physical body gets too weak to play or do much. Siblings can take responsibility for running the tape recorder with favorite music, or they can serve one meal a day as long as the little patient can still eat.

Healthy children should not be made to feel guilty if they continue to laugh and giggle, to bring friends home or watch TV, go to a dance or a ball game, just as no mother should be discouraged from continuing to go to the hairdresser or the parents to an occasional bowling game or whatever they previously enjoyed.

The worst thing we can do to the terminally ill child and the rest of the family is to make a morgue out of the house while the child is still living. Where there is laughter and joy, shared love, and little pleasures, the day-to-day difficulties are much easier to bear. If the little patient is overprotected, if every whim or desire is met, if everyone is expected to tiptoe around the house, the outcome is usually disastrous for the survivors.

When Bob was diagnosed as having cancer, every wish of his was met by parents who had much unresolved guilt and regret. The toys became more exclusive, expensive, and excessive. Bob obviously tested his parents and believed that he should get everything he could out of them. He barely played anymore but demanded more and more attention. He had never felt loved but he knew he could get material things "instead." Was it his punishment? His revenge for having been cheated out of the most necessary ingredient of life, the gift of unconditional love?

His brother Billy watched in amazement, and later with anger and envy, when his brother received literally everything he asked for. Famous athletes wrote to Bob and sent him autographed basketballs and baseballs. He was taken to Disneyland and to the Bahamas. He was flown to Tennessee to see the Grand Ole Opry and into the mountains of Colorado.

Billy began to resent his brother and started to test his parents himself. He asked for little things first, then bigger ones— always with the same result. Father's answer was always a very angry, "No, you cannot have it. We can't afford it." When he questioned why his brother got everything, the answer was a stereotype: "Would you rather have cancer?" No, Billy would not like to have cancer. He would not like to have the bone marrow needles. He would not like to lose his hair. But what had one thing to do with the other?

Billy started to injure himself weekly, but no one paid attention to him. The parents were too preoccupied with his sick brother. When he asked for a sandwich for lunch, his mother snapped at him, "Can't you see I'm busy? Fix it yourself." Billy started to wet his bed and got a spanking for it. Later, a few months before his brother died, a teacher noticed that Billy was very cruel to a handicapped child who attended school in a wheelchair. But no one noticed it beyond that remark in his school files.

Billy took me to my car as I left my house call on my first visit to their home. As I opened the car door, I asked him to sit with me for a while and tell me how things were going for him. He looked surprised, "For me?"

"Yes, for you," I answered. "Such illnesses are much harder on the brothers and sisters than they are on the patient." He looked sadly at me and responded, "Do you know that I have asthma? But I guess that's not enough."

So it is important to remember to also be good to yourself and to the rest of the family. Continue to share among all of them, and do not overindulge the little patient: You only leave him with guilt and a negative feeling about his true worth. "Why is it that I never got these things, and now that I have cancer, everything is possible?"

A terminal illness usually costs a fortune, and even the best insurance may not cover all the costs. There are many foundations which may help in a variety of ways, but we have too often seen families who were left with bills for $100,000 or $200,000 after the death of a child. It would be far more meaningful if such family problems could be discussed at the dinner table, so the other brothers and sisters could share the concern and be able to offer voluntarily, and without pressure or guilt, to give up certain extra pleasures in order to contribute to the family's welfare. They would be left with a sense of importance and pride.

Many little brothers and sisters have also been taught how to give oxygen or how to gently suction their little patient so they can offer contributions to the care of the patient, giving them the same sense of self-esteem. Those children will not wish their brothers (or sisters) to die in order to bring some semblance of a family life back into their existence. Children (siblings) who make such remarks in a burst of anger should not be punished. They are voicing a cry for help before it is too late, and understanding adults should spend some time alone with them and let them ventilate their frustration, sense of unimportance, and feeling of neglect.

Someone, preferably a family member or close friend, should spend some extra time with such children, taking them to shop, to fish, to play, or to a ball game, not only for pleasure but for the feeling that somebody still cares for them "although they do not have cancer."

Children of all ages who have been included in the home care of a terminally ill child are not shocked and traumatized by the final sight of a cachetic sibling, sometimes with a blown-up abdomen and blue marks on hands and arms. They see the sick one with different eyes; they communicate on different levels. Such sights shock only those who have not been part of the daily care of the sick child, but those visitors naturally will need to be prepared and informed before they enter the sickroom.

When a child dies, it is important that the family be allowed to be alone with the child who is making the transition. All brothers and sisters, regardless of their age, should be allowed (but not forced) to participate in this final being together. Many families have used this time for singing the child's favorite song, for a joined prayer, or for simply holding each other in a circle of togetherness before outsiders are allowed to come in.

Make your final good-bye and then take time out to rock your child, to wash him yourself if you choose, to dress and carry him out to the car which will take the body to the mortuary or whatever place is indicated.

While many families express a wish to move soon after the

death of a child, to get into another neighborhood "that does not remind us" of the tragedy or away from a streetcorner where the fatal accident occurred, this is *not* a healthy choice, and too many families have regretted such impulsive moves. To get beyond the pain, one must face and acknowledge it and move *through* the pain, rather than avoid it. Those who do fare much better in the long run and are able to face life's future windstorms without trying to run away from them.

To stay in the same home is also a blessing for the siblings, as their life has already been shaken up enough. They feel "in the way" during the last few weeks and months of the terminal illness of a sibling, and often their only support system is a school friend, a teacher or school counselor, or a buddy in the neighborhood. To uproot them at an intense, often unsettling grief period in their life is the worst thing we can do for them.

There are still too many families who wonder if the surviving children should be taken to a wake and a funeral. My question is "Why not?" Wasn't it their sister or brother who died? Why should they be excluded from this final farewell ritual which serves as the only sort of closure and beginning process of "letting go." The funeral is a public acknowledgment that a person significant in our lives has died. It is a ritual that signals acceptance of this reality and puts the physical body in a final place that can be visited later on, in order to make the separation gradual. The wake and funeral serve important purposes in the grief process, and those who are excluded from them feel that they are not an important part of the family.

If a sibling has much unresolved business concerning the child that died, he or she may refuse to attend the funeral. This choice is a sign of unfinished issues and should be respected as important. Children should never be forced to attend a wake or a funeral, but they should be encouraged to attend as a matter-of-fact reality, as they would share a meal with the family. If they refuse, the reason is often fear, guilt, shame, or latent resentment toward the deceased or the rest of the family. Whatever the issue, someone should later, after the funeral is over, try to discuss it with the child in a totally loving and not judgmental way. Much preventive psychiatry could be done this way.

We have taken many siblings separately to a wake, before the adults visit, without parents who might be ambivalent about permitting other children to see the open casket. With their permission we make a special visit, if the children so desire, to allow the siblings to see the body and ask any questions they may have. Many little brothers and sisters want to touch the corpse and are, naturally, allowed to do so. Many of them bring a special letter or love note with them, a flower or a favorite toy, and quietly "snuggle it" under the pillow.

These are very touching moments and show us the love and care the siblings want to share in this final moment. If it is not contrary to the family's beliefs, we tell the children that they can talk to their brother or sister, that they will continue to be aware of them, and that sometimes they may even visit them in their dreams. Those children leave relieved and matured, and will be better prepared to deal with future deaths in their lives.

The first few days after the death and the funeral will be busy ones. There are so many things to think of, so many relatives to accommodate, so many doors to be opened and closed, so much mail to be answered. This generally is good, since the busywork will give us moments of distraction and sometimes even a smile or laughter, which we need.

It is after the neighbors have stopped cooking and the friends and relatives have gone that the loneliness and real grief begin. At this time, be good to yourself. Don't expect your grief to last forever or to be done with in a certain time. In fact, don't think at all. Go through your days as best you can. Cry when you need to cry, beat the pillow if you need to express anger. Cook your meals or attend to your garden, your children, your dog, or your job as you have done before. It will be mechanical at first, but that's all right. You are entitled to grieve. Grief makes everything look darker—for a time.

Don't make a shrine out of your child's bedroom. But don't hide the photographs and reminders either. If you cannot decide what to do with toys, bicycles, or clothing, don't do anything. There is no rush about anything. Time is a human invention; in reality, it does not exist. Concentrate on the living, your mate, your parents who not only grieve for your pain but also for the death of a grandchild. Do things with your other children, so you can concentrate on living things and stop brooding for a while about realities that cannot be changed.

You will think for quite a while, "Is there anything I could have done differently? Is there anything that I omitted? Should I have noticed changes earlier, called in for another consultation?" Thoughts like this will haunt some parents for a long time, for guilt and fear are man's greatest enemies. Such thoughts are understandable, but you must remember that parents are never their children's doctors even if they have an M.D. degree. Parents are too close to their children to be their objective medical experts. Remember that all the guilt in the world is not helping a soul—least of all, it is not helping your child who died. Guilt will make you sick emotionally and, if you don't let go of it, physically.

Learn to accept slowly the things you cannot change, and concentrate on your living children and those who are part of your physical life. If you are lonesome, think of the thousands of lonesome people in your own neighborhood. Share your time and your love with them, and this will help you resist falling into the pit of self-pity.

There are so many group homes for unwanted children and teenagers where you could literally save a life, if you should dare to get involved with one of them. The suicide rate is frightening among them, and if you need love, give it and it will return a hundredfold.

Talk to your child who died, if it helps you. Share with

your child your progress and show that you can handle the windstorms of life, because the death of a child often is the teacher of unconditional love, and unconditional love has no claims, no expectations, needs not even a physical presence.

With love and blessings,
E.K.-R.

Chapter 2

The Beginnings of Life

AND A WOMAN who held a babe against
her bosom said, Speak to us of Children.
   And he said:
   Your children are not your children.
   They are the sons and daughters of Life's
longing for itself.
   They come through you but not from
you,
   And though they are with you yet they
belong not to you.

   You may give them your love but not
your thoughts,
   For they have their own thoughts.
   You may house their bodies but not
their souls,
   For their souls dwell in the house of tomorrow, which you cannot visit, not even
in your dreams.
   You may strive to be like them, but seek
not to make them like you.
   For life goes not backward nor tarries
with yesterday.

You are the bows from which your children as living arrows are sent forth.
The archer sees the mark upon the path
of the infinite, and He bends you with His
might that His arrows may go swift and far.
Let your bending in the archer's hand
be for gladness;
For even as He loves the arrow that flies,
so He loves also the bow that is stable.

—KAHLIL GIBRAN,
The Prophet

Not all children are expected with joy and excitement about
the miracle of a new life, the miracle of the creation of a brand-
new human being. At the time of this writing, fifteen million
children are starving to death, not all of them in faraway conti-
nents where we can put them out of our minds. There are
desperate children, hungry and needy children, all over the
world, on every continent, in every country, in every city.
Abortions prevent the birth of hundreds of thousands of
babies, but they do not solve the problems. Until our attitude
toward LIFE changes; until we are able to make a new and
stringent commitment to the QUALITY OF LIFE; until we practice what so many give only lip service to, and we redefine our
concepts of LIFE and LOVE, our society's problems will not be
solved.

In some parts of the world (I have traveled and worked all
over this planet), children are a natural part of life. One baby
after another is born, and the family and tribes take care of
them, feed them, nourish and raise them in an almost com-
munal fashion. Children can always find someone who cares
and who will share moments with them, someone who instructs
them in the arts and crafts, and who teaches them how to
survive physically, emotionally, and spiritually. Children are
viewed as an asset, as they will ultimately become the provid-

ers of all needs, including food and care for the elderly; in this view, children prove the universal law that "all benefits have to be mutual."

The more children such a family or tribe has, the more they are guaranteed survival in their old age. As the next generation of adults, the children will take care of the harvest, of trade, of the maintenance of the village and the survival of its inhabitants.

The modern world has changed enormously in the last half-century. Since the advent of modern transportation, of the material philosophy of life, since technology and science have replaced our old spiritual values, life has changed and affected especially the upbringing of our children.

Do you remember when families lived in the same communities for generations? When everyone knew the pastor or rabbi, the doctor, the teachers, the grocery store owner, by their personalities and often by their first names? When children had a sense of belonging, and the whole community awaited the birth of a newcomer? When the elderly would knit and sew to prepare the children's first outfits by hand? When neighbors were ready to help in the delivery and welcome of the new baby?

In America in the 1980s most of us don't even know when a neighbor has delivered a new baby or if she has disappeared for a couple of days and then returned, although by chance we may hear that she had a miscarriage or a stillbirth.

How different this is from the days when aunts and grandma came to attend the young mother when she had her babies. Then older brothers and sisters were able to look in awe at the size of the newborn's tiny toes and fingers, hear the baby's first cry—the sign of life—and see the new baby take its first meal at its mother's breast. These are scenes imprinted in the minds of little children that they will never forget. These are moments of sharing, learning, growing, and awe.

Now couples often decide it is better to have a career and security first, and perhaps a child later. They prefer to save for a house or a condominium before "being tied down" by a youngster. They want their freedom to travel, to socialize, to move, and they say they want to experience life and freedom before having kids.

They move from city to city, from job to job, and when an often unplanned baby arrives, the couple may have no family support system nearby, no grandma who knits the baby's outfit, no parents who will take care of the household, no familiar doctor or midwife, no support system of loving care and old familiar faces. Childbirth today frequently means hired help, a new physician, a large hospital, delivery by whoever is "on call," and often, induced labor for the convenience of the system.

When, some years ago, I worked in the delivery room of an upper middle-class hospital in the United States, almost three-quarters of all the babies were delivered by inducing labor and, much too often, by low forceps, simply to speed up the process and not waste too much time ("Time is money!") waiting for a slow but natural and conscious delivery. Very few babies were a healthy pink color; too many were bluish. Almost all mothers were sedated to the point that they had no awareness of the miracle in which they had just participated. Often, hours later, they asked me sleepily if they had a boy or a girl!

In the meantime, the fathers had returned to their jobs, proudly distributing cigars to their co-workers. The baby would be suctioned, washed, diapered, and put aside to accustom itself to its new environment, devoid of the warm, comforting contact of human skin. Every baby animal makes its start in life by clinging closely to its mother for days, but not the human baby—at least not in our modern hospitals, in our "advanced" technological, hurried society where time is money and efficiency is treasured above all other values.

Thus Americans begin life in an often highly depersonalized atmosphere, in an institution where the mother is in one room recuperating from anesthetics, episiotomies, or an induced labor, while the baby takes its first breaths in the hands of the caretakers and then is whisked away to a sterile nursery. Fathers resume their jobs after a few hours spent away from their desks, grandparents are informed of the joyful event by phone, and siblings are kept waiting at home for Mom to come back with the new addition to the family. Since the children already in the family have not been part of the miracle, they learn to associate this time with tension or a temporary abandonment, an interruption of their life-styles. They will therefore view the newcomer as the source of all these unpleasant changes.

Life will soon resume its old ways if everything goes all right, if mother and child are well, and if there are no complications clouding the horizon. But what happens to families when Baby or Mother are not all right? How do we prepare the parents and the siblings for this event?

Laura's Story: Loss and Loneliness

Laura expected her first child. At first her husband Billy was not thrilled by the news. Instead of an excited hug of appreciation and love, he seemed to be shocked. He wanted to advance in his job, he said. He wanted to remain mobile, travel, see the world. Was she sure, he asked, or just late with her period? Maybe it was the change of climate, since they had just moved from New York to the West Coast.

Laura became depressed; she had no friends in their new neighborhood and did not want to burden her family with sad letters. She stopped working when she was seven months pregnant and kept to herself in their small apartment, reading and thinking. She felt very alone—isolated and depressed—and her relationship with her husband seemed drastically altered. Billy was a good provider, often took her out for evening meals, and was courteous and attentive. But there was something missing: She wanted so much for him to share her excitement about the coming baby who was moving inside her.

However, Billy would never even put his hands on her belly. It was not that he felt embarrassed; it was almost as if he wished this intruder would disappear, so that he would not have to share his life with a third person. Laura put her hands on her belly, feeling the soft movements, and became aware of a tear rolling down her cheek. Since they had moved, she realized that she had only two people she could talk to: an older neighbor lady, who also lived alone, and the mailman, who occasionally rang the bell when he brought a letter from her family back East.

The days passed, and she grew more excited about the baby. Her physician asked her if she wanted to have tests to determine whether the baby was a boy or a girl. No, Laura replied, she wanted to be surprised. She wanted to be awake when the baby arrived, and in preparation she read every conceivable book on delivery and newborn baby care. Soon she was going to have a child; she would no longer be alone within these four walls. She prepared a crib, decorating it with rainbow colors, and started to look around in toy shops, with teddy bears and baby clothes on her mind. She even learned how to crochet while waiting for that still all-too-distant delivery date.

Only a few days before the calculated day of delivery, Laura felt sick. Her doctor told her it was probably a virus and recommended that she rest, advice she thought was odd as she had done little else for the past few months. Except for her regular exercises and walks, Laura had been home-bound all this time. She had never overexerted herself and had eaten only a minimum of very healthy foods, which she had actually learned to enjoy. She had neither smoked nor taken any alcohol. She had not gained any excessive weight, and her blood pressure and general health had been excellent. So there were certainly no signs for concern.

She was just in the process of completing her crocheted blanket when the thought occurred to her that "it was terribly still" inside her. How long had it been that way? Had she blocked the fact that there had been no movements lately?

Wouldn't the doctor have said something to her during her last checkup? She tried to put her fears away. She watched television, tried to read, called her husband. But she could not verbalize what was on her mind.

The next two days are still like a large, fuzzy black cloud in Laura's mind. Even today, two years later, she is unable to put all the pieces together. The blanket she finished that day is still in a closet, wrapped and untouched. The few baby toys she had bought to cheer herself up are still in their original boxes, also in the closet. All Laura remembers is that she could not talk with her husband about her fears, and that when she turned to her physician, he examined her and had her admitted to the hospital for a checkup, only to discharge her without any discussion, avoiding her desperate looks and asking her to come in a few weeks later "if nothing unexpected" happened before then.

Well, nothing unexpected happened, but the expected did not happen either: Her baby never moved again. It had died. A few weeks later labor was induced, but the dead child could not be delivered, and they finally had to decapitate it before it was possible to take it out. Laura vaguely heard the nurse talking about this; she remembers being in her room alone and hearing night nurses talk about decapitated babies. She wanted to scream, but she could not. They gave her Valium, and she has never felt herself since.

She remembers hearing the paging system in the hospital, a voice from far away announcing: "Mothers, get ready for your babies." And in every room around her, new mothers got ready to feed their babies. Laura looked out the window, where she saw a young mother in a wheelchair with a bundle of joy in her arms, a beaming young father opening the door of a car to take them home. Now, that's all she can think about. The days go by, but she is neither living nor dying.

Her husband still works at the same firm, where he is up for promotion. They will be moving again soon to another state. Laura has nothing to do; she gets a letter from home once in a while, and Valium helps her make it through the nights. Billy still takes her out for dinner occasionally, and she still keeps her home clean, dusts the furniture, watches TV. But her husband does not want to talk about it.

She has never seen her physician since the delivery of her dead child. Another man did the discharge examination and follow-up. They said that this was routine in large medical centers. Her husband's only comment about the delivery concerned the size of the bill. He remarked that he would have had a heart attack had they not had excellent insurance and, "Aren't you glad I took this job, so we are provided for?"

Laura's case is not unusual. Many thousands of people have no real help in times of crisis, no one who is willing to talk with them and share the pain, frustration, rage, and anguish in a healthy way. There are hundreds of thousands of people who have been given and are still given Valium as a substitute for human care, for the externalization of emotional pain, and who are left neither dying nor living. And so we have to ask ourselves why we have become so callous, so uncaring, so unwilling to take some time out of our busy schedules to help those in need to solve and deal with problems when they happen. Instead, they are given drugs to cloud their consciousness, to sedate the emotions, to prevent them from living fully so they can leave their pain behind and experience life once again with all its beauty, all its challenges; yes, with all its pains and its gifts. *Why?*

Martha's Experience

Martha was in the process of a divorce when she realized that she was pregnant again. She was deeply hurt by her husband's refusal to reconsider another trial period for their marriage, in order to give the children and their old commitment another chance.

Most of the next eight months were spent in lawyers' offices, in irate arguments between Jon and herself, in accusing phone calls from her in-laws, and in sleepless nights of worry about how she and the children were going to manage on her meager support money. When Martha went into labor, she had to call a neighbor to mind her toddlers, who were deep asleep and would certainly be troubled on awakening to find that neither Dad nor Mom were there. In a state of near panic, Martha was wheeled into the delivery room. Twelve hours later, she gave birth to an adorable little girl, whom she gratefully named after her neighbor, who seemed to be the only person there when she needed someone urgently.

Martha was able to sleep finally, to rest, and even to smile again. But her happiness would not last past that day. When she awoke from her peaceful slumber, a physician she had never seen before entered her room; he looked anxious and somewhat in a hurry. He introduced himself as one of the pediatricians and notified her in what seemed to her a cold, matter-of-fact manner that her baby was seriously troubled. He used language that she could not comprehend and tried to explain to her that there was a congenital defect in her daughter, one that might leave her paralyzed and unable to have bladder function. In short, surgery was indicated, but they could not guarantee that it would be successful. At least her baby had a chance to survive, and eventually would perhaps learn to move around in a wheelchair.

Martha was in a daze when a social worker visited her and asked if her ex-husband should be notified. Much later she would learn about the problem that babies had who were born as hers was with *spina bifida*, of shunts, of fears and hopes, of waiting in vain to have a baby brought in to be fed, cuddled, hugged, and eventually wrapped in a blanket to take home.

Martha was still in a recovery period when several physicians came to make rounds, examined her, and were ready to leave when she finally screamed for some explanation. A nurse reprimanded her and asked her to "control herself." Martha was furious—it seemed suddenly as if the whole world would cave in on her. She wanted to beat something, to scream, to cry, but no one seemed to take notice. An injection put her into a dazed state of mind, and she slept. She woke to the hazy questioning of a psychiatrist who did not even introduce himself, and she remained mute. Then she insisted on seeing her child. She fought physically to get up and leave the room. Another injection made her quiet—temporarily.

Martha's baby died before she was ever able to see her. The staff made this decision, regarding Martha as "too disturbed" to see her baby. The baby was buried, and she has never even seen the grave. The social worker took care of everything, she was told.

Martha was eventually discharged, but not before weeks of struggle with psychiatrists, nurses, and social workers, all of whom seemed to want to tell her what was best for her. When Martha got home, Cathy, her three-year-old, acted like a stranger. Cathy clung to her neighbor and cried when Martha wanted to lift her up. Two-year-old Johnny seemed more interested in his new toy than in his mother and almost casually glanced up when she entered the room. Pots and pans all seemed to be in different places when she went to cook dinner. Everything was strange and out of place, as if it belonged to someone else.

Martha, like so many other mothers, sedated herself with Valium and "cheered herself up" with alcohol. A year later, the children were turned over to their natural father, who asked for custody when he realized they were neglected and beaten. Martha was left alone in an empty house filled with empty bottles and never-ending nightmares.

It was her neighbor, again, who finally brought Martha to one of our workshops, and who saved her life and her sanity. It takes only one human being who cares!

The Gordons

The Gordons were the happy parents of four children, and they all were excited about the prospect of a new baby. They had four girls, and they were praying for a son—although another female would naturally be just as loved, just as lovable. The family had a big celebration dinner on the day Mark came home from the hospital. Rarely has a newborn been surrounded with so many helping hands as this beautiful seven-pound boy, who was the new treasure of the family.

The older children were allowed to diaper him, and even the smallest was permitted to hold him in her arms. He was welcomed, pampered, and beloved by the whole family, who regarded him as the greatest blessing they could ever receive.

On the day before his second birthday, Mark seemed cranky, and his belly seemed larger than normal. But no one wanted to pay attention to this—it was a happy day, and everyone dressed up to go to church. After church, all the friends and family members were to meet for dinner.

When Elly dressed Mark on his birthday the next morning, she noticed what seemed to be a tumor in his belly, but she quickly dismissed the idea, thinking of his doctor's recent reassurance that he was a healthy baby. But a few days later her anxiety recurred when she touched him during his bath and felt something that seemed like a tumor. Her drive to the doctor's office remains forever in her mind. Should I have brought him in earlier? Could they have saved him? These were some of the tormenting thoughts that would haunt her for months.

A Wilms tumor was verified in Mark, and weeks and months of worries followed. (A Wilms tumor is a kidney-based cancer, which can be cured if detected early so that the kidney can be removed and chemotherapy given to destroy whatever cancer cells have already spread. The statistics of survival improve rapidly, but not all children are diagnosed early enough.) The children were no longer able to touch Mark's belly and tickle him. They no longer were able to play and giggle with him. He was put on chemotherapy after he survived the surgery. His belly carried an enormous scar; he looked tired and became extremely vulnerable to infections.

Mark's third year of life was filled with visits and stays in the hospital. His physicians and nurses were wonderful and worked hard, but in spite of all their efforts and prayers, Mark died before he reached his third birthday.

At the very end, when Mark started to have blood in his urine and his little lungs were full of tumors, Elly and her husband asked for permission to take him home. They put him in a big bed with pillows all around him, with a view into the children's playroom. "Loony," the stray dog who had always been so fond of the children, sat on the foot of the bed and seemed to hold absolutely still, as if he knew that every vibration could be painful.

Mickey Mouse and teddy bear and Bozo, Mark's favorite clown, were sitting next to him, and his four sisters took turns staying in his room when they were home. Elly and her husband alternated staying awake during the nights, and Peter's boss gave him permission to take as many days off from work as he needed to be with his son.

Father John came to give Mark the last rites, and early one evening when the sun just started to sink behind the horizon, Mark closed his eyes and stopped breathing. Loony silently jumped off the bed and hid under it. Elly and Peter held Mark in their arms, no longer afraid to hurt him. His four sisters each picked a favorite toy to put in his casket, and on Good Friday his family put him to rest.

To Lose a Beloved One
A Prayer for Baby

Never to have known you, but to have loved you.
Never to have held you, the way mothers do.

With you I bury my hopes and dreams
For an unknown child I'd never seen.

But also I bury the love in my heart
And the sadness of knowing that we must part.

And I pray to God to do for you
All the things that I would like to do.

And to keep my baby safe from harm
To laugh and frolic in springtime's arms.

Sent by a friend in 1977.

* * *

What is it like to lose a child? Who helps whom during such a crisis? How can we be more sensitive to the needs of those who are faced with one of life's greatest tests? How can parents who lose a child ever again resume a normal, happy life?

Life was created to be simple and beautiful. In the challenge that life brings there will always be what I call windstorms—big and small. But from experience we know that all storms pass, that after every rain the sun will shine again, that spring follows even the coldest winter.

When parents have gone through the loss of a child or the diagnosis of a severe handicap or terminal illness, such thoughts are neither helpful nor believable. An apparently friendly statement like "It was God's will" or "At least you had him for a little while" is not only tasteless but infuriating to most newly bereaved parents.

No one can successfully shield another person from the pains of life; no one can take our grief away. No one can truly console a parent who has lost a child or make the grim reality disappear. But we can help them and be available to them. We can be there when they need to talk, when they need to cry, when they have to make decisions too difficult or complex to decide on their own. And we can help prevent many of the disastrous aftereffects of such painful losses by a far more sensitive and listening attitude before the death occurs, whenever this is possible.

In Laura's case, the depression started long before the tragic death of her baby just before delivery. Laura had never been able to deal with her husband's inability or unwillingness to express any joy about their expected newcomer. Instead, she withdrew as she had always done as a little girl when she felt rejected. Billy, Laura's young husband, was entirely concentrated on getting ahead in his job and was ambitious to travel, to see the world, and to be free enough to do so.

Billy had been greatly influenced by his father, who had said to him many times, "Get ahead." No one had ever encouraged him to have a family, and his own early memories were filled with admonitions to study, to make good grades, and to be first in his class. Billy never thought about other people's feelings and was quite oblivious of his wife's depression and, indeed, her different focus toward having a family. He regarded himself as a good husband who provided well for his wife and who took her regularly to eat in nice restaurants to get her out of the house, which seemed to be devoid of life and excitement.

When Laura began to realize that her baby no longer "kicked," she was unable to share this tragedy with Billy, since he had never even said he wanted the baby. She suppressed her anger and denied for quite a while her knowledge of her husband's feelings. She was afraid that he would be happy about the baby's death, if he knew, and she could not deal with such a reaction.

Laura's physician also avoided her, just as her husband never wanted to talk about mutual issues and questions. Again with her physician Laura was unable to assert herself, as she never had before, and therefore she couldn't share her innermost fears, to prepare herself for the shock. She was sedated and unable to grieve, unable to experience the depth of her pain, and thus unable to start living again.

Martha, who lost her newborn baby to *spina bifida*, would

have been helped a great deal if someone had taken time to sit quietly with her and prepare her for the news of a congenitally malformed baby who had little chance of survival. She could have been given a chance to talk to other parents who had experienced this trauma and who had survived in spite of the pain. She could have been helped had she been given a chance to externalize her frustration and grief, her anger and rage over her husband's desertion after the discovery of her new and unexpected, unwanted pregnancy. She would have had a chance to return in a healthy state to her two children had she not been heavily sedated and thus unable to deal with her suppressed feelings.

Visits from her children during Martha's early confinement could have prevented the unnecessary estrangement between the mother and children. As it happened, she was absent too long without having had a chance to prepare her children for a separation, and she returned to them a stranger, shaken and heavily sedated with tranquilizers, unable to reestablish a mutual and meaningful contact with them.

Martha's ensuing alcoholism and the lack of any support system prevented a healing of the trauma and added new problems and tragedies for all concerned.

How long is it going to take until members of the healing profession realize that Valium is as great a killer in its own way as cancer? How long is it going to take until we teach the prevention of such tragedies by replacing drugs with a sympathetic listening ear, by a human being who has his or her house in order and is not afraid of letting a patient express his or her pain and anguish, to make room so that a healing process can take place?

The Physical Quadrant

During the first years of life, each child needs a great deal of pampering and nurturing. And so it is when we have a terminal illness. Our first and primary need is for physical care. We cannot be concerned with emotional or spiritual issues when we are in pain, when we itch, when we are smelling bad and are unable to take care of our needs.

Terminal care of any dying patient has to consider the physical needs of the patient first and foremost. A paralyzed patient who is unable to speak has to be checked for the occurrence of a bowel movement or a wet bed before any visitor, social or professional, is brought to them. Old people who are at the end of their lives need to be touched, nourished, pampered, turned, cleaned, and dressed.

All human beings have these same needs, which come before anything else. Mothers and fathers of premature babies should always be allowed to touch and hold their infants, to have eye contact with them, even if the babies must be kept in incubators and later in bassinets. This bonding is necessary for a nurturing mutual relationship; it is a consolation and happy memory even to those parents who lose their children prematurely.

Bereaved parents whose children were taken away from them at birth and who were not allowed or able to hold and touch them have a much longer grief period and often stay in a stage of partial denial for years. This is equally true for parents who have had a stillborn baby. Any baby, born dead or alive, should be given to both parents to view, to touch, to accept as their offspring. In this way they can face the reality of having had a child, and they know then what they have lost and can face that loss with appropriate grief. If they have been deprived of this physical reality testing, their grief is prolonged, and they may either deny the existence of this short life or be afraid to chance another pregnancy. Their fantasies of the "monster" they imagine to have delivered are usually far worse than anything they could have seen in their actual baby.

We have been blessed by being present on many occasions when mothers were presented with defective infants and expressed their joy over their "beautiful baby." Beauty is, naturally, in the eyes of the beholder, and it is important not to project our own views and value judgments onto the parents. If there is a gross malformation or an especially grotesque appearance of any part of the little body, this can be covered with a diaper with an explicit explanation for the parents so they can make their own choice to view all or only part of their baby.

The Fear of Having More Children

The fear of having more children is a very real one for many parents, especially young mothers who have already gone through the death of a child. If the death occurred as the result of an accident, the parents were completely unprepared for it and may not even have been allowed to view the body of their little girl or boy. If a parent was the driver in a fatal car accident, he or she may not only have to deal with guilt and remorse but with tormenting questions of how the accident could have been avoided. Indeed, the parent may have been blamed for the death of the child.

If the parent was injured or in shock after an accident, he or she may have been taken away in an ambulance and not even been told about the fate of the passengers. As one mother so vividly describes it: "We started to skid on the slippery road, and I tried desperately to control the car. I screamed at the children to tighten their seat belts, but I don't know if they heard me. I don't even know if all this is true. Maybe I will get discharged from here and see that my legs are not amputated, that my son is not dead, and that my little girl is not paralyzed and in a coma."

This mother was rushed to the hospital, where everybody was concerned to save her life and the life of her little daughter. Her daughter never regained consciousness, and her son was dead at the scene of the accident. They were able to save the mother, but only after the amputation of both her legs. She never got to see the body of her son, who was buried while she was still on the critical list in the hospital. Her husband visited her before and after seeing his daughter, who was not expected to live. Nobody wanted to talk to her about her losses, about her self-blame or guilt, about the horror of having lost both children and both legs.

Well-meaning visitors tried to cheer her up: "You are young, you can have other children." She felt like throwing them out of her room but was unable to muster up enough courage to tell them to stop. She hated it when friends came and talked to her about their children, resented their happiness and their need to bring up what was for her the most painful subject. She was afraid of and for her husband. She couldn't communicate to him the sorrow she had inside, the guilt over contributing to the deaths of their children. She was obsessed about the last moments before the accident and tried to explain and understand it, but it all seemed to be in vain.

Her husband had not deserted her, had not abandoned her, had not reprimanded her, but his silence was far worse. He never asked her about her wishes concerning the boy's funeral, about the critical condition of their little Beth, her feelings about spending the rest of her life in a wheelchair.

She felt bad and undeserving of even his visits, and sometimes she would have preferred it if he had just come out and screamed at her, blamed her, accused her—rather than the stoical silence which must have hidden so many feelings.

We saw this father after one of his visits and asked him why he had showed so little emotion. With a surprised look, he explained that he had been explicitly instructed by his wife's doctor not to upset her, not to cry in front of her, and especially not to bring up the issue of the children and amputation. He thought he had done a good job!

We encouraged his wife to bring up the issues that troubled her the most, and husband and wife were finally able to hold each other, cry together, and share their concerns. If we do what feels right inside and don't let other people tell us what we can share with another person, the chances of solving conflicts and sharing the pain and joy are far greater.

Nick and Nelly: Overcoming the Fear of Having More Children

Nick and Nelly were so looking forward to spring and the little child they felt would complete their family. The winter had been long and cold, and then the snow began to melt. By the brook near their house the first spring flowers started to show. It was a perfect day to go into labor, and Nelly was happy when the day had arrived. It had been a difficult pregnancy; she had experienced problems keeping her weight down, and now the waiting would soon be over. Their three-year-old daughter had been well prepared for the arrival of a sibling, and she was very helpful in fixing up the room that her little brother or sister would soon occupy.

In spite of Nelly's objections, her doctor felt it would be best to "put her to sleep," and so she missed the actual moment of her son's birth. But those thoughts were soon forgotten when she was back in her room and a nurse brought this adorable frail infant and put him in her arms. Her husband's face was beaming: Now he had his son! For a brief moment they were together, just the three of them. They did not need words; it seemed that their happiness was complete at this moment. If only Nick had brought Lauri with him; they both felt she should really have been a part of this first togetherness. But Nick had promised to tell her all about it, and, besides, he had to run along. There were the birth announcements to be written and mailed, and the baby-sitter had to leave early tonight.

When Nelly was alone in her room again, she drifted into a happy and content half-sleep, thinking what it would be like when the four of them would be able to go to the beach in the summer, and her parents would come and visit from Europe....

And then she awoke. She had had a terrible dream, or was it not a dream? She was aware that she had drifted off for a while, but she could not possibly have slept more than a few minutes. She looked at the clock and rang for the nurse. "How is my baby?" she asked frantically. But the nurse only smiled and said, "Why, don't worry. Everything is just fine. He is wonderful," and left as quickly as she had come.

Nelly wanted to call Nick, but he had just left and had been so happy. She did not want to upset him. Anyway, what was wrong with her? A few moments ago she felt like the happiest mother in the world, and now she was on the verge of tears for no good reason. She remembered a neighbor who went into a terrible depression after having given birth to a baby. Maybe that was the matter with her. But she could not go back to sleep, and the thought haunted her that there was something terribly wrong with her little son.

When she brought her new baby home, everybody was excited except her. The baby seemed very slow and did not seem to have much of an appetite. He was much more lethargic than her daughter had been at the same age, but Nelly dismissed those thoughts quickly, for she did not want to alarm her family. Her daughter was like a little mother to the baby; she counted his toes and fingers, wanted to hold and touch him, and was almost afraid of this tiny little bundle, smaller than her largest doll. Nelly slowly prepared herself for the possibility of seeing a psychiatrist at her next checkup; there must be something drastically wrong with her!

On the second day at home she knew differently. The baby became more lethargic, and even her husband noticed that "he was not right." They also discovered little red dots on his arms and legs, and decided not to wait any longer but to take him back to the hospital. His sister waved good-bye to him: "Now, come back home soon! I will be lonesome without you." And then her dad's car disappeared.

The little girl could not understand why her parents did not come home for dinner. She did not understand that her baby brother had a serious infection and was fighting for his life. She never saw him in the neonatal intensive care unit, where he was put on a respirator, so small he was barely visible behind all the equipment, the tubes and the oxygen bubble.

The baby boy died when he was less than a week old, and Nelly and Nick's world seemed to stand still. Nelly felt tremendous rage and anger at God that she could not express till she finally let it out on her husband and her little daughter. She got angry at Nick for having mailed the birth announcements when "everybody knew" that something was wrong with their son. She told her little daughter to shut up when she kept asking questions about her little brother, and yelled at her when she woke Nelly up in the middle of the night after Nelly had finally found some rest. Nelly was furious at the nurse who had "lied" to her when she asked about her baby's health, and most painful of all, she was angry and unforgiving to herself that she did not insist on a consultation before she took her son home.

Why did she not listen to her dream or intuition or whatever it was? Why had she not discussed it with her husband? Maybe the baby could have been saved!

Further, Nelly blamed herself for not having rested more during the end of her pregnancy, for insisting on cleaning the house herself and doing a strenuous early spring cleaning before she went to the hospital. She even blamed her daughter for bringing playmates home who might have been responsible for bringing in an infection. She knew better than this, however; her pediatrician had told her that newborn babies are at risk from many infections because they do not have an immune system of their own. She blamed herself for not having nursed him, since that seemed to help babies fight infections.

When Nelly began to lock herself in her room and neglect her child and marriage, Nick finally brought a friend home who was willing to counsel them. This friend and his wife had gone through a similar experience after having waited for fifteen years for a baby, only to lose her when she was four days old. No, they never blamed God, but they were on the verge of a divorce when they decided to stop blaming anybody and to help and console each other instead. They had since adopted three orphans and seemed to be a happy family. And, who knows, they said, maybe God is looking for parents who really want children before he assigns them as parents to the unloved and unwanted!

Nick and Nelly have since added two more healthy children to their family, and although they still look at their little son's photograph in the nursery, the throbbing pain is gone and the painful memories have faded. They have joined a group of the Compassionate Friends to help other parents to survive the death of a baby. Nelly said the other day in a letter to me, "You know, sometimes I think I never would have learned what compassion and caring are all about. Why do some of us have to go through so much pain before we learn those lessons?"

All of us in life have to be tested and go through windstorms, but with the help of a friend we are usually able to come out of it—ever so slowly—richer in understanding and wiser about the hardships of life.

Chapter 3
Sudden Death

A BEAUTIFUL COUPLE from New Hampshire shared the following letter which will hopefully reach others who must deal with the issue of sudden death—an issue too often neglected. This father—V.B.—wrote to me after reading my first book, *On Death and Dying*, which dealt with the care of the terminally ill patients and not with families affected by sudden death.

"*On Death and Dying* was very good, but it leaves a big space for people of my experience. [We were] a normal family with a son twenty-three months old one day, then a tragic accident [happened:] Our son wandered from the house and fell into a pond on October 27. He was pronounced dead at the hospital at 1:30 P.M. My wife and I went home to start the arrangements, and we were called by the hospital at 3:30 P.M. His heart had started up by itself, and they were asking to take him to General Hospital. We agreed and went with them to the hospital.

"Our son never regained consciousness and died on October 29 at 7:30 A.M. I think that a book [is necessary] concerning sudden death and how to cope, survive, readjust, or what-have-you. Psychotherapy has helped both my wife and me to cope and to refocus our lives. But it was a while before we sought out help.

"[A book on] sudden death could deal with the destruction that strikes at a time like this. It could deal with the loneliness and the hopelessness that people experience. I don't have to tell you what [a book on] sudden death could be about, just that I think it is overdue as an aid to the survivors.

"I know that I would see people coming that I had not seen in, say, a year, and they would ask how my son was and how was the Mrs. And I would feel dirty and guilty to spoil their day by dumping on them the bad news that our son was dead. They would feel bad for asking, and I would feel bad for telling, so I used to duck and avoid people who did not know of the tragedy. Also, people at work did not know how to treat me after they knew about the death. Most would just avoid me so that they would not feel the pain. It is as if they gave their $2.00 for the flowers and did not want to get too close for fear that it might happen to them.

"Day-by-day affairs take on new meaning since the whole world has just come to an abrupt end, stopped, halted. . . . You feel like doing nothing, etc."

* * *

One million children disappear every year in the United States, and of these one million children, 100,000 end up somewhere in a morgue without leaving any clue as to what they experienced between their moment of leaving their homes until they met their death somewhere away from home.

Parents who lose a child by a sudden tragic death or by murder need to find a safe place where they can finally open up and share their feelings; where they can scream if need be (without being stopped or tranquilized); and where they can put into words the "unspeakable." In our bereaved parent workshops (as well as in our life, death, and transition workshops), young and old bereaved people begin to let go of the anguish and the often gruesome details of the last memories of their murdered children—also the memory of courtroom appearances, police stations, and the nights of waking up screaming for their missing children. No one will be shocked when they do so, no one will become so uncomfortable that he or she has to leave the room. Criticism and judgmental attitudes in such workshops turn into understanding and compassion.

The groups who share their pains also share their hopes. Many find indications of their child's inner awareness of impending death; and in sharing that special aspect with others who had a similar "hunch," they find not only consolation but a stimulus for further understanding of the spiritual nature of man. Through spontaneous drawings and other types of creative art, poems, and other at first "insignificant" statements made by their children, the family becomes aware of hidden messages, of the symbolic language used by little ones— messages that are often unraveled *only* after their deaths. Fathers find hidden Father's Day cards after a fatal accident; another child leaves an "I love you, Mommy" note on the kitchen table; others reveal their inner knowledge of impending death in their choice of subject and color in spontaneous drawings.

At the end of the workshops these parents can sing and laugh again, and also share happy and funny memories of their youngsters. Thus life somehow starts again for such parents— in a new and different form, but it is life, often expanded through the services parents and grandparents offer to others who must deal with the same or similar tragedies. Bereaved families reaching out to others similarly bereaved—that is naturally how all the self-help and service groups started, such as Parents of Murdered Children, Compassionate Friends, Candlelighters, etc., who reach millions of people all over the world at a time of need.

Here is an excerpt from one of our bereaved parents workshop meetings. It sheds some light not only on the courage of these fathers and mothers, but also on their enhanced and increased understanding of life and man's inner strength and inner knowledge. Hope and peace are the results we work to attain, to replace the most intense inner rage and incomprehensible grief and pain.

One couple shared the story of their little eight-year-old girl who died by a freak accident during a trip overseas, and how they missed the cues that they might have been better off not going on the trip at all. After the death of their little girl, they found "evidence" that their little daughter had prepared things to leave behind, as little messages of love:

"We spent a week and brought our two oldest daughters, seven and eight years old, to visit the friend. We spent a fair amount of time with this couple, who had recently split up and were trying to get their marriage back together. We went to the airport. I travel thousands of miles a year, but this was the first time I've ever been bumped off a flight. Our flight was oversold, and both of us felt very ill at ease about going. So we talked about getting bumped off the flight, about whether we should really go, because we were really not up to going. But then we said we should go, because the children were real excited and we were anxious to go.

"Our daughter had the freak accident over there. She fell and hit her head and had internal bleeding. We picked her up, started mouth-to-mouth resuscitation and got her breathing again, and raced to the hospital, which unfortunately was eighteen miles away. We kept her alive for twenty minutes. She died on Wednesday. Our seven-year-old daughter had a birthday on Friday, the funeral was on Saturday, and Father's Day was Sunday.

"Some of the unusual things that happened were: On the airplane going, our daughter, who obviously never did this before, wrote a thank-you note to the lady we were going to stay with . . . which was highly unusual. And she wrote it for both daughters. It was very unusual that she would ever do that on the way . . . to a vacation. . . . 'Thank you for inviting us. . . . We love being with you. . . . With love, L. and A.' She had never done anything like that. . . . We thought it was unusual, but she wrote it on the plane going over and gave it to her sister, saying, 'This is to give to W.'

"So our seven-year-old daughter knew that L. had done this particular card and found it for me a little over five weeks later. We were going through L.'s drawers and we found a second Father's Day card just five weeks after Father's Day, which again had been done prior to our leaving for vacation. . . . Why she did a second card, we'll never know, but the card was unusual—it was Noah's ark. . . . It says . . . 'Dear Daddy, Happy Father's Day. Thank you for the lovely year you have put in for me. I love you very much. . . . Love, L.' It was very unusual. She didn't sign the one that said, 'Dear Daddy, You're smart and I love you and I'm glad you're my daddy. Happy Father's Day. I love you a lot.' She just signed it 'Your oldest, with a lot of kisses and hugs,' but this particular card found five weeks later was very unusual."

Another mother shares memories of her teenage daughter who was killed in an accident: "I looked at her pictures after she had died. . . . From the time that she was eleven and a half until she died, she was like five different people. Every year she changed. Her whole physical presence kept changing, and the summer before she died she organized her life. She took care of everything. She made a list of people that she needed to go and make it right with, and she went to see them.

"I took her out to dinner about ten days before she died. She had not been doing well in school. She was an A student, and she had not been doing too well. She was fifteen, and she had skipped a grade. She was a girl who had skipped a grade because she was longing so to get on with her own life, and we talked about her future. I said, 'What are you going to do?' . . . and she said . . . 'Well, Mom, I don't want to go to [another school], and it's hard for a kid my age to get a job. And besides, my life is almost over. . . .' All three of those statements were said with equal energy; not one was more important than the other one.

"And of course, as a mother, I said, 'What are you talking about? You're only fifteen!' I had no concept at all that on one level she really knew what was happening. . . . I had no foreknowledge that this being who just happened to have passed through me was this teacher, this incredible teacher. And she made her rounds. . . . Everything was in total order; she spent the last couple of weeks ironing everything. I couldn't believe the order in her room. . . . This is a fifteen-year-old child, you know. I was just amazed. And she didn't take any identification with her, and so I see it as an act of love because she knew. She knew when she left to go in the car that she would not be coming home again; she didn't want me to be awakened at 1:30 in the morning to be told that my daughter had died, and I didn't find out until 3:00 the next day.

"She always took her identification with her, but this time she didn't and I found it . . . her little book, right next to her bed. This is what she wrote: 'I wish I could solve everyone's problems for them . . . or even try to help them—meaning my fellow human friends, brothers, and sisters, all on the same plane—to see the discomfort. . . . The pain suffered by you yourself is the pain you not only caused consciously. . . . It can be healed the best by you, yourself, from your heart, spirit, and bodily points of energy. Just be in touch, keep in touch, come in touch, go in touch, stride in touch, and ride in touch."

* * *

The father of a murdered child, an eleven-year-old girl, was able to share his experiences and memories, something fathers usually have less opportunity to do than mothers in our society:

"My daughter was kidnapped in December, along with another little girl. I found the first little girl murdered, and the next day we found my little girl. My daughter painted a watercolor for her mom's birthday of the same month, which she gave to her; I have it framed now. My daughter gave me a lot of messages that I see now and have in my mind. . . . She asked me one time, 'Dad, do you believe in reincarnation?' She was eleven when she was murdered. I said, 'Well, honey, I don't have any real strong feelings either for or against it, but I don't really have anything that I can say yes or no. Why?' She said, 'Well, Dad, I have this really strong feeling that I was eighty-three once,' and so that's just one little message that she gave me.

"Before she died she made this birthday present for my wife. It's a picture of an ocean and a wave. In the right lower quadrant, which is supposed to reveal the immediate future, is a black rock; it fills out the whole corner and has her signature on it. The big sun on the upper portion and the dark blue and yellow . . . I'm beginning to understand now. . . . The wave breaking over the rock is in light blue, and there is a rainbow. We didn't understand other than the fact that it was a gift for us. It wasn't until after I heard Elisabeth talk that I realized that, in her spontaneous drawing the day before her death, my daughter had really let us know that this was happening. . . . And this has been a real great comfort to us. I wanted to share it with everybody because it means a lot to us."

Another parent pitched in at this point and said, "May I share my paintings from my daughter, because of something that I have learned today . . . that makes me feel a lot better." She then proceeded to share paintings done by her daughter, who committed suicide, and also poems that she wrote when she was fifteen.

A mother of a nineteen-year-old added her memories of the creation of little characters that her daughter did before her fatal car accident. "My daughter was five feet seven inches. She was flat as a board. She had a sister who was three years younger and who was built like Carol Doda. She'd say to me, 'What did you do to me, Mom. I wasn't in line to get big boobs.' So she created all these funny boob-people and aspired to do work with children in wallpapers, batiking, and ceramic. She left me a wonderful legacy. All her ceramic vases and urns or whatever she made had an Egyptian mask. She was killed in an automobile accident on the Golden Gate Bridge. She was in a terrible accident where the car rolled three times just months before her fatal accident. While having her car rebuilt, I lent her my car, and three months later she was killed. She swerved to avoid another accident that just happened, and as she came out of her first swerve there was a pedestrian crossing, so she swerved again, lost control, and hit the divider ten yards beyond.

"My son was killed six and a half months later, but a week after his sister was killed he wrote a letter to God. He said 'Dear God, I know you're not Santa Claus, but for a gift for me for Christmas could you please let me know that my sister is all right? I know that I will be with her someday, but in my vocabulary someday is a long way away. I love her very much, and I want to be with her. Please let me know she is all right.' . . . The day after his seventeenth birthday he was killed in exactly the same way. He was with her three days before her birthday and the day after his. She was nineteen and he was seventeen the day before he was killed. . . .

"At the memorial service there were young people . . . there was absolutely the greatest outpouring of love that you can imagine. . . . My son was an artist in his own right and a writer-cartoonist, and every person that stood up at that memorial service said that he had given them the gift of turning a negative into a positive.

"My youngest daughter, who was ten at the time, was also in the accident with her brother. . . . She has the wisdom of a ninety-year-old. . . . She was knocked unconscious, and when she was coming out of it she found a dog nipping at her arm—his leg had been torn open. She looked over at her brother, and realized that she couldn't do anything but that she had to get help. So she got up and started hiking. They were

miles from anywhere, on a dirt road, and she was screaming
and yelling for help. Realizing that the dog was really in bad
shape, she had the presence of mind to take her top off and
tie a tourniquet around the dog's leg. Then she hiked out in
that kind of shock. . . . So there's always somebody when you
need them the most. . . .

"I get firmer and firmer convictions to hang in there because
they're in a much better place than we are. . . . You see, I
believe that they have a very tight spiritual bonding that is
expressed in this love and explains my son's desire to be with
his sister. It is also my sustaining belief that we are on this level
of life to accomplish a mission, and when that is finished we
are able to go home. . . . We then live in peace and tranquility
and never suffer pain, anguish, fear, or negativity again. I feel
it was God's blessing to me to have been my daughter's and
my son's mother here on earth."

A mother, whose son was accidentally killed by electrocu-
tion, shares the following:

"About a month before my son's accident, he was always
leaving notes on the table or something. I got up to go to
work, and he left me a note on the kitchen table. I had been
grumbling that, oh, I just didn't want to go to work, just
wanted to stay home and sleep late. So the note said: 'Dear
Mom, I love you.' I really feel the Lord was trying to tell me
something . . . because all month I had a very strange feeling,
and I can remember that day writing in my diary . . . 'Thank
you, Lord, for my son's writing that to me this morning. I
really needed that.' And I did. It really made my day.

"After the accident, as soon as I walked into the emergency
room, all I can remember is his feet. It seemed like we were
there forever. Finally, I said I wanted to know what was going
on. So my friend and I followed the nurse. . . . Someone came
out and said he was gone. But I was strong. . . . It was about six
years later I had to deal with the loss, and that's why I try to

tell people to deal with what's going on with them at the time."

Facing Crisis Alone

Most troubled are those whose support system is not available at a time of such crisis. Since we started working with prisoners, we have met many mothers who had to face the sudden death of a child alone. They felt like widows for quite some time, except that widows have a support system and receive sympathy when they lose their husbands, while wives of prisoners are shunned, avoided, and have few outreaching hands to support them in times of crisis, as if they had been partners in crime.

Mrs. L. had just returned from an especially depressing visit to the penitentiary when a neighbor informed her that her son had waited over an hour for her, but had finally left to go fishing. She paced up and down the floor of her small, confining apartment where they had moved recently to make ends meet. She did not know anyone in the community and felt vulnerable and alone.

She thought of calling her mother, but she would only hear the same stories she had heard so many times in the past: "Leave your husband. He is no good, and he never will be." How could a mother be so judgmental of a man who had gone through so much hardship in his life? she thought to herself. Her husband was not a bad man. He was just weak and got himself into fights too quickly. He had pulled a knife on someone who insulted him, and in the ensuing struggle the man got badly hurt. She prayed to God he would not die.

A few hours later the phone rang. She hoped that perhaps it would be her mother calling anyway. But it was a strange voice, and her heart sank. Who is this? What do you want? The stranger asked about a boy who had been in an accident. He asked her if she knew where her son was. No, she was not sure; he had gone fishing. Her head started to spin; her mind became fuzzy. "What happened? Tell me! I need to know."

But the man at the other end of the line simply told her to come to the hospital.

The bus took forever to arrive. People got off and on at every stop as if they had all the time in the world. She finally got to the hospital, and the girl at the reception desk asked her what she wanted. She was sent alone clear across the hospital to the emergency room. She got lost, started to run, was screamed at for almost running into a patient on a stretcher, but moved on without saying a word. By the time she arrived at the emergency waiting room, she was in a panic. Here she was kept waiting, with no information and no reassurance. She had no idea whether it really was her son who was brought in.

Finally, she could no longer sit. She went through a door where she saw some nurses laughing and smoking. They did not even pay attention to her presence. She moved on, pulled curtain after curtain. Behind some of them were stretchers with people on them, old and young, black and white . . . all waiting.

Then she heard some noises in an adjacent room, and without knocking she walked in. Some nurses and doctors were just disconnecting some tubes from her son's arms. He had his eyes half open, some blood was on his nose and on the corner of his mouth. That's all she could see. Somebody yelled at her to get out. One of the nurses grabbed her arm and pulled her away. She was fighting now, struggling to reach her son, to hold him, to shake him, to tell him that he would be all right. But they would not let her. He was dead, they told her.

She was sedated. Her mother came to take care of the funeral arrangements. She still has that haunting vision of having been so close to her son and of being pulled away from him, before she was able to touch him. She still hears her neighbor's voice, "He waited a long time for you, but finally left to . . ." Then her tears well up, and she is still waiting. Waiting for what? Waiting for her mother to call, to understand, to be there when she needs her. Waiting for her husband to be released. Waiting for the sun to shine again in her life. But she is like most mothers: She cannot believe yet that the sun will ever shine again, that her mother will really understand one day, that justice will prevail, that her husband will return home.

Reaching Out for Help

Some parents, in the depth of their agony over their abused and murdered children, receive help through the works of spiritual leaders like Ram Dass and Stephen Levine, who take them to a higher understanding of life and death without minimizing the nature of their agony and loss. The following is an excerpt of a letter exchange between the parent of a child victim and Ram Dass:

"When our eleven-year-old daughter was abducted and murdered, a deep communication opened with Ram Dass.

"I see our daughter as a soul who was actively engaged in her work while on earth. Her last three years in particular showed me the flowering of a shining being—caring, loving, and reaching out to the members of her family, many friends, and relatives, young and old. She was always giving little 'love' somethings to everyone. To make you smile, to help you feel good, to show she cared. She had learned somehow to bear her defeats and frustrations and not be intimidated or slowed by them. The petals were opening and reaching for the sun. She was not a clone of her parents. She was the best of us and the strongest of us. The wake of our daughter's death leaves the many beings who knew her, and a surprising number that didn't, torn open to this teaching."

This was Ram Dass's response to these parents, which was published in the Hanuman Foundation Newsletter in the hopes of reaching other parents:

". . . Your daughter finished her brief work on earth and left the stage in a manner that leaves those of us left behind with a

cry of agony in our hearts as the fragile thread of our faith is
dealt with so violently. Is anyone strong enough to stay conscious through such teachings as you are receiving? Probably
very few, and even they would only have a whisper of
equanimity and spacious peace midst the screaming trumpets
of their rage, grief, horror, and desolation.

"I cannot assuage your pain with any words, nor should I.
For your pain is your daughter's legacy to you. Not that she
or I would inflict such pain by choice. But—there it is—and it
must burn its purifying way to completion. You may emerge
from this ordeal more dead than alive—and then you can
understand why the greatest saints, for whom every human
being is their child, shoulder the unbearable pain and are called
the living dead. For something within you dies when you bear
the unbearable—and it is only in that dark night of the soul
that you are prepared to see as God sees, and to love as God
loves.

"Now is the time to let your grief find expression—no false
strength. Now is the time to sit quietly and speak to your
daughter, and thank her for being with you these few years
and encourage her to go on with her work, knowing that
you will grow in compassion and wisdom from this experience.

"In my heart I know that you and she will meet again and
again and recognize the many ways in which you have known
each other. Your rational minds can never 'understand'. what
has happened. But your hearts, if you can keep them open to
God, will find their own intuitive way.

"Your daughter came through you to do her work on earth
(which includes her manner of death). Now her soul is free,
and the love that you can share with her is invulnerable to the
winds of changing time and space. In that deep love, include
me, too."

Dealing with Hurtful Emotions

Sudden deaths often leave parents and siblings in a desperate
state of guilt, even deaths that occur suddenly after a long

history of illness. One parent, in the depths of such feeling, wrote:

"Please give me the information I need to help myself and the other parents in our Compassionate Friends group to deal with the guilt . . . the ifs . . . the absence of a final parting while Jessie was still alive . . . being able to tell him verbally we loved him before he passed away. Did he suffer? No one can completely answer that one, I suppose. Does he survive beyond death? Is he lonely for us . . . sad? If I had a sign, a clue that he is better off now than before, it would help. These questions torment all of us parents because we can't find any answers right off here. My son was waiting for me to see him that morning . . . he never saw me, and I was oh, so close by . . . he saw his own death instead. I have to live with that thought for the rest of my life. . . . He needed me and I wasn't there. How does a mother deal with this? I *could* have been with him. . . ."

In an article written for a publication printed especially for parents who are losing or have lost a child, I have offered the following counsel:
"Margaret Gerner
Editor, National Newsletter
9619 Abaco Ct.
St. Louis, MO 63136

"My dear Margaret,
"Thank you for your letter of January 22 and your request to help you with your National Newsletter for bereaved parents. Since I just came back from Europe, Egypt, Jerusalem, Alaska, and Hawaii, I thought the only way not to have to look at my 2,000 unanswered letters is to send you an article right now, so here it is. . . .

Dear Friends,
Margaret Gerner, your editor of this beautiful newsletter, has asked me to write a few words to all of you who are mourning a child or who are in the process of facing

the reality of an impending death of one of your children. As you probably know, I wrote many books (*On Death and Dying, To Live Until We Say Goodbye*, and the more recent one which deals mainly with dying children, *Living with Death and Dying*), and you know of my twenty years of working in this field.

There are many things I could share with you, but perhaps the most significant is the progress we have made in the last decade in helping not only families during their long and arduous journey through a terminal illness with a child, but also those thousands of parents whose children have been murdered, committed suicide, or met a sudden accidental death. Those families have not been privileged to have time, in itself, a healer and a preparator. Time is a healer because it gives us moments for reflection, and an opportunity to say the many things we have not said before. It gives us a chance to undo things we regret and to concentrate our loving energy on those who are in the process of leaving us.

Time is a preparator, because it allows us at our own speed to come out of the shock and numbness, the anger at our destiny, at mates, siblings, yes . . . even at the dying child or God, a natural human reaction. We need the time to bargain with God and ultimately to react to the many losses which we call the "little deaths," which precede our final separation. The little deaths are the losses of children's beautiful hair when they are on chemotherapy, the need to hospitalize them when you can no longer care for them at home, their inability to walk, dance, kick a football or play soccer, go to a prom or come home with their friends, giggling and laughing and making plans for the future. When all these losses can be mourned as they occur, the final grief work will be minimal.

And then comes, naturally, the final preparatory grief, which is silent and beyond words, as we are finally facing the reality that we will never see them in a wedding gown, that we will never see them at their graduation, and that we can never look forward to grandchildren. And thus, the families mourn those things which will "never be." Our little patients also wean off and want to see fewer and fewer people, in order to be able to let go. This is the time when peace and serenity can prevail if we know when to stop life-prolonging procedures, when to take them home and simply love them until they make their final transition we call death.

Many of you who have lost a little one in a sudden death have not been privileged with this extra time and I want you to consider not only the tragedy, but also the blessing of this sudden death. You will never have to deal with the anguish and agony of long and painful medical procedures; you will never have to worry about the effects on brothers and sisters, who are unfortunately often put in a secondary position, while the sick child is spoiled with material things, trips to Disneyland and all sorts of frantic "making up" endeavors, which are often more beneficial to those who survive than to the sick child. Many a sibling has asked for similar favors, only to be denied the requests with the cruel reply, "Would you rather have cancer?" Many of these brothers and sisters are left with bitterness, a sense of unfairness and tremendous guilt about their hostility placed on the dying sibling as a result of the unfair treatment by the parents.

I'm sharing this with you so that those of you who have problems with your other children will spend your love and energy with them before it is too late. I'm sharing this also with you in the hope that you *never* allow anybody to give you Valium at the time of such a crisis, as it will cheat you out of the chance to experience *all* your feelings, cry out all your pain, shed all your tears, so that you can live again, not only for your own sake, but for the sake of your family and all others whose life you can touch!

We have learned that those who were informed of a

sudden death do much better if they can externalize their anguish and their pain in a safe and preferably sound-proof environment as soon as possible after the sudden death. We have, therefore, encouraged hospital emergency rooms to establish screaming rooms where people can externalize their grief not accompanied by an all-too-busy professional, but hopefully by a member of Compassionate Friends, one who has not been taught by textbooks but by the school of life and who can compassionately be there to facilitate the shedding of tears and the emptying of the pool of anguish and pain, in order to start living again.

Our five-day, live-in workshops given by myself and the staff of Shanti Nilaya all over the world, help those who have additional guilt and unfinished business, which is especially painful when a child commits suicide. Suicide is the third cause of death among our children between the ages of six and sixteen, and a million questions will haunt those parents who wonder how such a tragedy could have been prevented. Such guilt will only diminish your energy and prevent you from living fully and from eventually helping others to face such losses.

We have had parents in our workshops who have lost all their children through cancer within six months and yet they require no psychiatric help, no Valium or other tranquilizers, and are now helping others to come to grips with such losses, just as the Compassionate Friends are doing all over the country and abroad.

If any of you are interested in joining one of these workshops, drop us a note and we will send you more information.

Remember that God sends to none of His children more than they can cope with, and remember my favorite saying: "Should you shield the canyons from the windstorms, you would never see the beauty of their carvings."

This never means that you should not acknowledge the

pain and the anguish, the sadness and the loneliness after the loss of a child, but you must also know that after every winter, spring follows and out of your pain . . . if you choose so . . . comes a great amount of compassion, increased understanding and wisdom and love for others who are in pain. Use these gifts to touch other lives and understand that *all* my work with dying children came out of the memory of the horrors of the concentration camps of Nazi Germany, where 96,000 children were put in gas chambers. Out of every tragedy can come a blessing or a curse, compassion or bitterness . . . the choice is *yours*!

To end this letter, I want you to know that our research in death and life after death has revealed beyond a shadow of a doubt that those who make the transition are more alive, more surrounded with *unconditional love* and beauty than you can ever conceive. They are not really dead. They have just preceded us in the evolutionary journey all of us are on; they are with their former playmates (as they call them), or guardian angels; they are with family members who preceded them in death and are unable to miss you as you miss them since they are unable to feel any negative feelings. The only thing that stays with them is the knowledge of love and care that they have received and of the lessons they have learned during their physical life.

Marilyn Sunderman, the world-famous portrait painter of Honolulu, Hawaii, was in the process of painting a picture of me. She paints, inspired or channeled through high guidance, and she was amazed to see that out of a started portrait of the "55-year-old death and dying lady" emerged a unique and beautiful picture of a little child looking up at a butterfly. She was told to make this picture available to chapters of the Compassionate Friends, and it is perhaps the greatest gift we can give to all of you, namely the knowledge that our physical body is only a cocoon and death is really the emergence of the indestructible and immortal real part of us, symbolically speaking, the butterfly.

As the children of the concentration camps at Majdanek scratched little butterflies with their fingernails on the walls before entering the gas chambers, so did your children know at the moment of death that they would emerge free and unencumbered into a land where there is no more pain, into a land of peace and unconditional love, into a land where there is no time and where they can reach you at the speed of their thoughts. KNOW THAT and enjoy the spring with new flowers coming out after the deadly winter frosts, and enjoy the new leaves and life bursting forth all around you.

Chapter 4
Head Injuries and Coma

Head Injuries

STEPHEN HAD FINALLY GRADUATED from high school, and his parents breathed a great sigh of relief. He was the oldest of five children, and perhaps because his brothers and sisters had come so soon after his birth, no one ever seemed to have enough time for him. He was often compared to his younger siblings, all of whom seemed to have more of a sense of responsibility than Stephen. The parents had hoped that he would set an example of "the older brother," but that expectation was never fulfilled.

While the younger ones in this family did fairly well in school and completed their homework, usually before dinner, Stephen had to be constantly reminded. He was called the "scatterbrain" by his sisters who loved to tease him. His father often blamed him for having "a brain like a bird." "What will ever become of you if you don't use your brain?" his mother hollered at him furiously when he returned without doing the errand she expected of him.

He left the house one day, and nobody thought much of it when he did not return for supper. "Our forgetful kid is probably still walking around trying to remember what his mother asked of him" was his father's unconcerned remark.

An hour later the phone rang. After answering it, the father fell silent and the color seemed to disappear from his face. "Yes, we will be right over. Isn't there anything else you can tell me? Is he alive at least?" the mother heard him say.

Half an hour later they were in the car driving frantically to the local hospital. They exchanged few words. They were in a state of shock and numbness. All they knew was that Stephen had been in a car accident, that they had not been able to get him out of the wreck for over an hour, and that he had just been admitted to the trauma unit in a nearby hospital.

Pictures of the last few weeks with Stephen flashed into their minds: the pride they experienced when he had been able to graduate from high school after all. The graduation photographs had just arrived; Stephen had not yet seen them. He looked so adult and happy in the tuxedo he had rented for the prom. He was so thrilled when Pat had accepted his invitation. He had finally had his first success—and now this! It wasn't fair.

"Slow down if you don't want to be killed, too," Mrs. K. heard herself saying to her husband. "Killed? O my God! Not that, please God, let him be alive! I don't care what he will have to give up, but *please, please* let him live!"

They arrived at the hospital, went through a maze of hallways and corridors, and finally arrived at the admissions desk, only to be told to wait. In a daze, they were sent to another wing, another waiting room. Everything seemed to be unreal, and everybody seemed preoccupied with their own little drama. "Don't you know that somewhere in here my son's battling for his life?" the mother wanted to scream, but no one seemed to be concerned.

Finally a very young-looking doctor came out and introduced himself. Yes, the boy in the wreck had been their son. It took them "forever" to get him out of the wreck. A friend who passed by had identified him and supplied their phone number and address. Stephen apparently had just spent hours in his friend's basement to create a very special surprise for his father on Father's Day. He had just finished it and asked his friend to hide it away for the coming Sunday, and off he went in a hurry so as not "to make them mad if I'm late for supper." Those must have been the last words he spoke.

No, it was impossible to see him now. He didn't look very good. Yes, he was still alive, but he had little chance to make it. The words registered somewhere in his parents' minds. Minutes felt like hours, hours like days—waiting, not knowing, praying, hoping, and more waiting.

A mother who sat with her little boy in the same waiting room hollered at Mrs. K.: "What's the matter with your brains? Don't you know we have to wait for lab results?" It stung like needles. How often had they made fun of Stephen's brains, just because he seemed so often preoccupied with things they did not understand? Did they ever ask him what he was dreaming about?

They were finally taken to a back room where they saw the mangled remains of what a short while ago had been their proud graduate. His face looked puffed, expressionless. It was an odd, undefinable color, and traces of blue marks were all over him. One eye seemed to be at the wrong place, and dark-blue shadows were apparent under both eyes. "The eye is the smallest problem," another physician explained. "If we can keep the vital signs up, we will be able to operate on him. Dr. S. has been called for a consultation, and if he is able to come, he will be the man who will take care of the surgery."

There were tubes and machines and busy nurses coming and going. An old black nurse's aide quietly pressed Mrs. K.'s hand and gave her a glance. It took her out of her shock and disbelief. Someone actually cared!

They spent about ten minutes in a consultation room with the attending physician. Then they were encouraged to go home and "get some sleep." My God, who could think that parents could sleep after such a sight! Mr. K. called his oldest daughter to come take him home; he was too sick, too devastated to be able to drive a car.

Mr. K. had aged in a few hours. He could think only of his oldest son being wheeled into the operating room without the consolation and support of his family. He walked up and down from the kitchen to the living room, waiting for a phone call, waiting to hear that his son was well.

In the early morning hours the parents couldn't wait any longer. Why had no one called? Why didn't somebody let them know how Stephen was doing? Wasn't it their child who was fighting for his young life? They were almost physically sick when they arrived at the hospital. This time the hallways were empty. The silence was almost as painful as the noise of last night. There seemed to be no color, no friendly voice anywhere. They felt like robots, again referred from one place to another.

"Doesn't anybody know where Stephen is?" they wanted to scream, but at the same time they were afraid to make a nuisance out of themselves for fear of irritating the people they needed to depend on for the next few hours, days, or weeks.

They finally reached the third floor, where the newly-operated-on neurosurgical patients were taken after surgery. Stephen had apparently survived the operation, and the surgeons had not even come out of the recovery room. They were exhausted, but Stephen was still alive. Even so, his chance to survive as a functioning young man was less than one percent.

And again the parents waited in a small anteroom, waiting, praying, hoping. The next few days passed in an endless pattern of being allowed to see him a few minutes a day, driving home to get a few hours of rest, getting some food ready for the children, and answering the phone calls that started to come in from the many friends their son had.

It seemed that they—for the first time—got to know their oldest child. One boy shared how much Stephen had helped him a year before when his sister had drowned. "If it had not been for Stephen, I probably would have killed myself. I felt so guilty for laughing when she screamed for help, and then suddenly she disappeared under the waves and was gone." My God, Stephen had never told them of the many hours he had spent with his friend to help him relieve his guilt, to help him live again! How many times had they reprimanded him for not coming home from school to do his homework, when in fact he might have quietly been helping his friends in need?

There were dozens of young people standing around now in the hallways of this impersonal hospital, although they knew that only the next of kin would be allowed in to see Stephen. He could neither move his legs nor do anything that seemed to indicate that he understood what had happened in his world. For a while the hospital considered sending him to a nursing home especially geared toward the care of people in a coma. But at the last minute the parents of a school friend of Stephen's told them about a new organization for parents of children with head injuries.

The names and addresses of the organization that assists head-injured patients and families follow.

In California:

Southern California Head Injury
Foundation, Inc.
8050 Calmosa Avenue
Whittier, California 90602

Nationally:

National Head Injury Foundation, Inc.
280 Singletary Lane
Framingham, Massachusetts 01701

Coma

David was a healthy, robust nineteen-year-old whose life changed drastically in 1975, when his motorcycle and a car collided. He received immediate emergency treatment for his skull fractures, but remained unconscious, and shortly after admission showed decerebrate rigidity, an ominous sign that continued for a long time in spite of two surgical procedures to remove hematomas (bleedings).

After endless months of treatment, hope and despair, the family was able to take their son home. For seven long years the mother has cared for this young man who is paralyzed in all four extremities, unable to speak or follow any commands. With marked joint deformities, he lies in bed, unable to participate in any of life's functionings. He is a constant reminder to the mother that we of the medical profession sometimes overdo our attempts to keep young people alive at all costs, oblivious to the nightmares that follow when parents see the nonfunctioning body of their child lying in a bed year after year, turned by family and nurses, fed like a baby, unable to move arms or legs, unable to utter a word or respond to anything the family tries to communicate. The mother's letter speaks for itself:

"Dear Elisabeth,

"I appreciated your comments about my son David, but it is getting increasingly difficult to convince his physician that he is not to get antibiotics for infection—although none has occurred in recent months. One of the reasons for his fear in not administering is the recent case of the Attorney General of California suing two doctors who did not administer antibiotics, other medication, *or food* to a patient who subsequently died. While I have never said no food—nor would I—I am pretty set on no antibiotics; still, I do not wish to quarrel any longer with this man.

"I feel so defeated because I have run up against a brick wall time after time after time. Since your letter I have had examinations and tests taken of David. The examination was in October, and the tests the day after Thanksgiving. I saw the results of the brain scan, which was dreadful. The doctor asked me what happened to my son, and after I told him he pointed out that he had never seen 'such an abnormal brain' and of course it was a result of the accident as well as the two craneotomies.

"Since that time I simply cannot settle my unsettled feelings, and nearly every day I wake up crying or on the verge of crying—something I should have done *immediately after* the accident, not seven years later. I had no idea how terribly David had been injured, as incredible as that might seem. I had no idea the extent of the injuries; that is to say, I did not have the comprehension or understanding I have acquired during the past six months.

"To me, now, I find it incredible that with the injuries he sustained that he was pulled through—that we have had to suffer all these years. I hate to put it this way, because I had gone through considerable therapy to get over this kind of stuff, and it seems I've slipped horribly.

"Anyhow, I am looking forward to meeting you because somehow, I need to let go more emotionally. Sometimes I think I've got it, but lately I know I don't have it. It would have been much simpler for all if David had simply been allowed to die when he had his accident; that is to say, for his body to die, because I did have the experience that he left that night; the tests have proved conclusively that he has no higher cortical function, and I would think that this would mean he *is* gone out of the body.

"I find it incredible that his physician would even consider 'a little bit of antibiotics' just so people could say he did a good job—not to be criticized. I find it shattering to hear people say David could live to be 65 or older as he is."

* * *

Much attention has been given to the Karen Quinlan story: Some years ago this young woman slipped into a coma following an overdose, and was maintained on life-prolonging procedures. She is now, almost a decade later, still in a coma, a small bundle of a stiff body, lovingly cared for in a nursing home and still visited by her most devoted and wonderful parents.

Most of her brain is nonfunctioning. She can neither speak nor respond, nor move any of her extremities and yet—in all this long, drawn out tragedy—her existence has brought new awareness to the world, which otherwise would still be too callous and indifferent to bring such problems into the open.

Many institutions and professional, ethical-moral, and religious forums have paid attention to the issue of artificial prolongation of life, and I am sure hot arguments will continue both pro- and contra-life prolonging procedures in brain stem-damaged youngsters who don't have a chance to truly live.

They exist but don't live in nursing homes, extended care facilities, or at home and are a tremendous burden, financially, emotionally, and physically to families and care-givers. They do serve as reminders to the survivors of the preciousness of life. They do tell us to appreciate the moments we have to share with each other, to talk, to respond, to take time out to laugh and enjoy time with each other while we still have the chance. But how long do we need to keep such people alive at all costs? How long do we give them antibiotics?

All families need to make these heartbreaking and difficult decisions for themselves. If and when the science of medicine has depleted all the family's resources, such youngsters should be taken home as long as there is an adequate nursing staff available to nurture and move them, put them in a warm bath, and give them as many physical pleasures as are possible under the circumstances. We can always have a sibling play tapes from a cassette recorder or record player, old school pals can drop by, and the family can share as much of their activities with their unresponsive child as possible. We know that such children can hear, and frequent stimulation often leads to remarkable but—oh, so slow—improvements.

Families also need to know that it is important to differentiate between consciousness and awareness, the latter not being dependent on a functioning brain. While these children are intermittently out of their bodies for brief periods of time, they are totally aware of what is going on in their environment. When they return to their physical shell, their brain damage does not allow them to comprehend or identify what is going on, and they will "respond" only with a blank look, if at all. This is why it is so important to continue the normal life around them as long as possible.

After a while the friends and siblings stop visiting. They don't know what to say to a friend who never even looks at them. Husbands drop by less and less, if they live a separated or divorced existence (which we found in 80 percent of the families we visited), and it may well be that their own unresolved guilt and grief prevents them from facing it over and over again. This often leaves the mother as the sole responsible care-giver, a load too hard to carry.

When the condition remains stable and the child stops making any progress over years of good physical and supportive care, the parents should be allowed—together with the caring and nonjudgmental physician—to decide when no more antibiotics should be administered.

Once more people become aware that our physical form is not the person, but the cocoon, we may have fewer problems in letting go and less guilt that we did not prolong a life at all costs.

One woman wrote to me about her 3½-year-old daughter, who had a neurologically degenerative disease. She had recently slipped into a coma and could not speak, although her mother felt the girl could communicate with her. My message is that children who are in a coma are out of their physical body most of the time, and that during this time they can hear all communications that people may have with them, and they will understand the universal language of love and care. There is no fear, no pain, and no agony in their understanding of their life situation.

Chapter 5

The Natural Way to Prepare Children for Life

Let us put our minds together and see what life we will make for our children.

—AKWESASNE NOTES,
Mohawk Nation, via Rooseveltown, N.Y.

MAN IS BORN with five natural emotions (described in the chart on page 61), all of which we have a tendency to twist around until they have become unnatural. They drain our energy and leave us with buckets of unshed tears, repressed anger and desire for revenge, envy and competition, and problems of self-pity, thus contributing to physical and emotional ill health, and a great deal to our problems of violence directed at others and ourselves.

Fears That Limit Our Lives

Fear is a natural emotion, but people are born with only two inherent fears: the one, of falling from high places; and the other, the fear of sudden loud noises. These fears are gifts to us, since they preserve life. How many other fears do you have, and how many will you pass on to your children? Many people base their whole life's decisions on fears such as fear of failure and/or fear of success; fear of abandonment and rejection; fear of pain and death; fear of old age and wrinkled faces; fear of not being loved; fear of being too fat or too skinny; fear of the boss and of what the neighbors think. There are so many acquired fears that burden our lives and drain our energy!

Either knowingly or unconsciously, we pass our acquired fears along to our children and are not aware until it is too late that these cause indescribable damage and pain. For example, parents who are afraid to let their toddler ride a tricycle or their older child venture out on a bicycle will emotionally cripple their youngster and create another generation of people who base their lives on fear.

Natural Emotions	Distorted, Unnatural Emotions
Fear ⟨ of falling from high places / of loud, unexpected noises	Fears of failure, rejection, not being loved, success, suffering, violence, boss, neighbors' opinions, etc.
Grief: How we deal with loss, expressed by tears and sharing	Self-pity, extended bad moods, depressions, guilt, shame, self reproach, blame
Anger (takes 15 seconds): Brings about change, assertiveness, self-protection	Prolonged anger, rage, hate, revenge, bitterness, resentment
Jealousy: Stimulus and motivator for growth	Envy, competition, possessiveness, self condemnation
Love (unconditional): Care, concern, nurturance Ability to say no, set limits to help others become independent; self worth, self trust, self love	I love you, *if*. . . . leads to pleasing others to "buy" their love and/or approval (we call this prostitution)

Additionally, man consists of four quadrants. *The psysical quadrant* is the most important during the first year of life. That is when we need all the physical care we can get.

Mrs. T. was one of those "proper ladies" who always appear as if they have just come from the beauty parlor. Daily she went to her office dressed as if she had been invited to a luncheon at the White House; her handbag matched her shoes, and no one would have suspected that her life was filled with fears. One of her greatest fears had to do with the opinions of others, especially her neighbors. She had worked hard to have a successful career and was eager not to be known as "the woman who came from the wrong side of the tracks." She saved every nickel to spend on her clothing, and no one would have guessed that she had to count her pennies before buying anything else, including a membership in the local country club. This woman was a widow, and her husband had left her little after the hospital bills and the funeral had been paid for.

One of Mrs. T.'s daughters was married and worked as a cosmetician; the other was engaged to be married and lived with her fiance out of town—another reality Mrs T. did not want her friends and neighbors to know about. For the past few months, Mrs. T. had been involved in a constant struggle and nightly fight with her one and only son, Bob.

Bob was eighteen years old and he mixed with the "wrong kids," in Mrs. T.'s opinion. It was not that they were bad; these kids attended high school and spent evenings at home, often at Mrs. T.'s house, talking and listening to rock music. They were saving their money to start a band, and occasionally they took some girls to the movies.

But for the past few months, Mrs. T. had given her son "the business" every evening, when she returned home and saw him sitting in the kitchen on top of the refrigerator. Bob always looked unkempt and unconcerned, and what infuriated her the most was that he wore the same old gray T-shirt for days, "that T-shirt that he got from one of his girl friends, with an undefinable color, washed out and worn out." When she talked about him and his friends, Mrs. T.'s disgust was unmistakable. She talked about them as if they had personally hurt or insulted her, and she frankly admitted that—once started—she was unable to stop yelling at Bob until he left the room or the house.

One night after listening to a lecture on "Life and Death," Mrs. T. returned home to see Bob sitting in the same familiar position, wearing the same T-shirt that triggered her nightly rages. She gave me the following account about her moment of revelation:

"That night I came home, and there he sat with his friends. I was just ready to lash out at him again when I looked at him. It was almost as if I were seeing him for the first time. I suddenly heard myself saying, "Bob, if you want to wear that T-shirt, it's OK with me. Because if you should have an accident with your car driving your friends home tonight, I would bury you in that T-shirt."

If a woman is raised with the concept that she is lovable only when she looks pretty, and she receives positive reinforcement only when she looks neat and up-to-date, then like Mrs. T., she is likely to pass this value judgment on to her children and will feel terribly threatened when they do not follow in her path. It is interesting that Mrs. T.'s daughter, whom I never met, became a cosmetician and apparently "inherited" some of her mother's values.

Why should our children have to die—or why should we

have to imagine them dead—before we see the beauty of their lives? Why do our fears of what the neighbors may think—that we cannot afford to dress our children nicely—drive a mother and a son apart?

The Emotional Quadrant

Very young children have no fear of death, although they have the two innate fears of sudden loud noises and of falling from high places. Later on children are naturally afraid of separation, since the fear of abandonment and the absence of a loving caretaker is very basic and meaningful. Children are aware of their dependency, and those who have been exposed to early traumas in life are scarred. They will need to relive the trauma and learn to let go of the panic, pain, anxiety and rage of the abandonment.

These violent feelings arise often, not solely when a member of the family dies. Abandonments of all sorts happen thousands of times over in our society, and if the loss is not associated with the death of a loved one, few people will recognize this. The emergency support systems or shoulders to lean on will not be called into action, and there will be no sympathy visits by neighbors. So the child who feels abandoned in some manner is left vulnerable; his future mind-set could include a general mistrust, a fear of ever allowing a close relationship, an alienation from the person who is blamed for the separation, and a deep grief over the absence of love.

Rene was such a child, and he needed thirty years to heal. He was only five years old when his father told him to get into the car, because they were going somewhere together. Rene was very excited. His father had been drinking for many years; his mom had been in and out of mental hospitals, and there had been very little laughter and happiness in his life. And now his dad was going to take him somewhere. He did not dare to ask him where they were going. To the zoo? To the park? To a football game? He could not understand why Dad had come home in the middle of the week, but he knew that his mom was very sick again, because she had slept all day and never came down even to fix him a sandwich.

In the car, Rene and his father approached a huge building and parked. His father silently opened the car door and let Rene out. The father was very quiet; he did not even smile once. Rene wondered if his father was mad at him. He remembered he had fixed his own breakfast. He had even put the dishes in the sink. He was never noisy when his mom and dad had their fights, and he stayed in the den and out of the way. He had not heard them fighting today, and therefore Rene had hoped it would be a good day.

His dad took him by the hand and led him into a strange room with a funny smell. A Catholic sister came and talked to his father, but no one talked to him. Then his father left the room, and a short time later the sister left also. Rene sat very quietly and waited, but no one came. Maybe his dad had to go to the bathroom. Finally he got up, and out the window he saw his dad walking out of the house toward the car. He ran as fast as he could: "Dad, Dad, don't leave me!" But the car door shut, and he saw the old familiar car turn the corner—out of sight.

Rene never saw his mother again. She returned to the mental hospital, where two years later she killed herself. He didn't see his father again for many years. It was much later that a strange woman came to visit him one day; she told him that his dad had married her and that they had planned to take him out of the home of the sisters to see if it could "work out."

Rene tried to please his dad in every way he could. He painted the new house and worked every free moment he had to get a nod of approval from him. But his dad remained as silent as he had always been. This silence always brought back to Rene the memory of that nightmarish day when he had been taken away from home without so much as an explanation, much less a good-bye or last hug from his mom.

His father never said "thank you" or "I am pleased with you," just as he never brought up the reasons for Rene's placement in the home and the lack of warning. So Rene grew up trying to please, not knowing that the fear of rejection and abandonment was still with him in adulthood. But Rene was afraid of alcoholism, afraid of mental illness, afraid of getting close to anyone. His whole life consisted of work and more work to please his father. He never allowed himself to get angry, to speak up, to express displeasure. The only time his face lit up was at the sight of a parent playing with a child in the park or swinging on a swing in a schoolyard. He spent his free time in those places, vicariously enjoying the laughter of these children, unaware of why he could not experience love and laughter in his own life.

As a mature adult he took an opportunity to look at his pain, anguish, despair, and incomprehension of this totally unexpected abandonment in early childhood, and he emerged a free man. It took him only one week, touched by others who shared their agonies in a safe place where it was regarded as a blessing to get rid of old tears and anger. During that week, Rene felt loved unconditionally. This man has just resolved his conflicts and has begun to understand his inability to trust and relate.

If someone—preferably his parents—had talked with this little boy and made an effort to understand his play, his drawings, his sullen withdrawal and isolation, much pain and unresolved conflict, carried within for decades, could have easily been avoided. You think those things happened in the last century? No, they still happen every day in our society.

Many, many adults suffer from never having resolved the hurts of their childhood. So children need to be allowed to grieve without being labeled crybaby or sissy, or hearing the ridiculous statement "Big boys don't cry." If children of both sexes are not allowed to express their natural emotions in childhood, they will have problems later on in the form of self-pity and many psychosomatic symptoms. Grief and fear, when allowed to be expressed and shared in childhood, can prevent much future heartache.

Sharing the Emotions

Home care makes it possible for the last few days or weeks before a loved one dies to be, not a nightmare, but a shared and beautiful experience that leads to acceptance. Children can share in this care, helping by playing favorite music on a cassette recorder or by just being available for a visit. When they can express their grief, they often create beautiful things. One little boy whose grandfather was treated at home for his final illness wrote the following story in school after his grandfather died:

"I wish this story was not true but it is. My mother's dad died, he is going to be cremated over a hot fire, his ashes are going to be spread over a cool lake. I wish I were death: I would not let anyone die; I would let people live a wonderful life anywhere. My mother's father always went fishing for beautiful trout in the lake that his delicut [delicate] ashes will be spread over. I wish he would never die. I wish I weren't sad."

To accompany this story, he had made a drawing of a box in flames.

Children's Natural Jealousy

Jealousy, another natural emotion, is a stimulant for children to learn, to copy older children, to emulate them. It is made negative only by the reaction of an observer who either reprimands, corrects, or belittles the child for his very natural response.

Once, when I brought a children's story to the home of a second-grader, his little five-year-old sister spoke to me just before I left the house. She climbed on my knee and whispered, "Aunty Elisabeth, next year when you come back to visit us, I am going to read this whole book to you." There was a sense of anticipated pride that sooner or later she too would be able to read. She would ask her big brother to show her some of the letters, and soon she too would read. This is an ordinary jealousy, but such a normal desire for attention can create a special problem with siblings of terminally or chronically ill children.

Many brothers and sisters have responded with increasing negativity to their terminally ill siblings when parents react to the illness with excessive pampering. We have innumerable cases where the sick child was treated like a hero, where famous people were asked to write or visit them, where gifts and privileges were given to them far in abundance of anything the siblings could ever hope to receive. With parental guilt and overindulgence, it is no surprise when many of the brothers and sisters start acting out—begin to be whiney and eventually develop psychosomatic complaints—in order to get some attention and a share of the privileges.

Many brothers and sisters have wished their sick sibling dead, just to get back to "normal" life as they used to know it before the illness struck. Then when the sick sibling dies, guilt and fear are companions of their days and haunt them at night so they can't sleep. With the parents busy preparing for the arrival and accommodation of relatives and arrangements for the funeral service, the surviving child's behavior may go unnoticed. No one seems especially concerned when the child does not want to attend the funeral, and little do grownups comprehend the inner turmoil such children can go through.

In my group meetings with siblings of terminally ill children, we always talk about jealousy and unfairness. Some of the little ones have great potential for becoming effective psychiatrists! When a little girl came to my office asking desperately for an emergency consultation, I asked her to sit down and tell me why she was so upset and in such a hurry. She told me rather matter-of-factly that tomorrow was her birthday, the first one since the death of her sister. She then went on to explain how she had always envied her older sister, because their mother had allowed her to do anything and everything. And when she, Laurie, complained, Mom would always say, "If you were the oldest, you could do that too." She eventually reached a point when she was daydreaming of her sister's death so then she could be the oldest and number one.

After her sister died, Laurie never again thought about her guilty daydreams until now. She realized, since tomorrow was her birthday, that she was now the oldest and number one. But she could not really enjoy it until she had an answer to her question. But what was her question? Well, she just needed to know if little children grew up in heaven. My very spontaneous answer was, "Well, I don't know why they should not continue to grow. We all grow through life, and I guess we never stop growing and learning through eternity." This was enough to relieve Laurie's mind; she walked out happily, ready to enjoy her forthcoming birthday. Yes, children are so simple, so straightforward, so honest. If we adults could only learn how to become this way again!

Some readers may remember earlier discussions about a little boy at La Rabida, a children's hospital. This boy who needed a kidney transplant was seen shooting little girls down with an imaginary gun. The nurse was very upset with him since she failed to understand the symbolic language of this child's behavior. He had been waiting in vain for a cadaver kidney, but everything seemed to go wrong. Only once had his father taken him out of the hospital for a one-day trip, and on that very day the boy missed a kidney that might have matched. Now he sat day after day, week after week, month after month, waiting for someone to die so that he could get a kidney.

Is it surprising that this boy expressed his frustration by hurrying things along in an imaginary way by "shooting" at some other children? This is a good example of the symbolic language which children use—the boy was "acting out" his need to get a kidney. On my visit I took the boy down to the lake for a while, and together we threw rocks into the water. His emotions suddenly began to emerge as he threw one rock after the other, each one with more anger than the one before. On the way back to the hospital, he looked up and shared something he had never mentioned before. This was that his mom had stopped visiting him altogether since his body had rejected the last kidney, and she had since given birth to a baby girl.

Sadly, adults are often unable to listen and grasp their children's needs and to comprehend their symbolic language. Naturally, this little boy was jealous of the baby girl who he felt had replaced him, and he was angry that Mom was too busy with the baby to share some of her time with him. He was angry that no one was dying in order to give him a kidney so that he could live. He was also angry that the only good day he ever had with his father was the only day when a kidney became available to him.

In short, this little boy was angry over many understandable things, but children's hospitals are usually not good places to ventilate such feelings. He told me later on that any time he is quiet the nurses are nice to him, but when he is mad they want to ship him over to the other hospital. The "other hospital" was University Hospital, "where children are sent when they need an operation or when they are dying."

"I hope I die when they don't expect it, so I can stay with my friends here," he added philosophically. And there are still grownups who believe that children don't understand about death!

Many Aspects of Love

This brings us to another natural emotion: LOVE. What is love? How many people, how many poets have tried in vain to describe it in a few words? Love is the biggest enigma, the biggest problem, and the biggest blessing of all times. It consists of two different facets, both important—in fact, essential —to a full and meaningful life.

In the first year of life, as stated earlier, we need all the physical touching, nurturing, and pampering possible for a healthy development; this is part of love. We need the touching until we die. We need to touch old people more. We need to develop programs where the nursing home patient can be housed with the toddlers of working parents so that both can be touched, loved, hugged, and have an opportunity to share their time and space, their laughter and their tears. Old people would be less likely to drift into senility if they could rock a needy child, spoil a homesick child, tell them stories or build dreams together.

The little hands would explore old wrinkles and find them interesting and lovable. The children would experience unconditional love, a building block for life! It is the development of such mutual services that would help bridge the gap between the generations and do a lot of preventive medicine and psychiatry, and it would at the same time ease the burden of worried working parents. Children who have been touched and loved, rocked and hugged have a good foundation to pass this physical comfort on to others later in life.

Children who are kept in incubators, respirators, iron lungs, or other machines and tubes become inaccessible to touching, and this brings much hardship to parents. They must then find ways to touch the children's skin, wherever and whenever possible. At times a foot rub or a gentle touching of the head is the only possible physical contact, and it should be encouraged whenever it does not interfere with the life-prolonging or life-saving procedure.

The other aspect of love has to do with the ability to say no to a child's dependence and encourage individual development. A mother who ties her child's shoelaces until she is twelve years old does not express love but doubt in the ability of her child to master such tasks on her own. She will prevent this child from learning self-worth, self-love, pride, and self-confidence.

Parents who are unable to say no to a child and instead fulfill his every whim will not strengthen his character but weaken it. Such children do not feel loved and will not develop into confident adolescents who know their limits and can respect them. They will impress us as spoiled brats and will find it difficult to find friends who cater to them as their insecure parents did.

This becomes particularly important for parents of terminally ill children to understand; otherwise they may fall into behavior that disrupts their family life terribly. When parents suddenly realize that Peter is really terribly sick, that he may not survive, that he may never grow up to fulfill his own dreams, they may plunge into a variety of "making it up to him." They feel a mixture of grief and pity, guilt, sorrow, and endless questions about the why's of such a tragedy. The more they indulge the sick child, the more demanding he often becomes, and resentment builds up, not only in the parents but also in the siblings and other members of the household.

In this situation, parents are unable to express their anger at their child's ungratefulness and apparent lack of appreciation, so they often displace it on the other children, who then may ask for some little appropriate favors only to be angrily turned down. This vicious cycle of favoritism and resentment starts at a bad time, when the family is already under stress and has often almost exhausted their energy.

A truly loving parent who does not harbor guilt will simply limit the "spoiling" to more time spent with the sick child, to storytelling and the sharing of memories. If the child becomes limited in mobility or activities, a healthy family would discuss such issues and new problems as a challenge to their spirit of invention and, as a joint adventure, organize games or activities which can be shared by all—the little patient *and* siblings.

One of my most moving experiences was a house call to a little boy shortly before his death. He was blind already as a result of a brain tumor, and his little preschool-age sister gently approached me, explaining that he needed to hear me coming into his room so he would not be startled. She proceeded to present me with a variety of musical toys and instruments which she shared with him. Both parents had shared all the procedures and care with this little girl, and an atmosphere of genuine love prevailed without any sense of tension or anxiety. What a blessing for the little ones to have such early memories! She will grow up with the sense of security and feeling loved.

The Harm of Repressing Anger

Anger is another natural emotion which few adults understand. In its natural form it is a first expression of assertion of will, a simple "No, Mom!" and having an opinion of one's own. If it is accepted in its natural form, the child will develop a pride in his own choices and learn from his own mistakes. It will allow a child to develop into a decision-making individual with self-pride and self-worth.

Many children are provoking their parents' own unfinished business when they assert themselves. They will be bashed, spanked, beaten, belted, threatened, or at least sent to their rooms. Many children are locked up in dark closets or in cellars, or reprimanded in other brutal forms for saying no. Child abuse and child beatings are so prevalent that Americans have no idea how many inner and outer traumas children may be hiding even before they enter first grade.

Children who grow up without the opportunity of expressing their natural anger end up repressing resentment and rage, wishing to retaliate, wishing for revenge, and ultimately, genuine hating. They may appear very meek and obedient on the surface, but like a temporarily dormant volcano, this anger will erupt sooner or later. These are the children who keep up a good "front" and "out of the blue" become very vicious. In their early adulthood, such people may kill harmless, innocent people "for no reason," thereby beginning to express their rage and revenge after having it bottled up for years, sometimes decades.

Their parents' response to such unexpected crimes is total disbelief: "He was always such a good boy. I cannot believe that he did it." Why is this so important to understand? It is my hope that more young parents will begin to comprehend the importance of raising their children by allowing them the expression of natural emotions and showing them unconditional love. If this could be done with one generation of children, we could eliminate places of pornography, most prisons, and many other institutions! We could spend less time consoling families whose children were murdered, fewer hours trying to identify bodies of runaway children in cold morgues, and less time and energy trying to comprehend the ever-increasing number of childhood suicides.

A few examples may suffice to illuminate the problems we have created because of our ignorance and lack of understanding:

Leon was a beloved pediatrician and regarded as the sweetest man on the staff of a large hospital. He attended one of our workshops in order to improve his skills with dying children and counteract a slowly occurring "burnout," as he called it. In our introductory remarks we tried to explain to the group that burnouts are as impossible as the often-used excuse of "the devil made me do it." Burnout is simply a lack of understanding of our own unfinished business, and if we do not lay claim to it, look at it, evaluate its forms and origins, and get rid of it, anyone with similar problems will push our buttons. We then may overreact to it, and since this is not possible in a therapy or counseling session, on a hospital ward or with patients, we repress our feelings and add to the volcano within until it explodes one day in the wrong place, at the wrong time, and toward the wrong people.

During the second day of our "Life, Death and Transition" workshop (which is described in detail in *Working It Through*, Macmillan, 1982), Leon reacted to some screaming from a participant by suddenly hitting the mattress on the floor, and in a regressed state he acted out the beating and strangling of an invisible infant who had apparently brought him to the brink of homicide. After he had relived and actually acted out his homicidal rage by beating a mattress and strangling a pillow, he sobbed and shared a story which had troubled his mind for a decade.

Crying and expressing anger had always been an absolute "no-no" in his family. He grew up with the clear understanding that "good people don't cry, scream, or express anger." He was well-conditioned, and everyone who knew him referred to him as "the sweetest guy," implying "he could not hurt a fly." When he was a young intern, his wife gave birth to their first baby. He was overworked and overtired, felt exhausted by his gruesome schedule at the hospital, and was ill-prepared to take on the new responsibility of being a father.

Since his image had always been "a nice guy," his wife's expectations included that he would help her at night should the baby wake up. In his regressed state on the mattress he relived a moment of total rage that came as a result of his baby's incessant crying. He lifted his young son up in the air, thought of beating him to death, then strangling him, and finally made the gesture of throwing him through the window down to the pavement. In real life he had gone through all these motions and emotions, but a cold sweat and the realization of his homicidal rage stopped him before he could harm his son.

He had never shared the horrors of that night with anyone. Little did he expect that the whole scene would repeat itself one and a half years later when he was a resident and was expected to help with the care of his infant daughter. Leon went into pediatrics and made every conscious effort to become the most caring, loving pediatrician in the hospital. He repressed memories of those two nights and was not aware of the reasons for his professional choice until he came face to face with the "Hitler within."

A greatly relieved Leon shared his guilt, confessed his destructive desires, sobbed out his grief and remorse, and left the workshop in far better emotional and physical health as a result of this catharsis and understanding.

All the repressed little angers of life will eventually lead to a destructive acting out—from kicking an innocent dog to letting our frustration out on an undeserving student nurse, or actually killing a human being who unknowingly triggers some old hurts in us.

Unexpressed anger in little children leads to acting out in often gruesome and sadistic ways on animals, or on other children who are physically weaker or handicapped and who cannot defend themselves. And repressed anger, needless to say, is the cause of our overfilled prisons, our wars all across the world, and the ever-increasing rate of violence throughout our country.

Forgiveness

It is only when children are permitted and encouraged to express their natural anger that they can readily allow forgiveness to express itself. Rolando, a twelve-year-old child suffering from Werdnig-Hoffman's Disease, which affects the neuromuscular system, shared this wonderful experience which occurred a few days after his baptism at church. His baptism was for him a profoundly intense and moving spiritual event. However, certain things occurred which triggered a great deal of anger and brought on feelings of rejection. As he sobbed and trembled with his seething anger, his mother Ruth encouraged him to go into the back yard and "work it out." He asked to be taken from his wheelchair and placed on the ground, and he requested a large kitchen spoon. He then dug a hole and filled it with water. An hour later he called his mom and asked her to get his toy soldiers. She brought them out, fully expecting to witness soldiers clashing and being thrown into the water. Instead, what she witnessed was a sacred and deliberate ritual in which he took the water from the hole and anointed each toy soldier on the forehead.

Chapter 6

Loss as a Catalyst for
Growth and Understanding

A gem is not polished without friction, nor man perfected without trials. —CHINESE PROVERB

CHILDREN WHO GROW UP in a family where a parent has a terminal illness may react in a great variety of ways. Teenagers are usually more affected than very young children, and much depends on the philosophy of both parents and how willing they are to talk openly and frankly to their children about all possible windstorms of life. Children who have been allowed to participate in the death of a grandparent or relative at a young age are usually better prepared later in life when a parent or a sibling becomes terminally ill.

When teenagers respond to the terminal illness of a parent by becoming abusive, promiscuous, or unruly, they need the extraordinary understanding of a nonjudgmental person who can see their actions as a defense against the fear of impending loss.

One woman, who as a child had been callously dealt with by her parents concerning her baby brother's death, had borne pain from it ever since. She related:

"I wrote you a few years ago telling you of experiences in trying to accept life again after a suicide attempt. And I wrote two or three other letters talking about my illness. . . .

[77]

"Why I'm writing is because yesterday I spotted your latest book, *Living with Death and Dying*, and purchased it. I am only starting it, but I wanted to write to you and tell you of my first experience with death.

"I was ten years old when my thirteen-month-old baby brother Danny died. He had a viral infection and became dehydrated. My parents took him to the hospital, and he died an hour after admission.

"I had gone to school, and when I came home for lunch, I asked my mother how Danny was. She told me he was fine. Fine to me meant he would get well. I asked her when he would be coming home, and she told me that Danny had died. I turned around and walked into the living room and stood there. I remember thinking that it couldn't be true, that Danny couldn't be dead. Then I started telling myself that I shouldn't cry—that I was a big girl and big girls don't cry. My mother said that I stood there not moving for almost ten minutes before I came back into the kitchen and cried. I don't remember crying any other time than that once.

"We had Danny at home. I would get up real early before anyone else was up and stand in front of his coffin watching him. Sometimes I thought I saw him breathe.

"The day of his funeral my mother sent me to a neighbor's house. When I came home Danny was gone. No one had told me that he would be gone when I came back. I expected him still to be there. It seemed as if everyone was having a party, and I couldn't figure out why everyone seemed so happy when my baby brother was dead. Four months later we moved into a new house. To me it seemed like two weeks later. I have a complete total blackout of almost four months following his death.

"Thank goodness for your book. I think everyone should have that book. Children should be prepared for death or the experience of death long before they have to experience it, whether it's their own or someone else's. Danny's death was traumatic. It was the start of my becoming mentally ill.

"To me it seemed like my mother got my hopes up for Danny getting well, and then ripped them apart. I have never been able to understand why she told me Danny was fine. I asked her once, and she said that to her Danny *was* fine. He was no longer sick and in distress. But to me, at ten years of age, being dead was not fine.

"No one explained anything to me that I can remember. No one told me that after the funeral they would take Danny away, or I would have told him good-bye when I went to the neighbor's house. I wanted to go to his funeral, but it was decided I was too young for that. When Danny was buried, it was a big secret where he was. It was at least fifteen years later before I knew for sure where he was buried."

* * *

Sharing with Siblings

It is important that children, especially siblings, be allowed and encouraged to share the end with the sick one, if at home, and also to attend the funeral, unless this is against their own desire. One mother wrote concerning her three young daughters, two of whom were affected by the same disease that had recently killed their twenty-one-month-old baby brother. One of the girls, at age seven, had already been hospitalized about fifty times; another at age five, had experienced some four hundred hospitalizations for the disease, which involves rapid dehydration. Their older sister, age nine, so far had shown no signs of the problem.

After the baby brother died, this mother describes how she helped her daughters accept his death: "On the advice of the pediatricians, we took the children to see the baby privately at the funeral home. At that time M. wondered why he didn't sit up and talk to her, and she wanted to give him a kiss. The next day we took them to the funeral Mass at the church, but they didn't go to the cemetery. D. (nine) was very upset at the funeral; L. (seven) has not expressed any feeling either by word or action about the baby's death. L. and M. both know they have the same illness and we felt that L. would be the one most affected by his death. However, we felt that M. (five) would not understand, and therefore we were very surprised at her reaction on being admitted to the hospital three days after the funeral. She did not want to go, as she was afraid she would die. She didn't want me to leave her (which had never occurred before) because I 'left him and he died.'

"Ten days later she was transferred [to another hospital] by ambulance. . . . She was later transferred back. During this time she expressed a fear of dying and didn't want to go into the 'ground' with the baby even though she loved him. Sunday night when she returned home she slept fitfully and was walking around most of the night. Monday she was very quiet and would not go to bed that night. Finally, after much talking, she said she had to check her sisters to see if they were alright as she hadn't checked the baby and he died. She slept with us, waking up at least twice an hour. . . . We feel there are many things contributing to this as well as the death of the baby— her six-week hospitalization right after the funeral, being taken off all her medications which she has been on for three years, and starting kindergarten this week even though she has always gone to nursery school.

"As you suggested, I talked with her about wishing people away. After a while she said she had at times and I stressed that it had nothing to do with the baby's death. Today, she seems somewhat better, more outgoing, less fearful; she slept most of last night and I feel that she will be in her own room in the next day or two.

As I said before, the two girls know they have the same thing the baby had and L. has shown no emotion of any kind —is this normal? Our household certainly hasn't been a normal one with one or the other children constantly being hospitalized for the last four and three-quarter years. . . ."

In my reply to her, I told this brave mother first how much

I admired her for keeping her family together during such a difficult, long time. Her children "behave very normally considering the circumstances they live in. Young children sense the anxieties of their parents, but they also sense when they can calmly talk about these events." She did her little ones a great service not only by taking them privately to the funeral home after the baby's death so they could see him, but also by staying with her hospitalized daughter and reassuring her that she would not be deserted, a natural fear especially at a time of illness. She could also discuss the idea of a possible afterlife with her children, giving them the metaphor of the cocoon and the butterfly, so that they would not have to associate death with being in the ground, but rather up in heaven, where it is very beautiful.

*   *   *

When small children are sick or have to be hospitalized, they are most concerned about being separated from their parents. It is our belief that parents should be allowed to visit their sick children without any limitations.

When children reach age three or four, in addition to the fear of separation comes a fear of mutilation. This is when they begin to see death in their environment. They may see a car run over a cat or a dog and associate death with a mutilated, horrible body. Or they may see a cat tear up a bird. This also is the time when children become very aware of their bodies and are very proud of them. Little boys discover that they have something that little girls don't have; they want to be big and strong like Superman or like their own daddy. When blood has to be taken from them, they scream as if in anticipation of being mutilated. Very often parents bribe their children, promising them all sorts of toys if they don't cry and thus setting a precedent that is especially detrimental to children who have leukemia and similar disorders with remissions and relapses. Children sense very quickly that the louder they cry, the bigger the toy.

We are of the belief that children should be dealt with honestly and openly, that they should not be promised toys for good behavior, that they should be told when a procedure is going to hurt. Not only should they be told what is going to be done, but they should also be shown. We very often use a doll or teddy bear and allow the children to do the procedure on the teddy bear or the doll, so they know exactly what they have to face. This does not mean that they don't cry when they receive injections or when bone marrow tests must be done, but they know that you have been honest with them and they will accept the procedure much more easily than if you had lied to them at the beginning of a serious illness.

It is after this fear of separation and mutilation that children begin to talk about death as if death were a temporary happening. This is a very important concept and one that grown-ups should understand better. I think this fear of death as a temporary happening occurs at the same age children very often feel powerless in the face of a mommy who always says no. They feel angry, enraged, and impotent, and the only weapon that a four- or five-year-old has is to wish Mommy to drop dead. This basically means, for a four- or five-year-old, "I'm making you dead now because you are a bad mommy, but two or three hours later when I want a peanut butter and jelly sandwich I will make you get up again and fix it for me." This is what it means to believe in death as a temporary happening. My own child at four years old responded in a similar fashion when we buried a dog in the fall. She suddenly looked at me and said, "This is really not so sad. Next spring when your tulips come up, he'll come up again and play with me." I believe that it is important to allow children to have this belief, although from a scientific point of view it is not correct. It is like telling a child that there is no Santa Claus when he still needs to believe in Santa Claus.

One mother from California shared her five-year-old daughter's reaction to her brother's death. The mother related that she found it very interesting how obsessed her daughter was

with magic after her brother's death; perhaps she was looking
for a way to make it "all better." Nine months after her son's
death this woman was able to express how her daughter reacted
in a poem.

My Brother's Gone

Daddy says he's gone away
Mama says that he is dead
But he was here just yesterday
I'm not sure what they have said.

Daddy looks so very sad
And Mama keeps on cryin'
This whole thing's awful scarey
All because of brother's dyin'.

His teddy bear sits on his bed
His jammys are in the drawer
It's scarey sleepin' all alone
Be sure to close the closet door.

Daddy says he's in heaven now
I wonder where that's at
Mama says someday we'll all be there
But I'm not too sure about that.

I wish that I were magic
Then, you know what I would do?
I'd make him jump right outa that box
So he could run and play with me too.

But magic isn't real
At least that's what Mama said
So I guess I'll have to sleep alone
And Lancey will have to be dead.

As children get a little bit older, they will begin to see death as a permanent happening. They will very often personalize death—in this country it is the "bogeyman." In Switzerland it used to be a skeleton with a scythe. This is culturally determined. When a child is a little older still, he will begin to believe that death is a permanent happening: After about age eight or nine, children, like grown-ups, recognize the permanence of death.

*   *   *

One of the many, many letters we received from parents, in this case from R.S., a woman with cancer, illustrates how important family sharing and love are to both patient and family. This woman's openness, courage, and understanding brought her family through her own struggle with cancer, complicated by the raising of four children and the attempted suicide of one of them. As in most cases, when we go together through the windstorms of life we emerge with a sense of well-being and pride, as was the case with this family. Her letter:

"I apologize in advance for my typing—I have extensive nerve damage and it is difficult to control my fingers at times. . . .

"I attended a five-day workshop in Massachusetts a couple of years ago. It was a most thrilling experience. I have a terminal breast cancer and was diagnosed when I was thirty-three. My four small children were a tremendous support to me. I respected them with the truth, and they returned the compliment. I have been fortunate to be in remission and have been so for three years. My young children have now reached their teenage years, and I am very proud that I have lived long enough to watch them grow. I have been lecturing and writing articles to help financially. My husband and I were divorced two years after my diagnosis.

"Two years ago, my father contracted lung cancer, and it spread to his brain. After a two-week hospital stay, during which he was in and out of coma, he expressed a desire to come home. Against medical advice and cooperation, we brought him home. He lived long enough for his ten grand-children to find it in their souls to go to him and tell him how much they loved him and how much they would miss him.

"He was particularly touched by my young son, who had no other man to look up to and was very quiet about his feelings. My father had given him a baseball about two years prior to his illness. C., my son, had saved that ball on his bureau and had gone out to buy one from his allowance money. I didn't understand the meaning of his actions at the time, but when he visited my father he brought the ball with him. He asked my father to sign it. My dad was very weak and sometimes didn't even know who he was, but miraculously he woke from his fog and scribbled 'Love always, Bompa.' It was a tender moment shared by both. My dad died in my mother's arms two weeks later. Those of us who could get there in time were there to watch his spirit rise.

"At the workshop I attended, I talked to you about my older brother who would be responsible for my children when I die. He was never able to talk of my illness, nor the death of our younger brother (who died at twenty-three with a brain tumor). I trusted in God as you advised, and since the experi-ence of watching and participating in my father's last days, we have become very close. I thank God for my ability to live, and truly live, one day at a time. He never has failed me when the 'chips were down.'

"I have heard since that week with you of others who talk to 'spirit guides.' I was even told by one woman, who hap-pened to be talking to a group of us and knew nothing of my desires nor my illness, that she saw two guides near me. She asked me if I ever saw my guide, and I had to be honest that I had not. I have wanted to often. I feel so alone, and with four teenagers I often feel helpless. She called me on the phone the next morning really early, and she was out of breath. She had gotten my number from the program planner the night before.

She told me that she was 'visited' and was told that she should tell me about a dream she had. She saw what she called a very powerful guide in white, called Mary, and a little girl wearing a pink dress. She was told that I would need help in the near future and that I should call on these guides. I was very disappointed, for I have yet to feel a presence, much less see anything.

"I did, however, have a major problem within a week. My oldest daughter went into a severe depression and tried to overdose. She was in a coma for twenty-four hours. I feared for her life, for her mental capabilities, but most of all for her soul and mental anguish. When she woke, she asked for her psychiatrist. She had been hospitalized for several months earlier in the year. She said that now she felt good about her life and turned a corner in her attitude. She has accepted my eventual death with as much love as she can give.

"She became very involved with a drug abuse project in town (even though she was not heavily into drugs, she saw the potential for her abuse of them). She gathered her courage and went back to our 'small town' high school, which was very difficult for her. She has been able to make up last year's work and this year's work, and still come out with a B average—something her guidance counselor said would be impossible. She is graduating with her class in a couple of months and has been accepted by a local university to major in psychology.

"She spends time helping other teens in need of someone to take the time to sit and talk. She is quite a young woman, I am very proud."

Starting Over Again

"Dear Elisabeth,

"I'm sitting in my small one-room 'shack beautiful' on the banks of the Moose River in Concord, Vermont, reading my newly received newsletter. My ten-month-old daughter, Laura Mae, is babbling in her crib, moving jerkily as she exhaustedly 'props her eyelids open' for another minute of active life before finally (and hopefully) succumbing to sleep for the evening.

"Last year at this time I was looking forward to attending your lecture in Boston, after having taken part in an LD&T workshop in December. I was very pregnant and anticipating the birth with much anxiety, due to the loss [the year before] of my eight-month-old daughter Erin in a car accident and not knowing if I'd be able to love this child. I spoke with you briefly after your Boston lecture to try to resolve in my mind some things about the birth and death, including that I wanted to have a home birth. I wanted to tell you about the birth and about some of my 'progress' since we last spoke.

"I was unresolved about a home birth until it happened by itself, as I felt a giant burden of making a life/death decision and knew I couldn't handle the guilt if anything happened at home. But, after having been in the accident with Erin and being cooped up in the hospital after her death, I wanted to start this child's life somewhere positive. This cabin is my special place, so when my labor began at 11:00 P.M., I called the midwives instead of the O.B. doctor (I couldn't see waking him up in the middle of the night if I wasn't sure I'd go to the hospital). I figured the midwives could come and be with me while I was in labor, and I'd postpone the decision until a decent hour in the morning. Well, Laura Mae was born at 4:30 A.M. (the midwives arrived at 3:45 A.M.!), and she very sensitively cried with only her head born so I would know that she wasn't dead! She is a very different person/soul than Erin was.

"When Erin was born, I looked into her eyes and connected in a flash with wisdom, very telepathic. That's why she died so 'young'; she was an 'old' soul. Laura seems to be with me in a much more physical way; she's cuddly and makes me feel needed. She also is needful of all the love I have fastened inside me waiting for things to heal a little before I let it all out.

"Laura has relieved much of the physical ache left by Erin's death so that I could concentrate on personal growth in areas of the spirit. Ten days after Erin died, I had a 'vision' in which for four or five hours I was filled with incredible, overwhelming peace and love, during which time I experienced the solution to all worldy problems as unconditional love. At the end of the vision, Erin's face appeared as flickering points of light. She smiled, and then it faded to the then horrible reality of pain.

"Since Laura has filled the pain with her presence, I have been able to realize the potential of this gift more and more, trying to touch ever more often this place within of unconditional love which is God. I have been involved in healing myself through the auspices of a local holistic health clinic, where the most beneficial aspects were yoga and meditation, combined with psychotherapy (by someone who has attended two of your LD&T workshops!). Although I'm not disciplined enough at this point to do regular yoga, etc., at home in cramped quarters with a young baby, I still touch the place inside of me often enough to know I'm doing OK now, and trying to be patient and accept the slowness of the journey.

"The hardest part is not to judge myself for not 'doing meditation'—kind of like not 'going to church'—the everyman's way, which isn't necessarily the only way. I've even been able to stop my aching grief sometimes when I flash into the meditative space of love and experience calm and know I don't have to cry! I still cry, though, to help relieve pressure. It would be so wonderful to *always* be in that calm space, though.... Guess I'll have to wait until I die!

"I can't believe what's coming out of this pen . . . must be the result of 'cabin fever.' We still have lots of snow here....

"To celebrate Erin's life and some of the lessons I've learned since her death, I'm trying to get the courage to send 'Erin's Letter' (you *may* remember? I read it at the December workshop in New York) as a letter to the editor in the local paper. If even one person could be touched by it, it would be a help in this rural area of hard to come by touchings.

"I also have decided what *I* would like to put on Erin's yet to be made gravestone besides names and dates: LOVE IS ALL THERE IS.

"I haven't mentioned my husband V., who is on a very different journey through all of this. Hopefully, we will reach a point soon when we can share all of this together.

"Thank you for giving me confidence in my love for Erin and the experiences involved in her life and death."

The Healing Love Brings

In the summer of 1982, Erin's mother wrote again, and I will share some of her thoughts and feelings, because they will help others to understand the true meaning of "love is all there is."

"I think about Erin often as our marriage seems to end, against my will, which may be my worst enemy. She was our gift of love, and 'love is all there is.' The sign behind the altar in my childhood church school, 'God is Love,' is like a Zen koan—I suddenly understand it! Erin would have been three at the end of this month, and I think of her so often.

"I have read the letter of April 1980 [which follows] over again. I would have loved to have written [it] myself, but I have to give [my aunt] Pat credit for it. When she was typing this letter after the death of our child, the sun broke through the clouds and streamed in through the window onto her, making her certain that Erin had risen. Maybe she waited until she dictated this letter to let go."

And this is the letter that I want to share with you:

"Once upon a time, there was a little angel who lived in God's light. She was wise from living many lifetimes on Earth and from her talks with God and other angels in between times.

"As the saying goes, she was an 'old soul' whose progression to oneness with God was nearing perfection, but she wished to make one more journey to Earth. Her grandmotherly feelings extended to two beautiful souls who had come to Earth for further lessons in compassion, forgiveness, and understanding. The little angel had been with them on Earth before and felt she could influence them by joining them one more time for a short sojourn.

"While looking down from heaven she said to another angel, 'I will join them but for a very short time, otherwise my purpose will not be served.'

"Her angel friend said, 'Are you sure you want to go through the pain of passing again to help those two? I know you love them and have been with them many times, but you are so near to oneness with God now you don't really have to go.'

" 'But I must,' said the little angel, and she did.

"Oh! What joy she brought to the parents. They shared in her birth and marveled at her beauty.

"Her grandparents and great-grandparents saw that her eyes reflected the wisdom of the universe, and they pondered unto themselves on how such maturity and sense of being could be in such a tiny body.

" 'Oh! What an angel!' said great-grandfather. 'Oh! What a darling!' said great-grandmother. 'Oh! How precious!' said grandmother and grandfather. 'Oh! What a glory to have you!' said her aunts and uncle as they romped on the floor with the little angel.

"And then it came time for her to take leave and withdraw from Earth. The plan she made while in heaven for a sudden passing was as unalterable as the seasons and the tide. She had chosen a day recognized by many on Earth as Good Friday. This was an appropriate day, because her good friend Jesus had died on this day hundreds of Earth years before. She and Jesus often talked about soul progression and how hard it is for some people to grow. Jesus had taught her that when a person reaches oneness with God, that person experiences peace that passeth all understanding. The little angel wanted her loved ones to experience this, and her short trip was for that purpose.

"She knew from ages past that recriminations block growth and foul relationships, and that hate absolutely brings negative results. She knew that some situations offer the opportunity to show compassion, if people will reach out to each other with loving hearts. (She knew that love is all there is.)

"It is for this she wished before going into a deep sleep and resting in preparation for her ascension once again into God's light.

"Love, P."

The mother's commentary on this letter was: "I sometimes feel sad that I didn't write this letter, that it was my aunt who wrote it. But it seems as though Erin wrote it, because it seems exactly as my understanding of the vision I had about ten days after Erin's death. I 'know' that Erin is one with love, which is 'God.' "

Rereading this mother's and aunt's communications, it seems clear that Erin's short visit on this physical plane has had many ramifications. It was after her death that the family began much of their spiritual search and evolution, and it is not surprising to me that Erin's life, short though it was, can be the catalyst for the growth of those whose lives she touched.

Love Endures All Things

A letter from a minister's family in Michigan shows that it is possible to experience joy and growth in spite of the fact that two of this family's three children showed early signs of a progressive terminal illness. One child died at the age of six and a half years, weighing only eighteen pounds, and the little one was growing more spastic daily.

"In 1980, we had a little girl we named Joy. She is a real doll. Unfortunately, by January we knew she also has the same neurological disease her sister had. February 15, Bethany died at age six and a half—weighing eighteen pounds. Joy is progressing much more rapidly in her disease, and we are so fortunate to have her here in Midland at the skilled care unit of the hospital. She is really loved by everyone.

"Even after Bethany's autopsy there is no clue about the disease—it is a new one. Thanks to you I had the courage to try again. I have never known such peace. I no longer need to know the reason for all this. Love endures all things. We have learned a great deal from our experiences. We have to live on without these children. At least we have our memories of beautiful smiles, their perfect example of unconditional love, and our very real experience of loving them unconditionally.

"Marty, our son, is eight and doing well. He is so special and sensitive and patient with handicapped children. We're all so different than we would have been. We are so much closer as a family, too. I pray every day for the strength to get through all this. Joy has been declining rapidly the last six weeks, growing more spastic daily. She's a beautiful redheaded, blue-eyed, angelic child. Everyone falls in love with her on sight. . . .

"Joy has been having lots of breathing difficulties and spent January and February in an oxygen tent. She seems improved now. She is very fortunate to be in such a loving situation. The nurses and staff all love her so. We feel very blessed."

Finding Inner Peace

From the teachings of Black Elk comes the following about finding inner peace:

The first peace, which is the most important, is that which comes within the soul of men when they realize their relationship, their oneness with the universe and all its powers, and when they realize that at the center of the universe dwells Wakan-Tanka (God) and that this center is really everywhere; it is within each of us.

This is the real peace, and the others are but reflections of this. The second peace is that which is made between two individuals, and the third is that which is made between two nations. But above all you should understand that there can never be peace between nations until there is first known that true peace which . . . is within the souls of men.

The only way I know how to find the inner peace referred to above is through an honest, ongoing observation of our own behavior. Each time we notice ourselves being judgmental or resentful, we have to ask ourselves: "What is it that I react to?" If our angers and bad moods last hours or days, we have to become honest with ourselves and acknowledge that all bad moods serve only one purpose—consciously or not—and that is to punish. Whom do we want to punish and whom do we punish? It can be anyone or anything, but it puts the responsibility for our pain onto others, or sometimes just back on ourselves. We punish our children with silence or avoidance; we do the same thing with our mates, neighbors, or in-laws. The implicit message is always: I don't want to have anything to do with you.

Our anger can be directed at our destiny, at God, at the world. We will always find enough negative situations to enable ourselves to dwell in a pool of anguish and self-pity, blaming the economic situation of the country, the increased violence, the unemployment rate, the wars—but in reality, all these things are just good for our dissatisfaction and give us "permission" to be unhappy.

If, from time to time, we look at the blessings in our lives, at the warmth and care and love so many people respond with when there is a tragedy, at the fact that we can walk and talk, eat and breathe, then maybe we would reevaluate our bad moods and become aware that all negative thoughts bring with them more negativity, but all love shared returns a thousandfold.

"As a man thinketh" perhaps describes best how we are the creators of our own worlds. One of my favorite patients was a brilliant example of how to look at what we *have*, not what we don't have.

This woman was in her fifties when she was diagnosed as having ALS, a neurological disease that manifests itself with a progressive paralysis slowly ascending the body from the feet until it reaches the respiratory center, the speech centers, and eventually leads to death. This woman's family had earlier decided to respect her wishes to stay at home if humanly possible, and to be cared for in her own familiar environment rather than in an institution. After a time, to help with the patient's care, one of her three daughters took her into the home which she shared with her young husband and soon-anticipated first baby.

This move, which was to a distant part of town, brought with it many adjustments for the patient's husband, who had always been a loving father and hardworking provider for the family. Now he felt unneeded and unwanted, able to visit his wife only on weekends when he was off work. His home was empty in spite of the fact that one of the other daughters visited often and eventually moved in with him.

The paralyzed mother accepted her illness with great faith and peace. She was paralyzed to her neck when her daughter called and asked me to visit. On entering the patient's bedroom, I expected to meet a depressed woman of my own age who only months before was able to putter around her garden, cook, and take care of her shopping. Now she was totally dependent on her children, and her speech was impaired so that I was unable to comprehend what she so desperately tried to share. Her daughter patiently assisted as translator, and the following dialogue will be forever imprinted in my mind and heart:

I asked the woman: "What was it like when you went to sleep one night, knowing that probably tomorrow you would no longer be able to move your arms, hands, and fingers? That you would never again be able to turn a page in a book or ring a bell when you need somebody? What was that like?"

With no hesitation she said, "Yes, one morning when I awoke, my arms were lying dead on my bedsheets. I couldn't move as much as a finger. I could not call either, as you know. My voice went at the same time. So I waited. My daughter finally came and took one look at me and left. For a moment I thought, 'O my God, what if it is too much for my children?' But she reappeared at the door, walked in silently, and without saying a word, put her three-month-old baby girl in my paralyzed arms and left us alone for a moment.

"I thought, 'What if I had been kept in the hospital? I would never have been able to see this grandchild, to hold her, to hear her sounds. . . .' I could not move my body at all, but I was able to turn my head slightly to watch how she was lying there in my arms, a total bundle of health and happiness. Suddenly, she lifted up her little arms and hands and discovered her fingers. With great delight and awe she moved all her little fingers, and I said to myself, 'What a blessing! I had all this for fifty-five years. Now I can pass it on to my granddaughter!' "

What would our world be like if all of us could make a little effort to bless the things we have, instead of cursing our destiny for what we do not have?

Chapter 7

Missing and Murdered Children and Childhood Suicide

Missing Children in America

IN THE UNITED STATES, as previously mentioned, one million children disappear every year. It is an almost inconceivable tragedy for a parent to discover a child is missing, not knowing his or her whereabouts, and wondering if the child will end up as one of the 50,000 children who are lost each year without a trace.

Thousands of these, especially our young runaways, end up used and misused, maimed for life and traumatized. There is no statistic available to tell us exactly how many are murdered, how many end up as voluntary and involuntary prostitutes, not only in our own country but exported overseas to places around the globe where corrupt men and women use them for their own greed and their own pleasures.

An ever-increasing number of these children are kidnapped by a divorced parent. Others are runaways. Many will eventually return home again. Thousands, however, are victims of foul play, victims of murder, suicide, or accidents. Too many others end up following fanatics who try to convince them that their life-style and religion are better than what they can find anywhere else. About one thousand each year are buried by strangers who are unable to identify the dead youngsters.

How long will we wait until we start a registry for lost children, until we start an international network of brotherly teamwork to save our children from things worse than death?

They are seen hitchhiking across the country; they have no money, no specific goals except to run away. Run away from whom? Run away from what?

Suicide among our children is steadily on the increase, not only by teenagers or drug addicts, not only by children whose life history is full of child abuse, beatings, and rejection. Some statistics have shown communities where thirty percent of all the teenagers have attempted or committed suicide. Suicide is the number one cause of death among teenagers and the third highest cause of death among our children between the ages of six and sixteen. As for reasons, there are plenty; for example, twenty-five percent of our workshop participants have been exposed to incest and molestations before they completed high school.

Those are sad figures, and they are on the increase in a country that has more wealth and more blessings, more benefits and resources than any other country in the world.

What are we doing to our children that they would rather die or risk the uncertainty of the life in the street than stay at home? What causes a little schoolboy to take his life? What memories and attitudes cause a seven-year-old to jump out of a window to his death?

What can you and I do to prevent such agonies in our children and in the bereaved families whose guilt and anguish are overwhelming?

We have worked with bereaved families of murdered children, and of those whose little ones ended their own short lives, and have come to the conclusion that much of the tragedy could be prevented if people could allow the natural expression of emotions rather than the suppression of them; if they stopped putting their children in a mold of expectations

by telling them "I love you *if* . . ." I personally believe the
word *if* has killed more children in our times than the war in
Vietnam. And so many Vietnam veterans returned badly
troubled from that infamous war that more of them have died
by their own hands since their return than fell on the battle-
field.

* * *

Alena Synkova, a little girl who was deported to Terezin
concentration camp two days before Christmas in 1942, and
who was one of that camp's few survivors, wrote the following poem:

I'd Like to Go Alone

I'd like to go away alone
Where there are other, nicer people
Somewhere into the far unknown,
There, where no one kills another.

Maybe more of us,
A thousand strong,
Will reach this goal
Before too long.

Fifteen thousand children were deported to Terezin concentration camp, near Prague. Most of the children died only
one year before the end of the war. Only one hundred children returned home alive. What did these children experience?
They knew better than adults about the cruelty of man and
about their destiny. They knew that those who had been
tested by the windstorms of life prior to imprisonment would
have a chance to survive the tortures, the nightmares, the
hunger, and the disease. They also knew that those who had
been pampered and protected by wealth or other circumstances would not have an equal chance. One of the children,
young in age but old in wisdom, described these thoughts and
left them behind for us, the survivors:

Who was helpless back in Prague
And who was rich before
He's a poor soul here in Terezin,
His body bruised and sore.

Who was toughened up before,
He'll survive these days.
But who was used to servants
Will sink into his grave.

Parents of Murdered Children

Parents of murdered children, their siblings, grandparents, and relatives have a much harder time coming to grips with the death of a child than those who were blessed with time for adjustment, time to prepare, and time to grieve. Not only are they bereft of this preparatory phase, no matter how brief, but they are also deprived of the chance for a last good-bye.

The first trauma is the period of time that starts when the child does not return home at the expected time. After initial anger and thoughts about an appropriate punishment, parents' feelings change rapidly to concern and worry. Neighbors are questioned and school officials are notified. Then a search begins in the immediate area the child used to frequent. This is often accompanied by the parents' first feelings of guilt and puzzlement, and an awareness of their lack of knowledge about their child's habits and whereabouts.

Friends can be of enormous help at this time. Friends who were rejected in the past as "not suitable companions" for the missing child have often been the best informants and have not shied away from staying out all night and searching for the missing friend. Parental attitudes about these young people then change very rapidly from a previous judgmental, derogatory view to one of loving and grateful appreciation.

Questioning by police and first thoughts about foul play may trigger some unexpected reactions—a sense of rage and impotence, feelings of despair and impatience. Horror and guilt are intermixed with feelings of losing one's mind, and this is only aggravated by well-meaning people who try to console or advise, judge behavior or offer sedation.

One of the mothers I worked with sat motionless in her living room, too stunned to move or even answer the telephone. When she did, she was reprimanded by her boss for not calling in her absence from work, although this boss was aware that her employee's child was missing. The insensitivity of people is sometimes overwhelming and only adds to the turmoil and despair at a time when families need all the compassion in the world.

One well-meaning minister came to Mr. and Mrs. P.'s home and opened the conversation with "I understand Sonja has left us. The Lord will take care of her." With a patronizing gesture he put both his arms over the parents' shoulders and asked them to pray with him. He was shocked when the father slapped his arm and the mother ran out of the room screaming.

The usual support system is missing in cases like this. When a child has a terminal illness, there are physicians, nurses, social workers, and hospital chaplains who have had contact with the family and who know the participants in the drama. Usually one or the other has been able to get close to the family and to the patient. Friends and neighbors are able to talk, share memories, and help each other grieve over the death of a child. In a common human bond, each has contributed to the sharing of joy and despair, hope and frustration. All this is missing when a child simply disappears.

Families then fluctuate between hope and despair, anger and guilt. They have no one to whom they can express these conflicting feelings. Consolations and expressions of hope are often rejected or misplaced. "Leave me alone" can be expressed in many ways, but it always implicitly says, "You are not helping me."

One woman, Rita, showed a "strange" behavior which was

cruelly judged by her mother, who constantly told her how to behave. Rita methodically went through her daughter's belongings. She opened every drawer in her daughter's room, as if she could find some notes or clues to her daughter's disappearance. She pulled special dresses out and looked at the trophies she had received for ice skating, as if she needed to review her daughter's life in every aspect before facing the possibility of her death. Yet this was Rita's own way of beginning to face the reality and of letting go.

The rest of the family, who watched her, were furious with her. Little did they understand that each human being has his or her own way of coping with stress. In the end, this mother was best prepared to deal with the shock of finding out her daughter had been stabbed to death in a nearby forest. It was as if internally she had already known and prepared herself. She had already prepared her daughter's favorite dress for the casket and put her daughter's unopened diary away to read in "some distant future when I am ready to do it."

The family of little Bella had other problems, ones that made the reality of a vicious and violent crime almost impossible to imagine. They lived in the "projects," a large housing complex for poor families. They had struggled for survival for too long, using alcohol heavily for as long as they could remember, seeing different fathers and boyfriends come and go.

Bella's mother had a date that evening, and Bella was in the way; there was no place for her to go. It was already getting dark and cold outside, and no one would venture out in this neighborhood alone at this time. The family had finished their meager meal, and Bella's mother felt an upsurge of rage at the unfairness that she did not have any free time alone with her newly found friend. The small apartment was full of kids, and at times they really "got on her nerves."

All she wanted out of life was a little happiness, a man who could provide for her and love her. She was told that she had a short life expectation, and she was worried about the welfare of her six little ones, who would undoubtedly be put in foster homes or in an orphanage. That thought only made her shiver, as it brought back memories of her own loveless childhood in such an institution. Now she had finally found someone who seemed to love her, who appeared to care, and who did not mind including the children on an occasional outing to the beach or to Coney Island. Life, it seemed for a short moment, was finally good to her.

She wanted a bedroom of her own. She needed some warmth and intimacy, but it did not seem possible. Just as her friend started to get close to her, Bella appeared and made some silly demands for her mother's attention.

"Why don't you get lost? Get out of my life!" she heard herself scream at her startled little girl. Bella ran out of the apartment, while her mother threw herself on the couch crying uncontrollably.

Later that night Bella was found, dead, sprawled out on the pavement of the apartment parking lot. Some boys were arrested later for dragging her up on the roof, raping her repeatedly, and then throwing her off the roof to the pavement below. Nothing of this "registered" in this mother's mind. She sat in a stupor during the interrogation of her boyfriend and her older children. All she could mumble was: "My baby, my baby." No words reached her troubled mind. In this crisis she passed on to her children what she had suffered from all her life: the feeling of being unwanted, unloved, rejected. Her guilt emerged later on when she "awoke" from the state of shock and numbness, long after the funeral.

She was convinced that she was going crazy, that she was an unfit mother, that she deserved to lose what little good she had in this life. But her boyfriend stood by her, and neighbors who had not previously talked much with her took loving care of and fed her children. They were not taken away from her, because of the help she received from some "Friends of Shanti Nilaya" on the East Coast. She was later able to get in touch with and deal with the "tons" of repressed frustration and grief she felt over the love that she had never experienced in her life, and was therefore unable to pass on to her children.

Seeing gruesome newspaper stories and pictures with detailed descriptions of the horrible sexual assault on her daughter almost brought Bella's mother to the brink of insanity, but another mother of a sexually abused and murdered girl appeared at a crucial time and helped her by sharing her own resolution to this tragedy.

Out-of-Body Experiences

Many people have shared with us during our lectures and workshops around the world a fact that comforted Bella's mother somewhat: that people in a life-threatening and painful situation such as Bella underwent before her death have the ability to leave their physical body temporarily. This is often experienced by those who fall from mountains, as described in the early thirties by Viktor Frankl, who was not yet aware of the phrase "out-of-body experience." Drowning victims also describe a sense of peace and equanimity, when pictures of life pass through their minds and there is no fear, panic, or anxiety. Those are the most frequent accounts of out-of-body experiences in life-threatening circumstances.

From our own material collected over the past twenty years, it seems that the younger the child is, the easier it is for him or her to "simply slip out of its cocoon," as one assault victim later described it. She was able to describe the assaults on her body, the repeated stabbings; she watched them happen with what she described as "no bad feelings, almost a sense of compassion and grief for him." She was later found unconscious and on the verge of death, with over fifty stab wounds all over her body. She survived and now works as a prison counselor, helping to prevent others from having to experience such outbursts of rage against humanity.

Aftermath of Violent Death

Finally locating the missing person is both a relief and an agony. It is a relief in the sense that the waiting, fear, and tortures of wondering what's happened are over; an agony because all hope of finding the beloved child alive and well is gone. If there is mutilation, a viewing of the body is often impossible or at least prevented by those who think it is better not to "disturb" others—how little they know about human nature and human strength.

Once the criminal investigators have done their job and the body can be released to the mortuary, a loving person should prepare the body in such a way that family members are allowed to see the remains, to face that reality: "Yes, this is my son, my daughter." We bandage the parts that are mutilated or expose only the parts that are identifiable, so the next of kin have a last opportunity for a personal good-bye.

We find that those who have had to face sudden death and were deprived of a view of the body have to go through a far longer grief process; they often stay in a stage of denial for years or decades. It is not a total denial, but a partial denial that finds a variety of expressions.

Families whose children have been murdered but whose bodies are never found almost always believe that the murderer's deranged mind may have made a mistake, that their child is still alive somewhere, a runaway or otherwise disappeared, but not dead. This happens even if the murderer gives detailed descriptions of the child.

The siblings of slain children also have a hard time and are often "forgotten" while their parents are in a state of shock and numbness that may last for weeks. In bewildered reaction, such children may be seen putting a fist through a pane of glass or kicking a football across a field in an angry daze. They may have nightmares or be unable to get their homework done. They may be unable to concentrate, going from one activity to another without any effective attention span. They may become very moody and behave unfairly with their friends, and when these friends react, they may feel misunderstood and deserted by their pals at a time when they need more compassion, not less.

Some friend who knows the family and who is not directly involved with the murder (and therefore is less emotional and/or judgmental) should take the time to talk on behalf of the children with teachers, the school principal, and/or counselors to explain the family situation and the children's reaction. The children need a friend, someone who will listen and talk with them at this time. They need extra patience, tutoring, and support rather than ridiculous expectations like the all-too-frequently-heard remark, "You should be over that by now."

How can you get this picture out of your mind? How can you forget that your sister was repeatedly raped, stabbed, or strangled? How can you concentrate on the history of World War II without thinking of violence and destruction and imagine the face of your killed brother or sister? Also, there is a fear that doesn't go away: If it happened to them, it could happen to me. Who do they expect me to be, a robot? A gym teacher or physical education teacher can be of special help to children whose siblings have been killed. The teacher can spend a little extra time in the gym with them, challenging them to hit the punching bag, to use karate, to scream or hit out their rage and impotence on an inanimate object, to let off steam with a bowling ball, a tennis racket, a football, or whatever seems right at the time.

Siblings also have to be prepared for parental shifts in mood that have little to do with *their* behavior. Just as their days during this time of crisis fluctuate from fairly bearable to impossible, so too their parents' feelings change from day to day, from numbness to unexpected outbursts of anger or tears, from a silent, passive indifference toward the world to an enraged and resentful "Get these kids out of my life; I don't want to be reminded!"

Alcohol and drugs are the greatest dangers for parents and young adult family members immediately after such a trauma. The fathers are often obliged to return almost immediately to work, for fear of losing a job but also as a way of pretending that life goes on as before. They throw themselves into work and return home later and later. Or they may be unable to focus their attention and be called up by a supervisor or boss and pressured to "pull themselves together." They may stop by the local bar for a drink or two, suppressing how they really want to respond to the boss's insensitivity. They will be walking "powder kegs," and the slightest provocation from a co-worker may make them blow up.

Everybody around such troubled persons may start "walking on eggs," and then in addition the bereaved suddenly feels isolated and deserted. The spouse may feel similarly or not understand at all, and be unresponsive for a long time to any physical approaches, which only adds to feelings of abandonment.

One man, whose child was purposely driven over by an enraged teenager in a car (the child had been caught scratching something on the hood), was subsequently unable to face traffic and drive a car. Later on he revealed that he feared he would kill someone if any car got too close to him.

These people do not need long psychiatric therapy. They are reacting in an understandable yet unhealthy manner to a mental accumulation of repressed anger, rage at unfairness, and other old "unfinished business." If they receive help immediately from those who have been trained by life, those who understand rather than judge, those who love unconditionally rather than have expectations, they will find a safe place to externalize their pent-up emotions, to shred a telephone book placed on a mattress, to scream out their sense of impotent rage, and they will feel relieved and free of the enormously consuming repression of all these "unacceptable and ultimately destructive feelings." This is the purpose of our workshops, of our mutual support systems, and of our screaming rooms.

Mothers of murdered children may be unable to go grocery shopping for a while, to take their children to the playground in a stroller, or to go out into "the world" at all, because it seems cruel and cold to them. They do not understand why people do not want to talk about their Susy, why they bring up trivialities and worry about the next election. They do not seem to grasp why neighbors stop coming by and old Joe no longer stops to chat when he delivers the eggs. They blame the world for going on as usual. And suddenly, sometimes slowly, they realize that they themselves acted no differently before the tragedy hit.

They may have moments of grim revenge, thoughts of retaliation, a need to get even with the criminal who took their child's life. At the same time they dread that the murderer will be found. They dread the possibility of having to face him in court, of having to restrain their feelings of revenge, their own murderous impulses, and their need to punish him themselves.

They are angry at the judicial system for being so lenient, so slow, so unfair, so prejudiced, so unempathetic to the victim's family. They remember stories from the "Old West" where men of the village took justice into their own hands and lynched people, and they start fantasizing about how they would like to destroy the murderer. They do not yet see that this reaction is similar to the reaction of the accused who, because of some unconscious or conscious feeling of unfairness in his life, finally became a murderer. They do not know at this stage that all human beings have within them the potential to be a Hitler, although they also have the capacity to become a Mother Theresa.

Questionable Cause of Death

One aspect rarely discussed in connection with bereaved parents is a *questionable cause of death.* Our society is still far from fair; our judicial system is still partial and often seems to create more problems than it solves. People with money, name, and prestige still have a far greater chance of committing crimes and getting away without punishment than people who are poor, Hispanic, or black, having neither the money nor the know-how to protect themselves. In fact, many "accidents" are not accidents but suicides. Other "accidents" are not accidents but murders. But since "accident" as an explanation is more acceptable than either suicide or homicide, it is often the easy way out. Things are smoothed over, and the guilty are convinced that as grass will eventually grow over the grave, things will be forgotten.

But bereaved parents cannot forget. They may sense from the beginning that the death could not have been an accident. They may have knowledge and suspicions that no one wants to hear. The authorities and investigators dismiss them and use psychiatric jargon to explain their "paranoia." They will pat them on the back with "I understand your grief and anger . . ." and other patronizing jargon.

No one will listen to parents who feel cheated by the justice system. Their rage and feeling of "crying in the wilderness" demand far more drastic action than the authorities are prepared to offer. And the more and the louder such parents cry for another investigation and justice, the more they will be a nuisance to those who want to go on with their business as usual. Soon they are labeled "unstable, emotionally upset," and are avoided as much as possible. If they lack the resources to hire a private investigator or a caring and honest lawyer, the parents will continue to brood and try to figure out ways to comprehend their child's death.

With the dwindling of funds for legal aid and other public services, this problem will increase. It is an important issue since it breeds discontent, repressed anger, and hate. In due time such repressed frustration and anger lead again to more violent action and to people feeling that they need to "take justice into their own hands." America's prevalent use of handguns may be one of the indicators about people's lack of confidence in our protective agencies and in our judicial system, whereby the little crooks end up in jail and the big criminals are free to roam the country, continuing their destruction.

Childhood Suicide

Suicide in children brings probably the greatest heartache to any parent. It is also one of society's greatest problems, occurring more and more frequently.

Although there are many "hot lines" where desperate people can call day and night and many suicide-prevention centers across the country, we seem to be losing the battle. Suicide among our children from six to sixteen is the third cause of death, and in many communities where we have worked, up to thirty percent of the teenagers have attempted or committed suicide. What is the cause, what can we do about it?

Not long ago, a grieving mother asked me in total bewilderment how it is possible for an eleven-year-old child to kill himself. It was beyond her comprehension, and yet she had the courage to ask, to find out, so as to try to prevent future tragedies of this kind in her family. I asked her about the events prior to her son's death, and she answered very simply, "Nothing happened. He came home from school with a long face. Nobody paid much attention, except for my husband, who confronted him shortly before dinner. He cannot stand long faces at the dinner table. To his father's inquiry, 'What's the matter with you?' our son confessed that he had brought home two bad grades from school. My husband was angry and said, 'So you don't care. If you don't care, we don't care.' He ordered the rest of the family not to look at my son during the meal. My son didn't touch his food and went to his room after dinner. When I tucked my other five children into bed, I tried to teach him a lesson. I skipped his room. You see, he was always a good boy. He was a very normal child who always did what we wanted."

Early the next morning they heard a shot and found him dead. Dead, because he brought two bad grades home from school!

I think this is the tragedy of our achievement-oriented society, that we tell our children a thousand times, "I love you if you bring good grades home. I love you if you make it through high school. God, would I love you if I could say one day 'My son, the doctor.'" And so our children prostitute themselves to please us, to buy our love—which can never be bought! If we could learn that our children are beautiful and lovable even if they do not always achieve, that bad behavior can be disliked and corrected without deprivation of love, there would be far fewer runaways and fewer children in our society who lack self-love, self-worth, and a desire to live.

There are thousands of schoolchildren who come home from school to a cold flat, an empty house, a cold meal, if any, and no one to talk to. A young teenager left a collage with the word "help" and many signs and symptoms of her depression around. No one looked at her clues until after her death, when it was too late. A little Indian boy gave a poem to his classmate; the poem told clearly that he was unable to bear being caged in at a very strict and rigid school. It was passed around two weeks after he was found dead.

Many young children have no recourses and no one to share their troubles with. Many little girls have lived through years of incest and physical abuse, unable to confide in a grown-up because of threats to her life if she did so.

From our first hundred cases of incest involving little children, more than half were threatened with death if they were to as much as insinuate that "something happened to them." Needless to say, they were petrified when left in the care of an abusing father, grandfather, or uncle, and several of them preferred to die of their own choice rather than endure the tortures any longer.

The great majority of people—if they are honest—will

admit to having ruminated at one time or another about "ending it all," about avoiding the misery of their existence. Dag Hammarskjöld expressed these feelings so beautifully in his book *Markings* when he said, "So! That's the way in which you can be tempted to conquer loneliness—and to make the ultimate flight from Life. No! It may be that death is to be your final gift to Life, but it must not be an act of treachery against it." If the desperate child has one human being who cares, one person who can hear the often non-verbal plea for help, a disaster can often be prevented.

A little boy who sat forlorn on a sidewalk here in Southern California finally consented to talk to me when I simply sat by his side and waited until he was ready. After a few moments of general talk, I asked him straightforwardly what he was running away from. He shyly lifted his shirt and showed me a chest covered with old and fresh wounds caused by a hot steam iron. He then almost matter-of-factly told me that his mother would punish him again when he went home, and that he decided to run away. He could not quite decide which direction to take, and I offered to take him home. When a car stopped at the curb, he suddenly took off like a jet and was gone. All my efforts at finding him failed. Do we know how many of our children are suffering and we live right next door?

How many of us have ever looked at our own judgmental attitude when it comes to suicide? Have you ever watched hospital personnel when a suicidal youngster is brought in for the third or fourth time to an emergency room? The anger and hardly disguised disgust when the nurses have to pump the same child's stomach for the third time because of an overdose of sleeping pills are often recalled by a young patient years later. Why do they make us so angry? Is it because we are overworked and would rather work late hours with someone who wants to live? Do we ever take time out of our busy schedule to find out what inner pains, loneliness, and agony preceded the suicide attempt? Do we ever really find out whether they have one human being who can truly help them when they are discharged? Do we try to get to know the true circumstances, the family, the friends—if they have any?

A little boy was brought to my home one afternoon to show me some of the pictures he had drawn. He was pale and monosyllabic and obviously wanted to please. He waited to sit down until asked, did not touch the cookies until encouraged, and took the sheet of paper only when I put it under his nose. While we were drawing together, he started to talk, first very hesitantly, then more freely, until I had put the puzzle together.

This boy was six years old and he had already tried to kill himself more than a dozen times. He was caught running onto the train tracks when a train approached, he tried to drown himself in a bathtub, and recently he had attempted to jump out of a five-story building only to be rescued by an observant janitor. He had been abandoned by his mother and shipped from foster home to foster home. He had been beaten until he could no longer sit. He had been locked up in closets for full days only to be punished for wetting his pants while he was in his dark imprisonment.

The last family he had stayed with was nice to him, but when the foster mother was diagnosed as having cancer, he was taken away again. A lovely couple wanted to adopt him, but they did not fit into the stringent requirements of the adoption agency. Husband and wife had different religious beliefs, and it was thought that this was not a good way to bring up a child.

When will we begin to realize that love is all that counts? When will we begin to realize that all human beings, like plants, need nurturing, light, love, and compassion and understanding to grow, to thrive, and in turn to become loving, caring parents for the next generation?

*   *   *

This poem was given to a teacher by a twelfth-grader. Although it is not known if he wrote the poem, it is known that he committed suicide a few weeks after giving in to her.

He always wanted to explain things, but no one cared.
Sometimes he would draw and it wasn't anything.
He wanted to carve it in stone or write it in the sky.
He would lie out in the grass and look up in the sky
And it would only be him and the sky and the things
    inside him that
Needed saying.
And it was after that he drew the picture.
He kept it under his pillow and would let no one see it.
And he would look at it every night and think about it.
And when it was dark, and his eyes were closed, he
    could still see
It.
And it was all of him. And he loved it.
When he started school he brought it with him.
Not to show to anyone, but just to have it with him
    like a friend.
It was funny about school.
He sat in a square, brown desk
Like all other square, brown desks.
And he thought it should be red.
And his room was a square, brown room
Like all the other rooms.
And it was tight and close. And stiff.
He hated to hold the pencil and chalk.
With his arm stiff and his feet flat on the floor, stiff.
With the teacher watching and watching.
The teacher came and spoke to him.
She told him to wear a tie like all the other boys.
He said he didn't like them.
And she said it didn't matter.
After that they drew.

And he drew all yellow and it was the way he felt
   about morning.
And it was beautiful.
The teacher came and smiled at him.
"What's this?" she said. "Why don't you draw like
   Ken's drawing?
Isn't that beautiful?"
After that this mother bought him a tie.
And he always drew airplanes and rocket ships like
   everyone else.
And he threw the old picture away.
And when he lay alone looking at the sky,
It was big and blue and all of everything,
But he wasn't anymore.
He was square inside, and brown,
And his hands were stiff.
And he was like everyone else.
And the things inside him that needed saying didn't
   need it anymore.
It had stopped pushing.
It was crushed. Stiff.
Like everything else.

Chapter 8
Alternative Treatments: Visualization

WHEN TRYING TO DEAL with long-term illness in children, such as cancer, many desperate parents have looked for help outside the typical medical scientific mode. Most parents have been rejected by their physicians and received a rather angry response from them, as if they had suddenly become "their enemies."

In the future, with the growth of new holistic ways of thinking and caring, more and more families will be able to help each other, finding care and help for their little ones and themselves, too.

Simonton has been a wonderful role model in introducing the techniques of visualization, a method very often used by cancer patients in addition to the chemotherapy or other more "acceptable" treatments. Since many adults feel that children don't understand the meaning of visualization, I asked one of the mothers who has used this additional help for her little girl to summarize her own experiences with the more modern methods, and here is her letter:

"The following is a brief narrative of my work with my daughter, Lyndsay, who was two and a half years of age at the time. We utilized many methods of holistic medicine and natural remedies which helped immensely. She was usually very cooperative and seemed to 'know' these things helped her 'well' time be much better. We had a beautiful last year together.

"In August 1979, I was informed that Lyndsay's cancer had returned and was very bad in the bone marrow as well as a large tumor in her abdomen. We resumed chemotherapy again, but I felt in order for her to survive we had to do something more. The year before I had attended a holistic health conference at the University of California in San Diego. One of the workshops I attended was with Steve Halpern, and I learned about the use of color and music in therapy. On and off for the whole last year Lyndsay fell asleep at night under a turquoise light and listening to Halpern's 'Spectrum Suite,' which came to be known as 'Lyndsay's music.' I chose this because it was quiet and nondirectional, and having experienced a 'Spectrum Suite' meditation at this workshop, felt it would be good to help restore balance and therefore health to the body—the light was for healing and had a tranquilizing effect.

"I started Lyndsay doing active relaxation with me. We would prop up some pillows and get comfortable—sometimes after a session of giggling and wrestling around. We would start by relaxing the feet, then the legs, and so on up the body—until 'the whole body is relaxed.' She would usually keep her eyes closed. I would sometimes ask her to tell me what she saw with her eyes closed, and she had an excellent imagination. To show her what 'relaxed' meant, I first showed her how to tense a muscle and suddenly let it go and get real loose—and also used her Raggedy Ann doll. She thought this was great fun, but would be very serious about it sometimes and worked very hard.

"After we got relaxed, I would lead her by saying, 'Now breathe in the magic from the air and send the magic all through the body—the magic will help make your "owie" all better and help Lyndsay feel all better again.' I would ask her if she needed to send the magic somewhere in particular, and she would usually respond 'my tummy.' She usually slept at night under a turquoise light, but sometimes during this relaxation I would turn on a pink light. We would talk about what love is and use the pink light as a reference point, and breathe in pink-love and send it all over the body—and that would make Lyndsay warm and happy. We would always be visualizing the owie going away and Lyndsay becoming 'all better again.' I remember asking her how the 'magic' felt, and she usually described it as 'warm' and sometimes 'tickly.'

"I had seen an article in the paper the year before about a Simonton-trained psychologist in Phoenix who worked with cancer patients and had mentioned something about working with children, so I called him and made an appointment for him to meet Lyndsay. The youngest child he had ever dealt with was fourteen, but he and his associate agreed to help me all they could—and did not charge me for the few consultations that we had. We fixed up a pair of soft yellow booties like mittens, and embroidered a blue face on one to represent Lyndsay's 'helpers' and a red face on the other to represent the 'medicine.' The psychologist was interested in the process, but his young intern associate was much more helpful. They also gave her a copy of the children's book, *There Is a Rainbow Behind Every Dark Cloud.* She was only a little past two and a half at that time, but she definitely related to that book and made comments all the way through every time we read it. It really helped her with her visualizations.

"Initially we used a green chalkboard with white chalk and drew a picture representing Lyndsay. We would do our relaxation exercise (or whatever part she would sit still for—she was always anxious to get to the board) and then go to the board. She knew that 'helpers' lived inside her and were a very important part of her body which we called 'white cells,' and that they had much power in getting rid of the owie. The helpers were depicted as round smiling faces with a long pointed nose and a big mouth. The nose would jab into the owie, and the big mouth would gobble some down until the owie was 'all gone.'

"I would (or Lyndsay would) draw a smudgy chalk mark on the board approximately where the main tumor was (just over the right kidney). She would then put on her mittens and really work to erase the owie until all traces were gone. Sometimes (just before chemo), we would make a mark where the medicine went in and trace its route to the site of the owie, and show it working to help get rid of the tumor. She would use both hands together and understand that the medicine and her helpers worked 'together' to make the owie go away—and help Lyndsay to get 'all better.'

"At the end of the sessions we would leave the helpers all busy at work and erase them, and then dress the baby in a pretty dress and draw hair on her, using colored chalk. A big smile was made bigger, and the final picture showed Lyndsay happy, healthy, and all better, with a new growth of pretty curling hair. One time when a photographer was there Lyndsay spontaneously went over to her and gave the 'baby' in the picture (herself) a big kiss. She did this several different times. Another thing she did one time when she was really getting into erasing on the board: she suddenly threw it down and jumped up and down on it—really 'getting rid of that owie!'

"It was hard for us to do this routine three times a day sometimes, since Lyndsay was at a baby-sitter's while I worked part time, but that was our goal. In between she would often climb on my lap and place my hands where it hurt. This seemed to make her feel better, and then she would get back down and go on playing.

"More often, however, she would utilize the lap of her 'Aunt Carol,' who was a friend who came by to baby-sit for her on occasion and give her 'healing.' Lyndsay seemed to know that Carol was the person to go to for healing, and on one occasion in particular she let it be known that there was no doubt about what she was doing or why.

"At the end of that last summer together and on our way back from a trip to Colorado, we stopped in Flagstaff to visit her adopted 'Aunt Carol.' Lyndsay immediately ran and jumped onto Carol's lap and very pointedly placed Carol's hands where she wanted healing. Carol told Lyndsay that she didn't need the healing, that her cancer was all gone. Lyndsay looked up at her and replied, 'No, Carol, the owie is not all gone. It has come back, and Lyndsay wants it to get all better.' It turned out that she was right, unfortunately, but she went to Carol every chance she got after that time for healing.

"There were other healers that worked with her also, and Lyndsay always seemed to let them know that she knew they were trying to help her and often gave them some acknowledgment of the benefit she received from the experience. Because of these experiences with Lyndsay, I hope that someday our health caretakers will not downplay the importance of the exchange of healing energies, because even babies and toddlers are especially open and receptive to this type of healing. Many times I and others have witnessed Lyndsay feeling punk and in pain, and after a healing session jump down from the lap feeling good and going back to her play, happy and apparently rejuvenated.

"We were getting ready to go to California to get some new medicine that I told her would really be powerful and help more than ever. We started using colored chalk at this time, coloring in her helpers with a bright yellow to make them 'stronger and stronger,' and would draw the helpers working away all over the body to make it perfect.

"(This is an aside—I was taking her to Mexico for Laetrile. I knew it was probably too late for it to help much, but the day before we left the hospital took an X-ray, and they could find nothing there at all! I did not intend for her to have Laetrile intravenously. Her veins were exhausted, and I felt since it seemed to be under control again we could go with the pill form. I promised her *no more shots*—this is *very* important—and I feel explains what happened a few days later.)

"When we went to the new clinic for the new medicine, she was feeling so good she even fooled the doctors there. We discussed her case, and they admitted they had not had much luck with neuroblastoma—as it was usually so far advanced when found. I made the decision to go with the pills only—I did not know it at that time, but she could have had Laetrile by rectal implants, and I could have learned to do it myself. I did not have the money to stay there for the three-week routine but felt I did not have any choice because I had promised her no more I.V.'s. They encouraged me to try another new medication which was something that might help trigger the immune system to be more effective. Since her cancer was one that is believed caused by a congenitally faulty immune system, I agreed to try it. It turned out to be a very painful shot in the leg. Because these shots were needed daily and I was staying with a friend back in San Diego, they showed me how to give the shots and said I could do it so I wouldn't have to come back every day. Then after that she could go on the pill form of it.

"The next day was the beginning of the end. I can't stand shots myself, and I had a terrible time giving her a shot. Of course she fought me. I had to hold her down, then ended up hitting a vein, and it bled some. It was very traumatic, and I was sick at my stomach for doing that to her. Nothing I could say helped. She looked at me in total desolation and disbelief and would not talk to me—but looked at me as if to say, 'Now you too, Mommy?' Thereafter she would not touch her chalkboard again. As a matter of fact, I saw her several times in anger put her fingers in her mouth, wet them, and claw the face of Lyndsay on the board. She turned the board to the wall and refused to work on it ever again. She became very withdrawn and seemed depressed and introspective, as if listening or feeling something going on inside her—she was in a 'different space.' I was terrified that she had given up. Within a matter of a few days she seemed to be experiencing pain and was feeling lousy, not eating and just lying around. However, while we were still in San Diego, and even after I had given her a couple of shots (which I promptly stopped), some friends came to visit, and she ran into the bedroom and brought out her chalkboard proudly—for all to see.

"We were gone only one week, and although there was no trace of tumor, according to X-ray, the day before we left she became terribly sick and had to go immediately into the hospital upon our return to Phoenix. She never had a chance to go with the Laetrile pills. Another X-ray showed the growth rapidly increasing, and an obstruction was feared because she could not even keep water down. The next day she was given a dose of a relatively new chemo drug, went into renal failure, then congestive heart failure, and died three weeks later—all resistance having been thoroughly destroyed. (Incidentally, we did use some liquid Laetrile via rectal implants during those last weeks, and it did help alleviate much pain and enhance general well-being—she was even still trying to eat the day she died. The night before she died the tumor appeared to have shrunken considerably.)

"I 'knew' the day she turned her board to the wall and clawed the face that she had turned her anger inward destructively, because now even her own mommy was hurting her (with shots)—I believe she gave up. Perhaps if she hadn't received the fatal dose of chemo, we might have had at least a few more months. She fought so hard and even asked to see the doctor and get some 'new blood' several times—because she knew the new blood helped her feel better. Her time with working on the board was cut prematurely short, but I believe it was a powerful and effective tool during the short time we did use it, which was perhaps two months. It seemed to be very important to her, and she looked forward to the sessions.

"In an isolated incident, she had occasion to see one of her X-rays at the hospital, and I showed her on the X-ray where the owie was. In the room was a huge Dumbo elephant painted on the wall with Timothy, the mouse, carrying a red flag and sitting on his nose. I told Lyndsay to imagine her helpers now carrying red flags like this and charging the tumor, like an army, and really mowing it down. She then used the red flags after that on her own. There were so many different little things that happened, it's hard to remember them all, but they were all important in the overall picture. Even though she did not have the vocabulary to communicate, she understood probably more than I'll ever know, and let me know in so many ways what was happening to her—and preparing me for what was to come.

"One day toward the end she scribbled all over her board—and was showing me where the cancer was. I tried to stop her from doing that because I felt it was negative programming, but it turned out several days later (through hospital tests) that she was right, and I was dumbfounded. I had never believed, at least consciously, that she would possibly die. She could have very easily died the year before, but I believe she knew I wasn't ready. And while I was doing everything in my power to help her live, she was gently helping me grow and understand. She simply would not 'go,' until it came down to the day I had to tell her it was 'OK,' and I had to literally talk her out of the body. I experienced my death and rebirth on the same day she did."

Special note: "Five days before Lyndsay died she experienced an unusual seizure. She had evidently inhaled a breath but could not exhale, and the air was stuck in her. She started to panic and was terrified. She threw her head back and started struggling to breathe. I had Shawna turn her 'music' up and said, 'Lyndsay, listen to your music and relax the body.' I kept my voice even and calm, and started the relaxation exercise.

"Her eyes were glued to mine, and she was trying desperately to follow instructions. We quickly went up the body, starting from the feet, and when we got to the chest area she was able to expel the air and start breathing. This was not an epileptic attack but might have been something similar, because her jaw was clenched and her body became somewhat rigid—but she was definitely experiencing respiratory distress.

She maintained 'eye contact' with me, however, and acknowledged she 'understood' what I was saying and quickly followed my instructions. I was holding her on my lap and told her not to be afraid and to 'let the body go and get loose and relaxed.' It also terrified me because I thought she was dying—violently—but I realized when she made and held eye contact she was asking for help and responding. I absolutely believe that her prior training with relaxation saved her life in this crisis situation, and helped her get control and let go of the fear."

* * *

A therapist who became very much part of a family at the time of their son's dying used hypnotherapy as an adjunct to his treatment. In his own words:

I suppose Jean told you something of my use of hypnotherapy with David, initially for control of vomiting, and later for control of pain and anxiety. This turned out to be an especially useful tool, with David being able to use self-hypnosis even during the last trip to Texas. He and his mother worked together very creatively even on a new problem—appetite control, related to high-dose steroids.

The several references in the Christmas Day tape to David finding his peaceful place relate to hypnotherapeutic work in which I suggested once to him that he might have a pleasant dream concerning feelings of comfort and safety. He then had a hypnotic dream concerning feelings of comfort and safety. He had a hypnotic dream of being an eagle that could fly easily from one safe and happy place to another. If at any time the eagle was disturbed, it could immediately fly away to another place still more comfortable, still more peaceful. David used this imagery subsequently.

These experiences with hypnosis were not only helpful for their immediate intended purposes, but also gave both David and his mother a sense of control and mastery that they had not had previously. Jean has told me how much she had dreaded feeling helpless and passive, having to rely on drugs or machines or experts—and how relieved she felt when she knew she and David had a tool through which they could become much more active in mastering difficult situations. (Of course, many people feel that a person in hypnosis is passive, but those who have experienced it know quite well that just the opposite is true.)

In the last decade we have seen many parents using meditation and visualization as hypnotherapy to alleviate pain and anxiety in their children with terminal illnesses, and we strongly believe that parent groups should encourage these additional means and get training and assistance so they can become acquainted and comfortable in its use, as long as they are themselves in a good physical and emotional state.

Guided relaxation and meditation resources are plentiful; for example, Stephen Levine's workshops and books, as well as his personal visits with dying patients, have been another most useful and beneficial help to many.

Steve Halpern's albums on music and color healing have been a great help to some of our patients, as well as Thomas Roberts' and G. Hendricks' books on relaxation for children. Both Dr. Charles Stroebel's book and his cassette tapes for adults (called *The Quieting Reflex*) use guided relaxation, and Liz Stroebel's stress management cassette program with children, called "The Kiddie Q.R." (Quieting Reflex), endorsed by the National Educational Association, can be tried for exhausted parents and children.

Any hypnotherapist who works in collaboration with the treatment team can tailor-make a tape or approach to adjust to any child's special need.

The Ronald McDonald Houses, which were created for the accommodation of children with terminal or life-threatening illnesses and their parents—who often come from faraway places to be near a well-known treatment center—could be accommodated with a library of resources of this nature, and with a group of volunteers to make the waiting time between hospital treatments a fruitful and growth-producing time. It would be mandatory, naturally, to screen these contributors in order to eliminate charlatans and unethical "do-gooders."

There is so much we could do for our children and family members if our narrow-mindedness and blinders did not constantly get in our way.

Chapter 9
Children's Inner Knowledge of Death and Their Symbolic Language

AN ANONYMOUS PRAYER credited to the Sioux Indians reveals the universal knowledge of death as a transition to a different form of life. It was sent to me by a friend who knew of my interest in the spiritual knowledge of ancient cultures.

Sioux Prayer of Passing

Never the spirit is born
The spirit will cease to be never
Never the time when it was not.
End and beginning are dreams
Birthless and deathless and changeless
Remains the spirit forever.
Death has not touched it at all
Dead though the house of it seems.

Children's inner knowledge of death has been verified to us in a multitude of ways. In my early days as a country doctor in Switzerland I visited many children with tumors, heart disease, leukemia, and other life-threatening diseases. In those days very little was written about this topic, and the village physician had to depend mainly on his or her intuition and common sense in response to the patient's inquiry.

One night I ended up my house calls by stopping at the home of a little girl who had been quite sick for months and who seemed to respond poorly to her treatment. Her parents and her older siblings were busy with the harvest, and her mother only occasionally took an extra break to look in on her little girl. The little one was therefore tended to by a great-grandmother who was almost completely deaf and suffered from very poor vision. From a practical point of view she was a poor caretaker, yet she proved to be the best possible nurse and companion for our little Susan.

Granny sat with Susan all day long, although it seemed that she took frequent naps whenever my little patient dozed off. She must have had some extrasensory perception, as she was always totally alert and attentive whenever Susan awoke. Then Granny touched her gently to show her that she was aware of her awakening, and would patiently give her little sips of fluid through her dried lips, without ever pushing her or forcing her to eat.

I could have watched those two for hours. I often listened to the old woman's stories, which she must have made up from a mixture of old memories and an inner knowledge of the things to come. Her eyesight prevented her from reading storybooks, but her stories were far more exciting and inspiring than any books I ever read as a child or grownup—and I have read many! Granny seemed to know things that were going to happen, and her stories always seemed to be preparations of things to come.

Susan asked Granny a million questions at first. Later on, the questions became few. On the last day of Susan's life, which Granny must have foreseen, Susan simply asked her if she would "visit her soon." No one except Granny would have understood that question at that time. She gently touched her great-granddaughter's hand and said, "But, naturally, you know my frail old body is not going to last much longer. But I guess it keeps going while you need me here. Soon we will be together and, guess what? I will be able to hear and see, and we will dance together."

Granny knew that I witnessed this conversation and gave me an almost impish smile. Did she know already that one day I would understand and really know what these two special people shared on that day? Did she simply acknowledge my presence and include me in her teaching, knowing that every bit of help was appreciated and that those special, quiet moments made my work very beautiful and wonderful? How little I guessed in those days, thirty years ago, that it would be the very old and the very little ones who would become my teachers.

Granny got Susan's special dress ready and asked her mother not to go to work the next morning. There was such a wonderful understanding in this family. Breakfast was taken together, and a few moments after their morning break the father called to tell me that Susan had died.

As it was the custom in those days, the family washed and dressed Susan. The neighbors made a casket, and the village people came one by one to pay their respects. The body was kept in the "good" living room in full view of the kitchen and the dining room. Friends and neighbors, classmates and teachers came to say good-bye.

The village supplied the hearse and horses, and almost everyone walked behind the casket to the church and cemetery. The school children sang a song, the minister gave his sermon, the grandfather and one of the family's best friends said a few moving words, and the casket was lowered into the earth. Brothers and sisters, friends and neighbors put handfuls of earth on top of the casket and filled the hole.

Granny stood during the whole outdoor ritual and skipped only the meal held in the village restaurant, which was overflowing with relatives, friends, and neighbors. It was late at night when her family finally returned home. Granny had a little stroke, and on her begging was permitted to stay home to recover. I took care of her as much as was necessary.

My visits to this home became a treasure to me. They continued long after Granny had joined little Susan, and the family still sends me Christmas cards and looks forward to an occasional greeting from their "doctor across the water."

It is a gift to be a physician in the country, where life is still simple in many places and filled with love, work, sharing, and enough "grannies" who pass on their love, faith, and care to the younger generation, so they one day will be able to do the same for their children and their children's children.

I am sure, unbeknownst to me in those days, that Granny was one of my oldest teachers, and together with the many Susans I have cared for, they have imprinted on my mind that death can be as simple and as uncomplicated as life is—if we don't make a nightmare out of it.

Children's Symbolic Language

Another mother, whose sixteen-year-old daughter fell from a horse and died, shared a picture that her daughter had painted. The symbolism in this picture makes one wonder if the girl knew of her impending head injury, as do the poems that she wrote, which are not only touching but very revealing. The first one, without a title, was found the day after she died. It was on a loose sheet of paper she had put in her journal, which she had taken with her on her vacation.

I'm quite a child you know
Lost somewhere in between the lilies and the lace
and never in my life have I

approached you without
first retreating.
        All the better I believe
For you, at any rate.
        You wait, you'll see just what
I mean
     When I shatter into thousands.
     You've never been so scared
in all your life
And never so rewarded.

Mother

How do I touch you?
You are so fragile, so easily broken . . .
Yes, I do love you, but I am at the age of revolution
and how do I revolt?
If I leave you now, what will become of us?
Can't you see that I must love you from a distance?
I can no longer be your support;
My shoulders are burdened with my own weight as it is.
You frighten me now, weeping for your sons . . .
What shall you do when I, your only daughter, takes her turn?
Your love is strong; but rejection comes so easily.
How can I leave you and still know that you will feel me
                           by you?
If you ask for my touch, and I cannot give it to you,
   will you understand?

A Dream I Have Had More Than Once

I am walking through a parking lot, a large one in front of a mall of twenty or thirty stores. There is no one there except me. It is dark, early morning. I can hear every move I make echo. It's cool.

I see a man standing in the distance and, as I do, we are for a split second transferred to a sunny field, but then back again.

So quickly it's as if it was only in my imagination. I approach him. He is tall. His hair is blond, his eyes very dark. He is very tired. He is Jesus. I don't know how I know this, but I do. By now I'm within a foot of him, and I stop. He is wearing blue jeans, no shirt. His skin is very smooth. He looks very sad, as if he were saying good-bye to me, and then he takes both my hands and starts to cry. I start to cry, too, because I don't know *how* long it's been since I've seen him and even now I miss him. He wets the backs of my hands with his tears, then goes, saying, "You don't have to come to me for me to be here. I am here for you when you need me." When I'm alone again I sit on a curb of the mall and cry hard. I stay there till the sun rises, then get up, and slowly walk away. . . .

Wish

I wish for life when life is over,
I wish for death when death has come.
But being on the brink of both and neither
I wish only to complete what I've begun.

I am a myth, a vision of a vision,
I am a trailing shadow growing small,
An extension of mechanical precision,
A cry, a scream . . . a jump before a fall.

These were written by Mary Hickman in the spring before the summer of her death, and found after her death.

* * *

A mother from the East Coast shared another experience with us, and I will simply transcribe her unedited letter, which speaks for itself.

"My daughter woke up early that morning in a state that can only be called 'extreme excitement.' She'd slept in my bed that night, and I was awakened by her hugging and shaking

me, saying, 'Mom, Mom, Jesus told me I'm going to heaven! I
enjoy to go to heaven, Mama, and it's all beautiful and gold
and silver and shining, and Jesus and God are there. . . .'
etc., etc. She was talking so fast that I could barely follow
her. Almost euphoric. This scared me—first, by its strange-
ness. Surprise, not what you'd call a common topic of conversation.

"I was affected mostly by her excitement. R. was by nature
a calm, almost contemplative child, extremely intelligent, but
not a child much given to 'wildness,' bounding-about-silliness
that many four-year-olds get. She was also verbally skilled and
very precise with her speech. To find her so excited that she
was stammering and tripping over her words was very unusual. In fact, I don't remember *ever* seeing her in such a state,
not at Christmas, birthdays, or the circus.

"I told her to hush, slow down, not talk that way (mostly a
superstitious fear on my part). I'd had a 'feeling' since she was
born that she somehow wouldn't be with me long (I'd never
mentioned it to anyone but one close friend). I didn't want to
be reminded of it, and I didn't want to hear her speaking of it,
certainly not in this *sudden*, out of the blue, wild manner.
She'd never, ever talked of dying except in an abstract way,
not of her death before.

"I couldn't succeed in slowing her down. She went on and
on, telling me of this 'beautiful golden heaven, with wonderful
things and gold angels and diamonds and jewels, Mother.' And
how happy she was going to be there and how much fun she'd
have, and how Jesus had *told* her. Very emphatic, so excited
that she was difficult to follow. I remember her manner and
content more than her actual words, except for some.

"I said, 'Honey, wait, settle down now,' and begged her
back, 'If you went to heaven, I'd miss you, honey. And I'm
glad that you had such a happy dream, but let's slow down and
relax a minute, OK?'

"It didn't work. She said, 'It was *not* a dream, it was *real*' (in
that emphatic way that four-year-olds have), and then, 'But

you don't have to worry, Mama, 'cause Jesus said that I could take care of you, and I'm going to give you gold and rubies and precious stones, and you won't have to worry about anything, and you'll really like the gold and rubies and precious stones. . . .' and on she went. (I'm putting in quotations only those portions I remember rather positively word for word; the rest of the conversation I remember well in gist but not in word-by-word context.)

"This is basically what she said. She continued for a while, talking about how wonderful heaven was (gradually becoming calmer), and when I again complimented her on her lovely dream, she said it was not a dream but was 'really, really real,' and laid in my arms for a while and said I shouldn't worry 'cause Jesus would take care of me, climbed out of bed, and ran off to play.

"I got up, too, and fixed breakfast. We had a normal day, but somehow between 3:00 and 3:30 that afternoon, R. was murdered (by intentional drowning).

"The conversation with my daughter that morning was so surprising that I mentioned what I called my daughter's dream to at least one other person that morning. This person remembers the conversation. One of her first thoughts when she heard the news of R.'s death was 'How could R. have known?'

"My personal belief is that it is *not* possible for people to know the future—the laws of physics will not bend. It was *not possible* for R. to have known that she was going to 'go to heaven.'

"And yet this did happen. My daughter woke in a very unusual state of great excitement and claimed that Jesus told her she was going to heaven (I honestly don't remember if she said 'today'). And she was dead that afternoon. I can't explain it.

"We did not have a religious household as such. My daughter went to church with us twice, and of course we read stories of Moses and Jesus and Mary and Joseph. They did attend a Sunday school irregularly. I tried to teach my children love and respect for all, kindness and caring, rather than a religion, because I had no way to teach them what I do not know. I've studied and learned, prayed, meditated, and for the life of me I do not know!

"When the girls asked about heaven, I always told them I didn't know what happens when we die. They heard the word 'heaven' somewhere else. To my knowledge, R. hadn't heard of 'golden streets of heaven' or any other such concept. We'd never discussed that.

"She just woke up one morning, claiming she'd seen Jesus and told me about 'heaven' and said she was going there. And died within about seven hours.

"I can't explain it."

The Spiritual Quadrant

If people doubt that their children are aware of a terminal illness, they should look at the poems or drawings these children create, often during their illness but sometimes months before a diagnosis is made. An example of this is the poem of a little girl, written six months before her death, two months after the diagnosis was made. Although she was told that she had anemia, the little girl was intuitively aware that she had only a limited time left on this earth. It needs to be understood that this is often a pre-conscious awareness and not a conscious, intellectual knowledge. It comes from the "inner, spiritual, intuitive quadrant" and gradually prepares the child to face the forthcoming transition, even if the grown-ups deny or avoid this reality.

Time

Watching the seconds,
Go by.
Wasting and passing time,
Stalling, killing, sleeping on—
Time.

Experiences, loves, moments of death,
Moments of tears, never to come again,
Gone—
    Forever.

Generations all explain time differently,
But by coincidence,
It becomes the same,
    Time.

In memories, dreams, the thoughts of
That moment tick by as you think
Your final thoughts,
    of
        Time.

Courage and Poems

One brief motel room consultation in Australia resulted in a beautiful sharing between Chris, her mother, and myself, and I received the following letter after our time together, from her mother:

"I want you to know how much you have helped us. Since seeing you, Chris has had another two subarachnoid hemorrhages from Arteric Nerous Malformations. She is still well with no disabilities. When Chris's neurosurgeon said he may have to reconsider operating to prolong her life, she told him she wanted to die a normal girl with no disabilities.

"Her father and I have gone along with her opinion because she is nearly fifteen and has lived with this one-third of her life. She has told us the quality of her life here is more important than the quantity. She seems so full of contradictions, for she can and does talk of death, yet she refused an anointing because she said she was not sick enough and has what she calls her 'hopeful box,' with baby things in it.

"I fear I still cannot accept the possibility of her death as well as she seems to. I love her so much and don't want to lose

her. I fear I will, though she is a good little teacher and is
helping us all. . . . Yesterday I found some poems she has
written [that] I would like to share with you. I think she is
saying a great deal, but am not sure what she is saying. By
the way, they were done a few weeks before she went to
hospital."

Clouds

One day I layed down to sleep,
then decided to take a peek,
at the beautiful sky above
to see if I could see a dove.
The sky was cloudy, dark, and gray,
yet I could see far away,
that in the sky there were some
clouds which I could make some
pictures out.
There were sailships on a blue sea,
Little flowers and little bees.
Then I looked and looked again.
There I saw a lady standing,
There she was dressed in blue and
white, and there were flowers at
her feet.
Then as I saw her go a little
tear ran down her nose.
Then another and another till
I had to get my umbrella.

"I have enclosed some more poems Chris has written; the
last ones I sent you were written for a school project just
before Chris had a cerebral hemorrhage in March 1981. This
second lot was done for me as a Christmas gift. She doesn't
draw much anymore. The doctors tell us now that because of
the frequency of the bleeds they consider she has a better
chance if she has an operation.

"Chris's first reaction was shock. Tears, anger, 'Why in the hell can't they leave me alone? I'm well and happy and working with the children I love. . . .' And then later, after thinking it out very thoroughly . . . 'I'm sick and tired of waiting and wondering if and when the next bleed is coming and if it's going to be the big one. . . . I can't see that I have much choice,' and the choice was left to Chris. She is fifteen now, and it is her life. 'As I am now, I can't even drink tea or coffee in case it puts my pulse up. . . . I can't do anything strenuous. What could happen if I married and tried to have babies?' I replied that I didn't know but said with honesty that intercourse is a very strenuous activity. . . . She said, 'I thought that might be so.'

"Chris has decided to have the operation. Her twin sister is really frightened and is talking, which is a giant step for her. Like her father and elder sister, she has managed to ignore the fear that Chris may die. Chris is a good teacher, and she has been a tremendous help to me. She told her sister that God knows what she wants, and she will either be all right— perhaps little defects would be OK, because she would be able to overcome them—or she will die, and that's OK because 'I'd be well, normal, and happy with God.' Chris will not think about severe disabilities or brain stem damage. As far as she's concerned, that just isn't on, and she would rather die.

"Chris wrote this letter and poem about a friend in the hospital who died of leukemia: 'Dear M., This morning R. died. It wasn't really a great shock because everybody knew sooner or later that he would die. Late at night I would think of what I could do for him, so I wrote him this poem. I lay awake thinking should I give it to him or not. I decided not to, and then he died. I suppose just writing a poem isn't much, but that is all I could do. When I found out this morning that he had died, in a way I was glad; then I thought, What a waste, but he will make a beautiful angel in heaven.

" 'I am sure that children like R. are put on this earth for a reason, and God only knows what it is. You've just got to think of all the other children that live and not of all the children that die. I was sitting beside J.'s bed and thinking of R. I got really upset. I tried to say to myself—"Chris, J. is going to be OK." I honestly think I am going to be OK, it's just that it's so damn hard to let go and say "if it's God's will." It's all right for Him, He's OK. He's got the little children up there with Him, and He keeps sending more children down for cancer and leukemia to kill them, and the cycle just keeps going on and, anyway, "keep doing the good job." Keep smiling. Love an angel, Chris. xxxxx' "

Life

The road of life is bumpy
The road of life is steep.
There are ups and downs,
Happiness and sorrows,
    but the best of all,
Little children will get their rewards,
Of being little angels in heaven. . . .

Love

Love is everywhere,
you don't have,
to look hard
to find some
love to
place
inside your
heart like the
old saying goes
Love wasn't put into your heart to stay
love isn't love until
you give some
away.

"Luke is a seven-year-old boy Chris met in the hospital. He had his left leg amputated above the knee—cancer. Chris has never missed visiting him since she met him. She loves him dearly."

Luke

Luke is my friend,
a pal and a mate; some
people call him Luke the Spook.
I always remember him in my
prayers and don't call him
Luke the Spook, but my
little freckle face Angel from
heaven.

Is This What It's Really Like?

What is really down that tunnel?
Really it's like looking down a funnel.
Do I dare to open the door,
and find that that room has no door?
There is a bright light for me to see.
Is anyone really looking for me?
No, I've decided not to open the door.
Oh, how lovely everyone looks, they
are all Angels from heaven.
And I look at myself all
beautiful and nice. Beautiful
little children running everywhere.
No, don't be afraid, my friends.
Everyone is so kind around
here. I open the door and
let people in. There are
many coming in but never
going out because everyone
loves it here.

Sadness

Sadness is like a waterfall
without any water.
Sadness is having a meat pie
without any tomato sauce.
Sadness is having clothes
without a body.
Sadness is having a purse
without any money.
Sadness is a light bulb
without a light.
Sadness is a toothbrush
without any toothpaste.
Sadness is taking a shower
without any soap.
Sadness is something people
can live without.

Why?

Why do we have parents, and why do we have homes?
Why have we got two ears, and why have we a nose? Why do
babies live; why do babies die? Why do we die, and why are
we scared to? Why do we live; why are we living? The answer is, why not!!

Family

A family is always full
of love and good cheer.
That is why God puts
us here, to love and
cherish till death do
us part, and love
while there is still
love in our hearts.

One year later, almost to the exact day this letter was written, a mailgram was received:

"Dear Elisabeth, Christine is now a butterfly. My love, B.B."

Chris left the following letter and last will for her family:

"To Mum—

"I want you to know that I always loved you and I always will. I know I will go to heaven and I know I will see you when you die. I want you to always remember me and talk to me in your prayers. . . . I don't want to see you crying all the time. I will be happy in heaven and I want you to know that all your life. . . . Say sweet dreams, God bless, and I love you and thanks, God, every night to yourself because I will hear you. I love Dad, Karen, and Ann, too, very much. . . . I love you, too. You saw me through the bad times and the good times and I will never forget it ever. I love you, Mum, very much. . . .

"Lots of love,

"Your daughter always, Chris XXXXOX"

January 1, 1982

This is the last Will and Testament of me, Chris ————.

I give devise and bequeath unto my family my money to be put to good use, whether it be for my funeral or to the Mater Children's Hospital Appeal. The clothes that don't fit either my older sister or my twin shall go to the poor. My toys are to go to my nieces and nephews when Karen or Ann have children. Muffy is to be buried with me. My jewelry is to be shared out between Karen and Ann and maybe Mum. My dove and my ring are to be on me when I die. Dad's Mother's ring is to go to Karen [. . .] whom I borrowed it from. My collection of china is to go to my whole family. Everything else may be divided between Karen and Ann, whatever it be.

I will have flowers and lots of loud music at my funeral. . . .

"Chris did not finish writing her will as she intended to on May 4, 1982, because she went to the hospital with a hemorrhage and was unconscious, prior to her operation on June 4, 1982.

"These letters, with instructions for Mass, [and] the will were all in a bag Chris took to hospital with her.

"Here are some portions of the letters Chris wrote . . . she left us a treasure, worth much more than gold, a precious gift of herself, her love, and honesty. Her faith, which she fought to find, dear and true. Black and white, no shades of gray . . . a certain knowledge that God knows how she felt, and understood, clearly with unconditional love. They speak for themselves."

"To my family and friends,

"I hereby being in sound heart and mind now do out this note. . . . I know it will be hard but I think if God wants me to die he'll take me and if he wants me to live I will. Mum once said God made doctors and I said God made my mind to make up my own decisions.

"I think being left handicapped would even surely kill me, not being able to do anything. I would *love* to be buried in my special "going away" dress. I love it, Mum. Thank you for all you've done. You've been there all the time and I love you for it. Dad, I hope you face up to my death as a sign of God's love for me, and I love you too. Thanks a lot for everything, too. Karen, I know now that I was jealous of you because you are everything I'm not. I love you, just remember that. Thanks for everything.

"Last but not least I come to my little twin sister Ann. I love you so very much, just always remember that whenever you need to talk to anyone I'll be listening. I still want to feel wanted when I'm gone . . . I can say while I'm writing this that not one word has gone down on this paper without tears. I'll miss you all. I'll always remember and be watching over you all.

"Also I have to mention Cathy: she is my bestest friend and will always be. I'll have a talk to God about transferring her Dad to Melbourne. And when we are all born again it's going to be different. I would like Cathy to come to my funeral. I love her very much.

"Just think, I'll see Dad's Mum and Dad, Mum's Gran, Christopher, Mrs. Brady. Tell Joyce and Bill I'll look after Chris for them and thank them too. I love them both very much. If I missed out anyone just tell them I love them and will miss them all. Place a picture of all the family and Cisco with me, OK? I want Bernard, Father Tom to do my Mass and Aunty Jan and Aunty Barb to do a jazzy funeral. I want all my flowers to be yellow, pink, and white carnations and roses. NO *RED*. I don't want people to stop talking about me and I want everyone to be happy for me.

"Family, Thank you, I love you all very much. . . .

"Say Good-bye to Cisco for me. I love him so much.

"I MISS AND LOVE all who [are] mentioned in this letter

"Bye, your daughter, sister, friend, Chris

"XXXXXX

"Love you all."

*   *   *

Dear Dr. Ross,

"I have listened to you with great interest whenever you have appeared on television. You seem to be the only person I have ever met who has convictions as great as my own.

"I have two grandsons. The elder is very close to me spiritually. They are both so dear, do not mistake me. The elder, Jonathan, comes into my bed, and we talk about all manner of things.

"Not long ago I had a seventieth birthday, but for about eighteen months this little chap has stroked my wrinkles—not many!—and my upper arm—'so soft, Grandma, but there's nothing there because you are old.'

"We had a conversation that went like this:

J: Will you be an angel when you die, Grandma?
ME: I hope so.
J: People can't see angels, can they?
ME: No.
J: Could you die now, Grandma? Then you could be beside me always.

"We have talked about what we will do when we don't have to bother about our bodies.

"I told them both I do not want a gravestone, just a tree with beautiful flowers and berries for the birds and a dish underneath for water for the birds. They both are now trying to write 'Grandma' in their very best lettering to put on the dish! It's all very lighthearted, in fact a 'fun project.'

"The eldest one says, 'The others will think you have gone, won't they? But I shall know!'

"You can well imagine how I pounced on the opportunity for him to explain to his little brother and even his Mummy and Daddy so they shall not be sad!

"All this happened nearly two years ago.

"The *very day* you spoke of death, children, and rainbows I received this card. [The card was a drawing of a rainbow that goes down to a pot of gold at a house surrounded by flowers, birds, etc.]

"It is not his own death, even mine has been forgotten, but subconsciously there it all is on the card my grandson made for me. There is my rainbow—my flowers for the birds—but do look in the corner! My eyes filled up—a pot of happiness lies at *my* house! That is what I mean to him *now*, but the happiness also means the distress of parting has been removed.

"I hope this letter is not too long, but I too *know* and have been able to pass my knowledge on, a wonderful, privileged thing to do."

Chapter 10
How Can Friends Help?

AFTER THE DEATH OF A CHILD, the world seems to stand still, and if anything moves around us, it is not meant for us. We mechanically walk the dog, put a coat on our first-grader, and send him off to school; we absentmindedly put the coffeepot on, and we answer the phone in a daze.

When the florist comes with flowers, we remember vaguely to give him a tip. We nod a thank you when a neighbor brings some fresh-smelling, warm apple pie, but we are not really "with it." We want to turn the clock back; we want to hear Jimm's arrival with his usual loud and happy, "Hi, Mom." We want to see his muddy shoes again at the entrance, the ones he always brought back from his soccer games. We are waiting to hear him play the drums, his beloved drums! We do not want to believe that they will never again be heard, played by his oh, so beautiful, special hands.

We walk around in circles, picking up some laundry here and there, feeding the canary (did I feed him yesterday?), and looking out into the gray misty morning. Another day, another night. If I could only hear his voice, his laughter, walk into his bedroom and see that bundle of sleepiness under his blanket, all rolled up and content. And soon he would wake up, rub his eyes, and holler, "Mom, what time is it?" He, naturally, always knew what time it was. He just wanted to acknowledge that he was back in the world, awake again for another day of sunshine, music, sports, and oh, I should not forget, his first girl friend.

I want to call her up and talk to her about him, about the time they spent together, hear about his dreams and joys. But what would I say to her? Would we just sit and stare at each other? Would we just break into sobs and cry together? I have no energy to make a call; I can hardly move from one room to another. God, please let the time pass.

I open a letter on top of a pile of mail that came in yesterday, or was it two days ago? It was written in a delicate handwriting by someone whose name I don't recall:

"My dearest . . .

"I am so very, very sorry about the death of your son, but I am glad that you called to tell me. (Now I remember again who this is. My thinking has been terrible lately.) Your pain and despair have been old and familiar songs to me, songs so well remembered. And because I can remember so clearly, I can also tell you with complete certainty that the joy will come to you again, though it may seem impossible to you now. You will be able to look back and see Jimm's face, the funny little mannerisms that belonged only to him, the way his hair fell when it was just brushed; you will be able to hear his laughter and hold him close without feeling as if your heart is breaking.

"But this change comes ever so slowly, almost imperceptibly. And sometimes the time between now and then is so hard to endure. Your faith in life and happiness and the future may often waiver, but *grab* onto life and anyone and any thing that you need for help!

"You don't have to be strong or logical or sensible, or any of the things you think you have to be. For me, it turned out to be better when I didn't try to fight the pain but let it roll over me like a giant tidal wave and carry me along with it, until it spent its fury and dropped me gasping but alive on the shores of sanity. And, like any storm, it gradually died. The waves crashed farther and farther apart, and somewhere, without my being aware of it, life became worth living again.

"My dear friend, I am a strong swimmer. So when you find yourself being swallowed up in the backwash, close your eyes and feel my arms around you holding you up, and feel my love, one human being to another, one mother's love to another, reaching out across this continent to hold your heart in warmth and comfort while it heals.

"Every day my prayers will be for your pain to ease and for peace to come to you. You know that we are always given what we need, whether we want it or not. You will be given. Just keep right on reaching for it. It is there.

"It will always be here for you, available to you, at *any* time of the day or night, and despite the miles between us, we are as close to one another as the telephone or our thoughts.

"My thoughts are ever with you, and my love is now flowing to you, Sylvia"

The Loving Remembrance

After the death of an adolescent, a house that previously was full of young people, of the playing of drums and rock concerts, of the voices and laughter of teenagers, becomes terribly empty, cold, and quiet. It feels unreal, "like a morgue," as one mother described it. Life goes on, the mailman continues to come, but the lively sounds are no longer there and the doors no longer slam shut. That which used to be regarded as "a pest, a nightmare, an unbearable noise" is now sorely missed! Such bereaved parents wouldn't even mind the loudest drumming noise while they watch the news now, and the "If only I had told him once how much I really loved him" begins to emerge. The loss, the longing for the familiar now gone causes intense pain, and no amount of walking up and down the stairs between his bedroom and the basement will bring those sounds back into reality.

It is on days like this, weeks and months after the funeral, that the arrival of an old school pal can be the greatest gift. One boy came to the door of Mrs. L. and asked for permission to continue to play ball on their front yard, "like we used to do." God, was she happy to give that permission. Before long, other classmates came, and she saw herself busy in the kitchen, fixing cold drinks and snacks and laughingly bringing back old memories. "One day I have to tell Rick that he saved my life by doing that. I don't know how he knew. . . ."

I advised Mrs. L. to tell Rick *today* and not postpone it for tomorrow, as there might be no chance tomorrow. When she did, Rick told her in the most matter-of-fact way that it was her son who had told him that it was time to resume the old games on his front yard. He smilingly and a bit sheepishly told her that he only "followed orders" given by his old pal who "visited him occasionally in his dreams."

Helping with the Daily Tasks of Living

In Sandy Albertson's book *Endings and Beginnings* (New York: Random House, 1980), there are many beautiful examples of what friends can mean in times of stress. When a young husband was dying, his wife tried to visit him at least twice a day in the hospital, while caring for two little ones at home and nursing her infant daughter. Too tired and unsure about the priorities of life, she recounts the appearance of friends, although they were people she had never met before:

"Late one evening a woman from another Friends meeting arrived at our doorstep bearing a complete dinner for our family. I'd never met her, but she explained she had heard of us through other Quakers. I had little energy just then for building any new relationships, and I was grateful for the comfortableness with which this 'stranger' offered this gift to us without requiring ongoing response or involvement from us.

"Another evening, just as Robin and I had finished supper, the doorbell rang. It was a young mother whom I knew only slightly. She said, 'I have come to do your dishes,' and she did. Though I felt a bit awkward at first, it gets me smiling whenever I think of it now. There is a new level of trusting reached in a relationship when you can allow a friend to know your 'encrustations,' to vacuum your house or clean the bathroom."

Friends are also those people who sense that we need to get out of the house, the hospital, the atmosphere which reminds us of illness and death. These friends remember that we used to love to go to antique shops, to hear a concert in the park, to sit at the edge of the water and watch the seagulls and dream. Friends are people who quietly take us to those places, leave us there, and come back to pick us up in time to return to the grimmer realities of life. But the "space," the break we had, is a gift to and for ourselves that will help us make it through another day, another night.

The Man Who Came to Help
—by Madge Harrah

*"We were numb with grief. Then this quiet
neighbor appeared."*

Still in shock, I stumbled about the house trying to decide what to put into the suitcases. Earlier that evening I'd received a call from my hometown in Missouri telling me that my brother and his wife, her sister, and both the sister's children had been killed in a car wreck. "Come as soon as you can," begged my mother.

That's what I wanted to do—to leave at once, to hurry to

Madge Harrah, "The Man Who Came to Help," reprinted with permission from *Guideposts* magazine, © 1981 by Guideposts Associates, Inc.

my parents. But my husband Larry and I were in the midst of packing all our belongings to move from Ohio to New Mexico. Our house was a shambles. Some of the clothes that Larry and I and our two young children, Eric and Meghan, would need were already taped up in cartons. Which ones? Confused by grief, I couldn't remember. Other clothes lay unwashed in a pile on the laundry-room floor. Supper dishes still sat on the kitchen table. Toys were strewn everywhere.

While Larry made plane reservations for the following morning, I wandered about the house, aimlessly picking things up and putting them down again. I looked at all the tasks that should be taken care of—and I did nothing. I couldn't focus.

Again and again, the words I'd heard on the phone echoed through my head: "Bill is gone—Marilyn, too. June—and both the children . . ."

It was as though the message had muffled my brain with cotton. Whenever Larry spoke, he sounded far away. Curtains dropped behind my eyes. As I moved through the house, I ran into doors and tripped over chairs.

Larry made arrangements for us to leave by 7:00 the next morning. Then he phoned a few friends to tell them what had happened. Occasionally, someone asked to speak to me.

"If there's anything I can do, please let me know," that person would offer kindly.

"Thank you. Thank you very much," I'd reply. But I didn't know what to ask for. I was too confused to concentrate.

I sat in a chair, staring into space, while Larry called Donna King, the woman with whom I taught a nursery class at church each Sunday. Donna and I were casual friends, but we didn't see each other often. She and Emerson, her thin, quiet husband, were kept busy during the weekdays by their own "nursery"—six children ranging in age from fifteen years down to two years.

I was glad Larry had thought to warn her that she'd have the nursery class alone the coming Sunday.

While I sat there, Meghan darted by, clutching a ball. Eric chased after her.

They *should* be in bed, I thought.

I followed them into the living room. My legs dragged. My hands felt gloved with lead. I sank down on the couch, sitting in a stupor with my eyes closed.

When the doorbell rang, I rose slowly and crept across the room. I opened the door to see Emerson King standing on the porch. "I've come to clean your shoes," he said.

His words thudded against the insulation stuffing my ears. I asked him to repeat, to make sure I'd heard correctly.

"Donna had to stay with the baby," he said, "but we want to help you. I remember when my father died, it took me hours to get the children's shoes cleaned and shined for the funeral. So that's what I've come to do for you. Give me all your shoes—not just your good shoes, but *all* your shoes."

I hadn't even thought about shoes until he mentioned them. Now I remember that Eric had left the sidewalk to wade through the mud with his good shoes on after church the previous Sunday. Not to be outdone by her brother, Meghan had kicked rocks with her shoes, scuffing the toes. When we'd gotten home, I'd tossed the shoes into the laundry room, intending to clean them later, but I'd forgotten.

Emerson's request gave me something specific to do. While he spread newspapers on the kitchen floor, I gathered Larry's dress shoes, his everyday shoes, my heels, my flats, the children's dirty dress shoes, and their tennis shoes with the food spots. Emerson found a pan that he filled with soapy water. He got an old knife out of a drawer and retrieved a sponge from under the sink. Larry had to rummage through several cartons, but at last he located the shoe polish.

Emerson settled himself on the floor and got to work. Watching him concentrate intently on one task helped me pull my own thoughts into order.

Laundry first, I told myself.

While the washer chugged, I bathed the children and put

them to bed. Meghan seemed to be wheezing a little, so I assembled a first-aid and medicine kit for the trip.

While I cleared the supper dishes, Emerson continued to work, saying nothing. I thought of Jesus washing the feet of his disciples. Our Lord had knelt, served his friends, even as this man now knelt, serving us. The love in that act released my tears at last, healing rain to wash the fog from my mind. I could move. I could think. I could get on with the business of living.

One by one, the jobs fell into place.

I went into the laundry room to put a load of wash into the dryer, returning to the kitchen to find that Emerson had left. In a line against one wall stood all our shoes, gleaming, spotless. Later, when I started to pack, I saw that Emerson had even scrubbed the soles. I could put the shoes directly into the suitcases, knowing they wouldn't soil the clothes.

We got to bed late and rose very early, but by the time we left for the airport, all the jobs were done. Ahead lay grim, sad days, but the comfort of Christ's presence, symbolized by the image of a quiet man kneeling on my kitchen floor with a pan of water, would sustain me.

Now, whenever I hear of an acquaintance who has lost a loved one, I no longer call with the vague offer, "If there's anything I can do . . ." Now I try to think of one specific task that suits that person's need—such as washing the family car, taking the dog to the boarding kennel, or house-sitting during the funeral. And if the person says to me, "How did you know I needed that done?" I reply, "It's because a man once cleaned my shoes."

Choosing Life over Suffering

The following letter was written by a multiple sclerosis patient to her son, who had been taken away from her after her husband left her and she was unable to physically and financially support him. She had lost the use of her legs, her vision, and her will to live. She had lost her home, her marriage, and apparently, her only son.

Today, she has seen her son graduate from high school, after she herself struggled back to health and life. Her son has started college, after having moved back with his mother. This woman has enriched thousands of lives, because she has gone through the tumbler and has chosen to come out not crashed, but polished.

She works as a rehabilitation counselor with others who have multiple sclerosis and similar debilitating illnesses. Since she has been taught by life—her own life—she touches the core of their fears and anxieties and stands as a living example of "the beauty of the canyons" after uncountable windstorms. I remember when we first met, when she was at the end of her rope, when life seemed cruel and meaningless, when she felt that she could not cope with yet another loss. Death seemed to be welcome at that time. Yet she came to one of our workshops, she shared, cried, and laughed with others and emerged with the hope that she could try another day, another week, another month, maybe even another year.

Now, many years later, she gives me back what we gave to her. I send her my patients who feel at the end of their rope with multiple sclerosis and often, all they need is to see her shining face, hear her voice of confidence, and witness her radiant affirmation of life. She can see and work and walk again! She has enriched my life and given me the courage to keep on going when I felt I was at the end of my rope, and I thank her for that.

"Thanksgiving Day
"My dear son,
"Here is the letter I promised to write. While I'm still warmed up from typing, I will use the typewriter to make it easy for you. I spent Thanksgiving at work at the county hospital, catching up on long-postponed paperwork. It is so

quiet here today that it is hardly recognizable. No interruptions, no phones, no people, patients, doctors, referrals . . .

"Thanksgiving. For what? I was just thinking. Two weeks ago I would have been hard put to answer that one, except to say, 'Thanks for all the pain, suffering, and disappointments in my life!' Today, fortunately, my head is in a very different place. I can even make a list of thankfulness things: *Life*, 'good friends' (like you), health returning, great job here, people who care about me, who care about the same things in life that matter to me, people who are 'real' and 'honest' like you and your friends and mine. Lovable little children as yet undamaged by some of society's devastating influences. Soft, furry little animals like the kitten I had not so long ago. Lovely, refreshing flowers, trees, grass, ocean, seashore, birds, and breezes that make it a pleasure to be alive and aware. I feel good, even happy, for the first time in longer than I can recall dates. I'm glad I decided to live.

"My son, I hope you choose to *live* and fully so, enjoying all that you can create or find around you that is or can be rich and rewarding to you. I fear that you miss so much of what you could have when your head is in a bottle. I guess I've just recently had my own head in some sort of a bottle, awaking each day with fear or resignation or disquiet or purposelessness or plain *despair!*

"Finally, I pulled my head out and am feeling the delight in living each moment. Living not tied just to material things— one or two significant loved ones, future plans, ability to work, run, or walk—just living each day as it comes and enjoying the happenings, plus making things happen when I choose to!

"Maybe Thanksgiving (like living, loving, and age) is a state of mind and of heart. I feel *thankful* today just sitting here in my little cramped office with its familiar surroundings, thinking of people like you, my son, and where-I-am-in-the-world-this-moment-of-my-life! It is an unusually strange experience for me to feel all this as well as to be writing it at the same minute. I'm letting my thoughts flow through my fingers and the keys onto this paper.

"Warm feelings to you, C."

By sharing her letter with you, I hope that one day when you are in the midst of the windstorms of life, you will remember her words and know that what we make out of life is *our* choice. And when we really try, help will be forthcoming.

* * *

Another "Mommy" shares her recovery after the death of her little Karin in May 1978. She writes the following poem:

As the sun rises, and the day begins
    I think of you
As we rush around taking care of our
very important business
    I think of you
As we are so much in a hurry going nowhere,
too busy to stop and smell a flower,
hear a bird sing, smile at another person
    I think of you
Karin, Karin
    I always think of you
I'd call you my cookie pie
Because you were so especially sweet
And who would ever have thought I'd see you die
I told you, you were the light of my life
And now I am in darkness afraid and crying
Help me, oh help me out of the night
So I may see the light again
I saw you burned and in pain in your hospital bed
And I sat by your side until you were dead
I couldn't touch you because of your burns
I wanted to hold you and oh how I yearned
Karin, you touched my soul and we are one

Yes, you did jump high
And now you fly way up in the sky
And when you pass by just wink
And we'll say hi
Good-bye, good-bye, my beautiful butterfly.
I love you
Mommy

Recently, she wrote another note: "The pain was so great, I went crazy, but now things are no longer hazy. Now we are both free, and you have finally come back to me. Love, love, love" (with a smiling face in the loops of the *l*).

Caring Professionals Make the Difference

This is a letter from Nova Scotia, Canada, dated September 24, 1981. It speaks for itself, and it shows how a young couple, helped in caring ways by medical personnel, came to grips with the unexpected loss of their baby. The letter was written by the father.

"Our baby died two weeks ago, and I am just now reflecting on what happened. My most vibrant impression is the incredible luck my wife and I had on meeting the right people at the right time over a crucial period of twenty-three hours from the time we realized the baby was dead to the time we were able to see and touch him and say good-bye.

"We were touched by eleven doctors and nine nurses, a chaplain, two ambulance drivers, a funeral director, and many others. Not once did we experience anything but strong support and empathy for our situation and the ways we wanted to participate in this event.

"For an old sixties hippy with many of the old prejudices about traditional medicine still intact, it was very enlightening.

"Baby James died about September 9. Maria felt a little movement that day and dreamed about the baby being dead that night. The following day there was no movement, and

Maria felt very strange and tired and couldn't be comfortable with anything. That night when we were asleep, Maria started bleeding quite heavily for a short time. We bundled up the children and went to the hospital in Bridgewater, which is near to the cottage we stay in at the shore. We arrived about 3:00 A.M., and the attending nurses could not find the fetal heartbeat. The doctor on call could not find it either. They called a local obstetrician who asked that Maria be kept in the hospital and watched by a nurse. He would come in the morning.

"At this point we accepted that the baby was dead, even though there were more attempts to find the heartbeat. The first doctor imagined that labor would be induced, and we wanted to return to our own doctor in Middleton (fifty-seven miles away) for the induction and birth so we would be close to home and in familiar circumstances. Our home doctor was called, and he prepared for this subject to the approval of the obstetrician.

"At 9:30 A.M. the obstetrician came and examined Maria. From a physical examination he suspected that there were more complications than were first apparent. He said he would prefer to have an ultrasound done to determine if his suspicions were right, although he could do a surgical examination and then a Cesarean section immediately if necessary. He thought the baby was breech, and there was a placenta previa as well. He wanted Maria to go to Grace Maternity Hospital in Halifax. We agreed, and he phoned a friend there and arranged for her to take care of Maria on arrival. He was really calm and supportive, and I think we were extremely lucky to have met him. Everything that followed was just as perfect as possible medically.

"The nurse from Bridgewater insisted on going with Maria in the ambulance, and the doctor agreed. I thought this was amazing since it is about a 130-mile round trip. I drove our car to Halifax, which was really hard to do. As soon as I was alone I cried and cried and couldn't drive well. A friend came from Middleton and took the children.

"At the Grace they took a lot of blood and stepped up the intravenous which had been started in Bridgewater. Several doctors came at various times, and arrangements were made for the ultrasound tests. By this time it was Friday afternoon, and the surgeon wanted to proceed and needed as much information as possible as quickly as possible. The ultrasound showed no fetal movement, breech position, and a complete placenta previa. Although there was a lot of activity on that floor of the hospital, everyone was very caring and seemed to take a lot of time to discuss every aspect of the procedures with us. (In all there were eleven doctors and nine nurses involved with us, and none of them were resistant to what we wanted or uncaring about us.) I found the whole experience absolutely amazing.

"The surgery was scheduled for 6:30 P.M. The head anesthesiologist and his associate spent quite a while going over the alternatives and their side effects and advantages. Maria decided she would like to be awake mentally during the surgery, particularly since we wanted to be with the baby afterwards. She was prepared for a spinal block about 5:30.

"At 6:30 the surgeon came in and told us that another emergency required his attention. He came again at 7:30 and postponed our operation for the same reason. During this period of waiting we were well attended to. We realized that we could wait and just be together. Normally this hospital did two Cesareans a day, and most of them were predicted and scheduled. Since we had arrived, there had already been four, and two of them were emergencies. While we were waiting, a baby was born in each of the two labor rooms adjoining ours. All the other rooms were full and imminent. Even with this level of activity I felt that all was well. The nurses and doctors continued to care for us and take time with us.

"Since we had been waiting longer than usual, the anesthetic began losing its effect, and more had to be given. About 8:45 the surgeon came and said he was now ready to proceed. He asked Maria if she was ready, and Maria said she was nervous.

The doctor stopped and called everyone together. He wouldn't do anything until everyone was ready, and that included us. I was really impressed. This man, who was already working under a lot of pressure and with very high energy, continued to show an amazing amount of empathy. The surgeon said it would be difficult to administer any other form of anesthetic now that we had chosen one route, but preparations would be made to do so, and Maria could ask for release from her consciousness at any time during the surgery. This took a little while, but soon we went to the operating theater.

"Ever since we first came to the Grace I was encouraged to take part in what was going on. I was given things to do that involved me in the activities, besides taking part in the decision-making and being there to comfort and care for Maria. I was always asked to help when Maria was being moved around the hospital, and an orderly was never called once my ability to do some of the work was established.

"The operation took one hour and ten minutes. At first there were two nurses and three doctors in the room, as well as Maria and me. My main focus was being with Maria and staying in touch with her by touch and eye contact. I was still able to watch the operation. It was a routine Cesarean until they tried to get the baby out. Suddenly the energy in the room went up really high, and the surgeon sent people off to get some more equipment, another doctor, and blood. The energy stayed high for about four and a half minutes, and then the baby was out. Everyone relaxed, and the head surgeon did not proceed with the rest of the operation. Instead, they spent a couple of minutes reviewing what had been done. The decision had been his to make at the time, and now he wanted the others in attendance to integrate what had happened. He wanted to turn the I-decision into a we-decision. They could not remove the baby with a standard incision, and Maria's uterus had to be opened from top to bottom (rather than the expected small lateral incision). After everyone was caught up, they proceeded with the stitches.

"As soon as we were returned to our room, the hospital chaplain came and told us what the baby looked like, and then she brought him to us. We spent about an hour with him, crying, talking, holding, kissing, being at peace. Baby James was a well formed, normal baby. He was thirty-two weeks old (two months premature). He didn't show any signs of pain or struggle. Several times a nurse came to take the baby, but always left again without comment. When we felt finished, felt our last good-byes to this earthly form were complete, the body was given to the nurse. We had authorized an autopsy to try and discover the cause.

"My experience of holding and touching the baby was that he appeared to have a certain weight and feel when we first were with him that was not there when he left. This could be projected energy, but I like to think something really stayed behind with us or was released during our time together. I asked James to stay with our family in some form—an invisible member.

"We moved Maria to another floor that night, and we said good-night after she was given Demerol to help her sleep. She was given more during the night and the next morning. During the next few days she moved quickly from heavy drugs to lighter assistance until the third day when she stopped taking anything but penicillin.

"I started driving the two hundred miles back and forth to see the children, and managed to return to the cottage and bring our things home. During the next week I spent two days at home arranging for burial, building a coffin, and being with the children and friends. Maria's mother came and helped with the home.

"Maria started taking a lot of vitamin C, angelica, comfrey, mint, and vitamin E as soon as she could take anything by mouth. She came home six days after the surgery and is recovering very well.

"I was really impressed with the whole experience. Everyone was so supportive and helpful. A lot of my fantasies and prejudices about allopathic medicine and practitioners were re-examined, and I really appreciate that what we needed was available and was given to us in such a clear and caring way. The only time there was hesitation at the hospital was when I asked to see the baby after the autopsy. Even though this took some consultation with a supervisor and was highly irregular, I was eventually allowed to do so.

"I got a lot of support from our local funeral director, who brought the baby home for me and gave us space in his funeral home to do our own ceremony. We buried the baby ourselves with just the family and four friends present. The children helped build the coffin and dig the grave, and this seemed to help them absorb the event better. They were quite accepting of the whole thing, and we answered all their questions and attended to their needs as well as possible.

"When we thanked the people at the hospital we were told that our being there was really special, and our energy and love for each other and the baby impressed everyone and helped make it all happen the way it did. It was a really fine meeting of kind people."

"September 24, 1982: One year has passed since I put to paper this enormous event in our lives. At the time I wrote it only three days had passed since we had buried our Baby James. It was written primarily to share with friends, but also as a record of what really happened. This week our family has returned to the little cottages by the ocean which we left so abruptly in the middle of the night one year ago. It is a completing process for all of us. Four seasons have passed, and life continues. If anything, this death and crisis in our family has made us stronger and more committed as a family. We all still feel that James is with us in our daily lives as a memory and as some sort of reality, too."

* * *

Those who work with terminally ill children and their parents find that they must also work through the pain of loss. One social worker who had set up a program at an eminent hospital for children with cancer and their parents to share together, wrote the following:

"The beauty of these experiences and the individual beauty that I (usually) felt for my children and their families grew to love. In many ways I denied reality, for soon some of 'my' children died. And I found that I didn't mourn them. And more died, and then I began mourning the previous children.

"Well, seven children have died in the last seven months. I love, in some ways, these and other children. When it is appropriate, I do take them home with me for visits. Yet, now I'm getting scared. Scared of more losses. Scared of all the mourning that I put off. Scared at how bluntly we talk, at times, about death. And I'm scared of my own death. But this is how I feel at times, and at other times I really feel what I'm doing is good for the children and their families, and for myself. . . . I suppose that what I'm saying in this letter is that I'm feeling what my families go through. It's a growing experience, and I am finding out that growth can be painful. . . . How do you do it?"

In response, we answered:

Yes, I have gone through the same turmoil and the same tumbler a hundred times, if not a thousand times. There were many that I was with from the beginning to the end . . . many that I hoped from day to day . . . would die soon so I would not have to watch this long suffering . . . and many who died too soon, and I guess I was not ready to let go. With some of my children, I felt a deep sadness when they left, and as I did more and more of this work, it was more like releasing a butterfly from a cocoon and then going on to the next one and then the next one, and seeing them all as butterflies flying away from me, but knowing that they are in a good place and that there are others who have to be taken care of. Now I never again feel pain, I simply feel that I have done the best that I can: with some, a better job and with others, a lousy job, but nevertheless, the best that I was able to do at the given time. I think it will be the same way for you. Yes, you have to know that your own guides are always with you, and never more than two feet away from you, in their own invisible loving, caring, guiding way, they will lead you in the right direction.

Christmas with David

A Colorado family who had time to truly share and communicate with their young, dying son were also blessed with a compassionate therapist friend, who wrote what it was like to spend the last Christmas and the last day of David's life with the family. Those are Christmas gifts with real meaning, compared to the ones we buy in a department store! In her letter, she shared with me some of the special moments she experienced, the giving and receiving of gifts, the humor of the patient:

"I think I told you, I was with Jean and Norman and David almost constantly during David's last three days. Someone has said that David died 'in style,' and I think I do not know much better ways of saying it.

"People with a deep capacity for caring and sharing seemed to gravitate to David's room and, in one way or another, a self-selected group joined together, each doing 'his own thing' and yet showing utmost consideration for all the others. It was quite a remarkable group of family, personal friends, and professional staff joining together toward a common goal. I remember Norman weeping on Christmas Eve morning, saying he wanted me to stay and yet he did not want me to 'ruin my Christmas.' I said that I surely did not know what Christmas was all about if it wasn't a time for giving, and I think this attitude was shared by all of us who were there during those three days. Even David enjoyed giving, not only when he gave presents to his parents, but also when he made jokes and played humorously with the rest of us. He had once told me how much he enjoyed the humor of 'getting something nice from someone and then giving back to them something yukky.'

"Even on Christmas Day he experienced this particular pleasure, when I gave him a clean gauze to clean out his mouth after he had vomited blood. He cleaned his mouth and then grinned and laughed as he handed me back the bloody gauze.

"When I talked to Jean on Tuesday evening, she asked me to send along to you copies of some notes and letters she has written me. I am sure she told you about giving me David's lion puppet, which stands on my bookcase and sometimes helps in counseling children who face death. More than one child has noticed the puppet and has used the story behind it as a springboard for working on his own problems.

"Jean was especially moved by your talk on Monday afternoon as well as by the opportunity to talk directly to you on Tuesday. These experiences brought back for her many of the memories of David which she treasures so very much. She has told me more than once that she never feared memories, however poignant and painful they may be; rather, she feared forgetting. Therefore any experiences which bring back to sharper focus her memories of David are very precious to her. Tuesday evening, as she wrote a letter to you, she was very much in touch with all her feelings about David. I talked with her a couple of times that evening to help her put together materials for you, and she seemed to be weeping much of the time. But I think it is good for her. Certainly she felt so good after talking with you and looks forward to the possibility that she might be able to talk with you in the future.

"At Jean's request, I have had a duplicate made of the tape of David sharing Christmas presents with his father and mother on Christmas day. The tape ends with Jean saying 'It's OK.' She continued talking that way to David for another two or three hours, and when she knew he was at the point of death she repeated 'Peace, David,' to him over and over and over until he stopped breathing entirely. It was perhaps one of the most beautiful moments I have ever witnessed. I find it interesting that many have either felt sorry for me or criticized me for 'giving up my Christmas' last year. On the contrary, I felt that I gave up nothing and that it was surely the most meaningful Christmas I have spent in my life.

"David is so present in my mind that I have to write to you! I woke up feeling teary-eyed, like I wanted to cry about David, but generally I find it unproductive to lie in bed in that frame of mind—what I end up doing is missing the essence of Dave, the essence of the whole experience. So I got up, picked up a new book. . . . Started half reading, half looking at the unexpected snow—all in the full knowledge of the undercurrent in me focusing on Dave.

"The book is on Charles Williams, who is so mixed up in my David feelings that I can usually productively grieve or productively remember, experience Dave, life, death, emotion, love all in a nice ball of wax together, so to speak.

"You asked me how I feel to see others still cry for Dave—and of course I am glad that people still love him, and can experience him. And the question goes on, I suppose, 'Why don't I cry more, if others cry a little?' And the only thing I can answer is, 'Why does one cry for the dead?'

"The answer depends on who dies, and how, and why, and whether one feels negligent or responsible for the death, or whether one feels unfinished about the relationship—'I should have made amends, etc.'

"In David's case, a young person dying, one cries that it seems unnecessary—I rebelled at that all fall. But now the deed is done, and that which has been fought against with all of man's skill, has come to pass. How then to make meaning out of it? I am as bewildered by how one copes with accidental death, or violent death, as anyone, but this is not ours to cope with, by the mercy of God. We have only the strong memories that David died in calm, surrounded by the best care and love anyone could have. So no feelings of negligence, or broken relationship to mend. I could cry for his unfinished life, if threescore years and ten is most important, but if I believe that God is personal, and cares more for me and my loved ones than even I know how to, then how should I grieve that he is with God? And how could I doubt this personal God, after my experiences of the past month? And do I grieve for my loss of a son? Yes, if he were truly out of touch—but Dave is so real to me—not externally but internally—bound up in all that I cherish and wonder at and reflect on, that his reality is very present, very real, very full of meaning.

"And so I rejoice, mainly, that God should so bless me as to make meaning out of chaos."

Chapter 11
Letting Go

Shall the day of parting
be the day of gathering?
And shall it be said
that my eve was in truth my dawn?
—KAHLIL GIBRAN, *The Prophet*

LETTING GO is one of life's most difficult tasks. It starts when our little ones are born and have to be kept in the hospital for another day or two after their mothers are discharged, although we naturally counted on bringing our little bundle of joy home with us.

Years later, we learn how to let go of our children when they start kindergarten or school. Fathers seem to be less affected by the "preparatory good-byes," since they often leave the house before the youngster leaves for the school bus on his first "big" day. They hear the story about the event, but they were not there when the bus arrived, when an ambivalent youngster almost turned around to run back into mother's arms.

Then we have to let go of our children when the doctor decides that the appendix has to come out and they need to be prepared for surgery. These are all "little traumas," but maybe in a way they prepare us not to take the presence of our children for granted.

Writing to her own mother, a woman shares her feelings about motherhood:

[167]

"From One Mom to Another"

"Laura just left. It is 6:15 A.M., still dark outside. I thought I might go back to sleep, but no way . . . I am too excited.

"So, this is how it feels to be a Mom. Sometimes, I think, only another Mom can understand. Laura did not want me to take her to the airport; she wanted to take a cab and do it all herself. We hugged and kissed with lots of 'I love you's' and 'Have fun,' and now she is gone, doing it herself, and I am here.

"Laura has left before on other adventures—to camp, to her first day in school, even on an airplane once by herself when she was small. But, somehow it is different now. She is thirteen years old and wants to do it all by herself. 'Don't worry Mom, I'll be fine.' How I remember saying that to you!!!

"And, I really am *not* worried and am so proud that she wants to do it all herself. However, there is a leftover emotion that is difficult to define. I have an immediate instinct that you would understand that lingering feeling of, well, how it is to be a Mom.

"Laura will be gone for a week, and of course she will be back. But I know that she will be gone again and again, and each time she returns, it will probably be a little bit different.

"Maybe it is the gray morning rapidly turning brighter, or the sleepy quiet of the early morning house . . . I am feeling, for the first time, the perspective of time, of how my child's life passes through mine, and of how she will someday be gone, 'doing it all herself.'

"It is a good feeling. Laura is maturing and so healthy and eager. It is also an emotional knowledge that her time with me, as her Mom, as it has been so far, is really short, in the entire scheme of her life and mine.

"Where is she going, though? She is heading South to visit her grandparents, my parents, stepping back one generation for a time. That is right too, in the scheme of things, in her lifetime and yours.

"I started this monologue thinking of me and what it is like to be a Mom. Now, I am thinking of you and of your child, my brother, dead now three years. We don't talk about Alan as much as we think of him.

"I know that he is gone, and the time he passed through your life was too short. As many times as he left 'to do it himself' he always came back, and each time it was a little different. But Mom, that's how it is to be a Mom, even though his last departure was incomprehensible. Perhaps, from one Mom to another, I understand it all a little better now. The time we have with our children is limited; they must leave. The time we have with our children is forever, despite their leave. The time we have with our children is something to cherish.

"I hope that I haven't caused you to feel sad. A child's leaving is part of a mother's possession. And to have that possession, no matter what may accompany it, is not sad, it is incredibly special.

"I love you, Mom.

"Please give my child, also yours, a big hug and kiss for me. I do know that you cherish your time with her and also with me, your child. Perhaps that is why I *knew* you'd understand . . . so, that's how it feels to be a mom."

"Your daughter Netta"

* * *

Not *My* Son!

Cystic Fibrosis? What does that mean?
How long will he have it? Until six or sixteen?
Tell me, Doctor, tell me all that you know.
Is this an illness that he will outgrow?

Slow down a minute. Wait. I don't understand.
You say that he has to have treatments by hand?

I must pound on his chest three times a day,
to loosen the mucus that will not go away.

You say *Forever*? Till *death*? He'll have this disease.
Not *my* little Gary? Tell me different, oh, please!
Couldn't you be mistaken? Won't you run some more tests?
You've just mixed up his X-rays with another boy's chest.

Mist Therapy? Postural drainage? Enzymes and pills?
You're telling me this illness debilitates and kills.
There's no cure you say. Are you certain of that?
Oh, God! Not *my* son. No, not him. Not that.

This was written by D.A.G. in May 1974, when Gary was
three and a half years old and just diagnosed as having C.F. He
is now just entering his teen years.

* * *

The Grieving Process

The grieving process of parents can take many forms. It is
most important that no parent ever be told, "You should be
over it by now; it has been over a year!"

Family members who can talk together, who have been able
to share their experiences with other mourning parents, with
the hospital staff even after the death of a child, or with a
compassionate clergyman or relative, usually do much better
than those who hold all their feelings inside and return to
work, pretending that life goes on as usual. A father's account
of his grief period shows beautifully how little, precious memories become significant, how a favorite flower becomes a
source of intense feelings, how butterflies become symbols—
universal symbols of eternal life (something the children of
the concentration camps taught us). His son died at age six of
a brain stem tumor.

Notes on My Son's Death by a Father

Christian was my favorite of three sons. He was the middle son. I guess that is why. I felt he needed more attention. I loved him dearly.

As I write, the tears overflow my eyes. I can think of nothing bad or evil about Christian, and now everything of beauty outdoors reminds me of him.

He loved flowers (especially dahlias) and took joy in all things of beauty. I am reminded of the time he and I went to a yard sale. It was inside someone's house. He came across a cheap set of jewelry he wanted to buy for his mom. I tried to get him to look around for something of more practical use (there was a sterling silver ring or a small gold chain) but he looked around and kept coming back to the cheap jewelry. He insisted, and rightfully so, that this was "pretty" and he had to have something "pretty" for Mom. To this day Mom has never taken off that pretty chain. And whenever I see it, even though it is tarnished and has lost its luster, I can only see the chain as it is in Christian's eyes.

Lately the thought that comes to me a lot is "It is better to have loved and lost than never to have loved at all." I used to think this referred to man/woman love but I think it is more appropriate in reference to the death of a young son. Although I am hurting a lot I feel the six and a half years Christian gave us were worth it.

I still wonder what people without children do all their life. Some people have dogs or pets of one sort or another. Some people are into things, but these things of the world cannot please or occupy a person for any length of time, can it?

I also wonder now about anyone who is lonely or single or has no children. I wonder if they have had a tragedy because I have learned we are not the only people this has happened to. At our post here there are two other people who have lost young children recently (within two years). We were all at a party together a few weeks ago, and my wife was talking with

one of the women who lost a two-year-old girl to some disease
(not cancer). Her husband has shut the incident out of his
mind (tried to, I'm sure). He hasn't talked about it since it
happened. My wife and I both feel much relief after we have
talked and cried about Christian. This woman was crying as
my wife told how our five-year-old son occasionally cries because he misses Christian. . . .

It is easier to write now, but there are times when I can't
hold back the anguish, especially when I talk with my wife.
Christian's birthday is Thursday. He would be seven if he had
lived. That may be a tough day. In three more months we
move out of the country to a new job assignment. This gives
us an opportunity to get away from the house we know as
Christian's stomping grounds. It is still very difficult for my
wife to work out back because Christian was always an outdoor person and usually stayed out back until a friend came.
Christian made friends easily. It is easier for me to work out
back because I feel I am carrying out Christian's wishes.

I pray every day to Christian, but I know he cannot answer.
I am not sure of God despite a Catholic rearing. Funny how I
can still pray but have doubts about God. And the more I pray
to Christian and the longer he doesn't answer, the surer I am
that God does not exist, at least as most Christians believe.

My family and I use all the cliches when we think of Christian, but my most favored thought is that Christian was our
personal Christ. He was in my eyes, perfect, but human. He
came to us for a reason, and he died, never complaining. I wish
I knew what his purpose on earth was.

My mother-in-law died a few years ago, and I always
thought she had a purpose in life, which I believe was to see
Connie and me married. Further, I believe one of our children
is to fulfill a destiny. And I guess Christian's death was part of it.

Another thought that comes to mind is that Christian was
a very special person. He required little attention, strived for
perfection, and was a hard worker. And when a family is given

a very special person, [they] can't keep him for too long. He must be surrendered so he can help someone else. . . .

As I viewed Christian in his state of rest, I noticed the I.V. marks, one on each hand. They were black and blue now, and I thought again of Christ's nail wounds.

Sunday while on a car ride in our community we stopped to talk to a couple who are close to us. They lost a daughter to cancer (leukemia) about a year ago. However, when I first heard of this tragedy long ago, I never gave it much thought. Now that I have suffered the same fate, I feel like I should hug these people or be kind in some way. They only have one left. We have two. Thank God for our other two children. Without them life at this time would have no meaning. The loss of Christian could have been devastating.

The people in our community have been overwhelmingly kind and generous, thanks in part to my wife's popularity and community work. What a joy it is to know that people really do care. And care a lot.

When I planted the garden Saturday, I seemed to work like the devil because I know I was planting for Christian.

My five-year-old cries sometimes, and it is a sincere cry. He looks at us, and his expression says "It's OK to cry, Mom. I know how you feel." This is amazing for a child of five. He will not let you turn your head. He wants to see your face.

A month ago as we took a train ride here, we went underground, and our little five-year-old said, "Look, Mom, we are going underground like Christian is." There have been a few of these underground remarks from him.

Our eleven-year-old has not cried openly as many times since his brother passed away. I hope his holding it in doesn't do any psychological harm.

I worry that the children may have been exposed to too much at Christian's death.

One day when Christian was first sick, we were on an underground beltway and out of the deep blue Christian said,

"Mom, what is it like to be buried?" He had a fear of being by himself underground. Not about dying but about being by himself. Any thought of Christian suffering brings great anxiety upon me. I can recall when he did something very disturbing at home (while he was sick) and I ran after him and caught and smacked him. As I swung my hand, he pulled away and bumped himself on a piece of dining room furniture. I told him I did not care how sick he was; he could not do things like that. However, now I feel I may have been too harsh with him.

Now there is the helpless attitude. At the time when Christian was getting worse, around Christmas, we would read an article in the paper about Interferon or some other wonder drug and would busily make notes or make some phone calls to see if it was available for use with cases like Christian's. I wrote to a surgeon in Canada who told me the tumor was inoperable. Soon we realized that at our hospital they were capable of doing anything that almost any other institution of this magnitude could do. So we checked with all his doctors there.

Now we feel we should write the National Cancer Institute to see if we can help or check on those people.

I feel we are missing the boat in cancer research in one area. We should be taking more of a family medical history on people who die of cancer. I feel certain that if enough facts about a group of cancer victims were put into a computer, a correlation would come soon. I read in a newspaper about the Chinese detecting cancer of the esophagus by sending a team of researchers to the stricken area for two or three years to thoroughly document the situation. They studied all aspects of the situation there, and soon zeroed in on a mold which grew on a staple bread which they pickled. Anyhow, they seemed to find the problem in a very short time.

My wife believes that the seed of Christian's tumor may have been allowed to germinate due to his many ear infection problems. He had a lot of ear infections and many ear drum puncturing operations (myringotomy).

We can both think of many instances of being exposed to carcinogens. Mercury and X-rays when Connie was carrying Christian while she worked at a dentist's office. Chlorodane, which I sprayed about a year ago to kill crickets. And methechlorodane (used mostly to kill termites) spraying I did in and around the house seems like a dumb thing to have done. I now fear the stuff and will probably never use it indoors again.

At the last week of Christian's life we had the opportunity to have an experimental drug administered to Christian. It's called Cisplatin. It was supposed to have been absorbed by cancer cells more readily than normal cells. Then the tumor would die. At first they would not give this to Christian because he had a fever, but we convinced them that since it was his last chance, we should try it even though it might kill him. It didn't work.

For the overwhelming kindness and generosity shown to my family by the people of this community following the loss of my son I would like to say a humble thank you! And further, that I will strive to repay these graces ten fold. It is a pleasure to be sure once again that people really do care, especially the people of this fantastic community.

* * *

I recently received the following letter from J., Christian's father:

"Dear Elisabeth,

"We received your letter today and were very happy to hear from you. Thank you so much for your encouraging words. Your comments are, as always, soothing to both of us. I must confess, however, that I find it harder and harder to believe in anything. Being born and raised a Roman Catholic I was taught to believe. I want to believe. I feel I should, but after the death of Christian and all the prayers, thoughts, and energies that preceded, I find it increasingly difficult. I have worked things out for myself. However, I am troubled with the recurring thought that the reason I want to believe I will see Christian again is that I so desperately want to see him again, but I probably believe only because I was taught that way, or as I now recall the nuns' teaching methods, I was brainwashed that way. No disrespect intended.

"I cry only occasionally now. It's a great tension reliever. When Christian was taken from us, I used to picture him as being near in his old form. As time passed I envisioned him as resuming his old form only when requested. Then the time came when he told me he could no longer come to me in his old form, that he must join with the others, that I imagined him to be in the form of clouds. He would be part of a huge cloud. Now whenever I see a cloud I think of him. Also, I think of him whenever I see a butterfly, which reminds me of the reply I received, from the artist of the picture I send you, to an inquiry as to his wares: 'Why do you want a picture of a butterfly? Butterflies are free.'

"Also, whenever I am alone and see a bird, I like to think that it is Christian and he is just relaxing, roaming free, keeping an eye on us, but he knows that he is not allowed to change anything."

* * *

A part of the *grieving process* is a need to get a sign "of life" from our dead children. We want to touch them once more, see their smiles, hear their voices, but most of all we need to know that they are all right and not lonesome, as we are.

A mother whose young son died at Christmas had a beautiful dream the night before her son's birthday the following October. In the dream the mother and her son were together. She said to him, "You have not gone away after all." He replied, "I have gone away, but I am not alone."

The harder parents try to see or experience their children after death, the more unlikely it is that they will. Real dreaming about deceased children usually occurs a few weeks or months after the death of a child, when the agonizing pain and grief are lifted and the first quiet nights resume with normal sleep.

Those families who have had time to prepare for an impending death of a child may be more fortunate, as they have done most of their grieving during the last months or weeks of a child's life and thus may be able to "see" their loved one in a dream much earlier.

A young mother whose child was murdered in a most brutal rape and subsequent drowning returned home in a forlorn state of mind, after wandering around aimlessly for several days. When she was finally able to lie down on her bed, she noticed a bright light coming through the window and in it appeared her little first-grader, healthy, radiant, and smiling—with outstretched arms: "Look, Mom!" Her daughter disappeared after a few moments but the sight filled her with such peace and love that she was in a much better mental condition after this incident than the rest of the still frightened community!

I guess that visions, dreams and appearances of our loved ones who died depend a great deal on our natural need. I truly believe that we get what we need, and if we are unable to dream or otherwise become aware that our children have simply left us for a while, it may be a test of our faith and our trust. We get what we need, not always what we want. Much later on in life, when we look back at our windstorms we realize how much they have changed us, how much we have grown and become wiser in compassion and understanding!

One woman from Massachusetts, who lost both her husband and her four-year-old daughter to cancer within four years, had a beautiful symbolic experience after her daughter's death. Shortly before Brenda died, she told her mother that she would send a cardinal as a sign of assurance that there was, indeed, a heaven. On the very day of her funeral, more than a dozen of the striking birds appeared on the Boschetto's lawn, where none had appeared before. The cardinals' appearances in her yard occur almost daily and have tremendously strengthened Maxine Boschetto's faith in the continuity of existence. One more word needs to be said about "shopping around" for proof of survival. Many parents are so desperate that they would pay any price to get a "message" from their dead children. They visit psychics, have life readings, and go to any expense and travel to fulfill this wish. But these parents have the same gifts that any of the so-called psychics have. If they can be still, if they can trust, if they are willing to accept what is given to them and stop looking for external sources, they will find help and the consoling knowledge that they will see their children again. There are too many charlatans around willing to recommend someone for communications with their deceased child. Ask at night in your prayers or in your thoughts to get a sign from your child, and if you truly need it, it will be given.

You will also know at first, every butterfly, every cloud, every ray of sunshine is viewed as a signal from your child. Accept that without being too self-critical. It will help you to pay attention again to the beauty that is still around you and will always be around us, even after all our children have died. It is a natural part of the healing process.

* * *

Children who have been included in the death process and mourning within the family are able to let go and even write some beautiful letters to the deceased as their way of saying good-bye. Little Meagan was ten years old when her beloved Grandpa died. She drew a beautiful rainbow picture for him with an angel in a baby blue cloud (baby blue represents a "fading out of life" in universal symbolic language). She wrote in the upper left quadrant of the picture (over the angel), "To PaPa, this is your cloud to sit on." In the upper right corner she added, "A rainbow is so happy, so I want you to have a happy thing to remember us by." In a letter accompanying the drawing she wrote to him, "To PaPa, please be happy up in Heaven. We all want you to be. We all are praying for you to be. How is your house or cloud that you are staying on? Did you meet any presidents or famous people? Well, good-bye, be happy."

On the same day, this little girl wrote a Thanksgiving letter that many adults could learn from. It read:

What I Have to Give Thanks For

When I was a baby my real mother said she could not take care of me and give me a proper home. So she put me up for adoption. I have to give thanks for that because a nice couple (my parents now) came and wanted a baby girl. The one they described was me. So the lady showed me to them and they said they would provide a very good home for me and they did. So I have to give thanks for a very, very nice family.

I also have to give thanks for the world because if the world wouldn't be here I would not be here or my family. No birds, flowers, no people or animals. But we do have these things and you should be thankful too.

* * *

During the difficult process of accepting the loss of a child, some parents are able to find comfort in the positive accomplishments their children contributed while they were living and pride in their last achievements. One mother describes the great difficulty she (and all others have) in accepting the imminence of a child's death:

"Then, that horrible day on December 3, when the doctor stood in the hall and said 'I think you should know that at this point I don't think I will be able to cure John' [whose cancer was discovered when he was 14½ and who died soon after he turned 16]. . . . Well, my heart was very heavy and I was absolutely drained and I could not hold back the tears. John kept saying 'what's wrong,' and I just could not bring myself to say that to him. Not then.

"Somewhere along the line in December in the midst of my fears and anxieties, I managed to place a call to the American Cancer Society, saw a social worker and she helped—oh, how she helped. No, I did not have to tell John he was dying because of course he was and so are all of us so it did not have to be said. That was such a relief. And that very night I bought three books that helped me very much. . . . (The books she refers to are Dr. Ross's *Questions and Answers on Death and Dying* and *To Live Until We Say Goodbye*, and Doris Lund's book *Eric*.) . . . That very night I sat and read all of your *To Live Until We Say Goodbye*, and I cried and cried because my son was actually dying and I was going to lose him and I could do nothing about it. It hurt. I hated it and still hate it. But I realized this was normal and your books opened the door on many feelings and conversations with John, my daughters, my Mom and Dad, friends, and the Reverend from my church, all of which helped me so very much.

"No! It is not fair and it does not make any sense to us. Why should it? John was very special, from the day he was born, and was even more special now because he was going home to his heavenly father. And who could love him more, give John complete peace, make him strong again, and beautiful —more beautiful than we have ever known him? God, and only God, so I let go just a little bit.

"During the next couple of months, I devoured your books and I talked, cried, and reached out to John and to my family. . . . Each day that I read I let go just a little more.

"John and I never discussed the fact that he was dying, because he knew and I knew and he knew that I knew what was happening. He did not want to hurt us and he did not want to discuss what was happening, and that was alright. We didn't, but he knew I was there, that I loved him very much, and that he could say anything he wanted whenever he wanted.

"I was there by his side holding his hand through every single puncture, watching his pain and anguish and sending my love, in every breath I took, to him and through him. I know it and I believe with all my heart that he knew it too.

"We talked in our own way and both of us knew what the other was thinking and feeling—we were that close. I would not have missed that closeness for anything, even though it tore my heart and soul to pieces with every puncture. His pain and agony flowed through every part of me and my insides screamed and ripped apart a little more every time.

"It was through your books that I kept John home. On March 21, John was admitted to the hospital for extreme anemia and was given a transfusion. At the time we were with the doctor, I stepped into the other room and asked him if John was losing his battle and he said 'yes,' and no words can explain how I felt at that time. I cried and cried, and yes, I did it with John and in front of John. That night I stayed very, very late at the hospital with John and would have spent the night had he not rallied around and I knew in my heart that he was alright for the time being and would definitely come home the next day.

"On March 30, John turned sixteen and I knew he would not be with us much longer. However, I had reached the point of acceptance. John and I had said all we needed to say to each other in order to be separated and without horrendous pain.

"On April 3, John had his last puncture in the clinic. On the night of April 5 at 7:30 I held John in my arms, we cried together, and I helped him walk to the car for his last and final journey to the hospital. I promised him I would not leave him there alone and would stay with him until he came home. . . . They put him on oxygen from Thursday night until Saturday afternoon, and I did stay with him at the hospital, in his room, just as I promised him I would.

"We brought him home at 2:00 on Saturday afternoon, April 7, for the last and final stage of his journey here on earth. John was in much pain in the stomach, back, and shoulders. He had gone from 165 pounds to about 105 pounds and was nothing but skin and bones. He stood 6 feet 3½ inches tall, and 105 pounds just is not very much weight at that height. At this point John was very curved in the back from all the pain, punctures, and just everything.

"Still, no complaints. Just a simple 'rub my back,' or 'rub my shoulders,' or 'get me some milk,' or 'give me a cigarette.' That was it. He tried right up to the very end to be strong and do for himself. He even tried walking on his own from one room to the other. Not very well, because he was so weak and so heavily drugged—but he tried.

"On Wednesday morning, April 11, I sat on John's bed talking to him and rubbing his back and shoulders as we talked about the lady I work with, because she had been on vacation the week before. He asked if she was back and had she enjoyed herself. We also talked about his back and shoulders hurting. That day, at 12:20 in the afternoon John left us to go home to God.

"At last! No more pain, no more suffering, no more punctures.

"I was at work and my Mom called and asked if I could come home, and not really thinking, I said, 'why?' and pushed it until she said, 'John's gone,' and I screamed and hung up on my Mom. Oh, how I screamed, over and over and over. I did not expect to react that way, but it hurt so very much.

"My Dad came and picked me up and I went home and ran into John's room and held his arm and hand and told him 'I love you so very much' over and over and that I was going to miss him very much. I never said 'good-bye' because he will always be with me, in my heart; and someday I know we will be together again.

"Both of my girls took John's death very hard. My oldest daughter (thirteen) cried and cried and cried all day long way up into the night. The other one (nine) went into the entrance by the front door and banged her head repeatedly on the wall and as a result had a very bad headache for a couple of days.

"I held both girls' hands and we went into John's room and

stood at the foot of his bed so that they could see him and say whatever they wanted to say to John. They were both frightened, but on seeing John they felt better and not quite so scared.

"It was a lot of work, but I kept both girls very involved in everything from that moment until John's funeral. . . . When we went, family only, for the final visitation with John in the slumber room the girls again were very frightened. I held their hands and we walked up to the casket, and they were so filled with so many questions. Eventually we touched John and they were upset by the fact that John was so cold and so hard, but again, your book helped me to explain how John had left his earthly cocoon and because it was not needed it was not necessary for it to be warm, soft, and moving.

"Neither of my girls is afraid of death and they know that John is always with them, and that someday, we will all be together again.

"John fought a very courageous battle, and I am so very proud to be his mother, in life and in death. John kept his sense of humor through all his illness and was very strong."

A few months later, this mother wrote to me again, because as she said: "Some of the most important things I wanted to share were left unsaid. John radiated love, warmth, happiness in every breath, in addition to being a super fantastic person in so very many ways, and I want you to know this part of him also.

"I remember John as a fun-loving person full of life and the usual little-boy and teenage-boy mischief, but when I look back on these things now it was such good mischief and there is much humor to see, hold, and cherish forever.

"I remember sitting on the sidelines of a basketball game, when he was in the Gray-Y, laughing myself silly. When he should have been reaching up, he was bending down, and when he should have been bending down, he was—what else— stretching up. Or, just standing in the middle of the game watching everyone run and play as he yawned.

"Then there was the baseball game. That was really something. John got a hit and was so excited that the bat went flying through the air. After that game we stopped and I bought a bat and ball. John and I were in the yard the rest of the afternoon practicing dropping the bat after a hit instead of letting it sail through the air.

"We (John, the girls, and I) had many good tickling, romping, laughing sessions and many, many long walks and talks. John was very close to both girls and spent a lot of time with them. All three of them were close and shared many happy times together. Oh, yes, they fought and argued like normal brothers and sisters; however, no one else could say anything or do anything to any one of them without the other two jumping in to defend.

"John was an active member of the Boy Scouts and wanted to become an Eagle Scout. He was working toward this goal, but because of his loss of hair at the very beginning of his illness he became totally inactive . . . John was also active in the Youth Fellowships at the church until the loss of hair.

"During John's visit with my cousin last summer, he said, 'Before I die there are two things I want—to own a van and to make love to a girl!' When I found this out, I knew he had had one of those wishes. My parents had bought him a van in March as a sixteenth birthday present. It was purchased during the first half of March, and John was thrilled beyond words, even though too weak to really show much jumping enthusiasm.

"John worked very hard to get his learner's permit. Since he was not in school, and Teleteaching could not offer driver's education, he had to take a class through a private school. He had to be on his feet for four Saturdays from 9:30 A.M. to 5:30 P.M., and in his weakened pained condition that was very difficult—but he did it.

"John stood in the lines at the Department of Motor Vehicles all by himself when he went to apply for his learner's permit. I tried to get him to sit down and let me stand in the lines for him until I got up close to the front, but he would not go for it at all. He was determined to do this on his own, and he did, and this was within the last two months of his life.

"He was so pleased at his accomplishment. When we left the D.M.V. he took the keys from my hand (no resistance on my part) and he drove all the way home—not very far, but difficult because he was hurting and tired and had done a lot of standing.

"It was about a month after John passed away that one of his friends told me John had succeeded with his other wish—he had made love to a girl. We were in a show at the time, and I let out a whoop. There are just no words to describe how delighted I was at that moment to know that John had his wish. As a matter of fact, I was, until then, hoping, and praying that he had succeeded and believing in my heart that I would never know. How very, very wonderful for him, and I am so happy for his sake. He knew he was going to die, and he did something he really wanted to do.

"When John first became ill the Boy Scouts gave us a lot of support. My mom had called one of the Scout leaders to ask if he would please pick up a twenty-two rifle for John. He had earned his Shotgun and Rifle merit badge and my parents were going to give him the rifle for Christmas in 1977 (the month we discovered his cancer).

"When John came home from the hospital on the 20th, my mom called the scoutmaster—he asked if John was home, up to company, and if he could stop by to see John for just a few minutes that evening. Well, *all* the scoutmasters came over and presented John with his rifle from the troop. During the week between Christmas and New Year's, the scoutmaster took John and a few of the other boys shooting. John and I went to the shooting range several times. . . . Each time, we had a ball together.

"John gathered up enough strength during the last part of March to drive his van. Our birthdays are three days apart and he was determined to go shopping for my present himself. So, off he and Grandpa went in the van and from what I understand, he handled the van beautifully—better than my Dad could. John was so very proud of his van, and at least he knew it was there, he knew it was his, and he did get to drive it. I am very thankful for that.

"I will never forget the very first [hospital] admission. He was six feet two inches and went into the pediatrics ward because he was not quite fifteen at the time and still considered a child. In the waiting room, waiting for admission, he said he could not stay because he had forgotten something at home—dinner. Also, he could not go in because he had a headache and needed to go home and take some Anacin first.

"Funniest of all, was in his room. Lying on the bed he watched a toddler go by in the hall and turned to me and said, 'Do I have to put up with these twerps?' and just a minute later, was in the hall on hands and knees playing with one of those twerps.

"Sometimes John was so mischievous in such silly ways, and I guess I overlooked a lot too—he was mine, and I loved him, and I thought he was cute, funny, and lovable—and I still do. I guess especially during his illness I tended to overlook an awful lot, but I also learned that most of the things you let upset you are not that serious anyway and I have learned to overlook a lot of things with the girls, and also, to look at them through different eyes, if you know what I mean.

"Everything was always worked around John—his treatment and what he was up to doing. But, whatever we did was enjoyable. And he also had many outtings last summer with his friends that I know were very good and happy times for him. This I am also thankful for, for John. He had some good times to look back on when he could do nothing but lie around.

"As I have told you earlier, the Boy Scouts gave us much support during John's illness. The scoutmasters were his pall bearers, and the boys were there too, all in full dress uniform. . . . There were many youths at John's funeral—friends all of them. Scouts, church friends, neighborhood friends, and school friends.

"Just recently, the Boy Scouts had a family camp and invited all of us to the camp for the afternoon, dinner, and campfire. At the campfire, they did a Lost Scout Ceremony. It was happy, beautiful, and sad. At the very end of the campfire, they brought out their flag, and it is tradition in the Scouts that if they have no one to present the flag to, it is burned. They cut out two stars, one presented to my mother and one to me, in memory of John, and then they burned the flag in absolute silence—except for the tears many people were shedding.

"I am enclosing a copy of the poem that we had read at John's funeral. It expresses our feelings of love for John, in life and death:

To John, With Love

I'll lend you for a little time
A child of Mine, God said,
For you to love the while he lives
And mourn for when he's dead.

It may be six or seven weeks,
Or thirty years, or three,
But will you, till I call him back,
Take care of him for Me?

He'll bring his charm to gladden you
And should his stay be brief,
You'll have his lovely memories
As solace for your grief.

I cannot promise he will stay,
Since all from Earth return,
But there are lessons taught down "there"
I want this child to learn.

And there, with you on Earth
This child of mine I lend,
For the many souls that he will touch,
With the lessons that I send.

I looked the wide world over
In my search for people true,
And from the throngs who crowd life's way,
I have selected you.

Now will you give him all your love,
Nor think the labor vain,
Nor hate Me when I call around
To take him back again?

I fancy that I hear you say,
"Dear Lord, Thy will be done,"
For all the joy this child has brought,
All fateful risks we run.

We sheltered him with tenderness,
We love him while we may,
And for the happiness we've known,
We shall forever grateful stay.

But You came 'round to call for him
Much sooner than we'd planned—
Dear Lord, forgive this grief,
And help us understand.

*   *   *

Mike, a terminally ill teenager, left the following note on the night table the day of his death. His mother was so grateful for this message that she has shared it with us; it supports the ever-increasing conviction that children do better if they have open and honest communication with their families, as this young boy was fortunate to have.

The time has come,
My Job is done, now it's
The Time is for a
nother one, The gates
will open, open soon
 I now will go.
See you Soon.

Time, Time will never
Stop, Everlasting time,
Love, Love is Eturnal,
Fouever more Love I will
always love you.

His mother wrote, "I have watched with sadness parents who could or would not be honest with their children about their cancer. They have missed so much. My son and I talked openly about his death. He was able to tell me, 'I am scared.' I was able to say, 'I know, son, but you won't be.' My son taped messages to those he loved, family and friends. He helped plan his funeral. He gave a few things away to friends before he died. We were left with a great legacy—we are lucky. I hope to be able to help other parents to look at their children, to listen to them and to learn from them."

* * *

Another mother shares the experience of bringing her daughter home to die:

"When the doctors discussed my eleven-year-old daughter's diagnosis with me almost a year ago, my whole world shattered as I tried to figure out why cancer had struck. I knew that I had to try to alter the original prognosis of six months. I thought the answer rested with a New York doctor. . . . Having had no experience with cancer, and with so much being related to me daily, I hurriedly packed and went to New York with my daughter and she received chemotherapy.

"I was horrified when I first saw the pediatric outpatient floor; a whole new world of critically ill children unfolded before my eyes. My shock heightened as my daughter, Djenab, started taking the drugs which made her painfully ill. In that first week, I knew chemotherapy wasn't the answer. I started investigating the disease and other therapies such as diet, vitamins, etc. During that period I accepted the fact that the disease (which Djenab had) is incurable, although some people experience remissions.

"In the meantime, we were living in an apartment costing $950 per month, which fortunately for us became unavailable; so we had to seek out different lodgings. By 'accident' we ended up at the Ronald McDonald House, where our lives took a definite turn for the better.

"My daughter met other children with her particular ailment who had also undergone amputations (she had lost a leg by this time), and she realized that she was not alone. In spite of cancer's presence, we laughed, went to football games, plays, game shows, and museums, shared experiences, and gave each other the support we badly needed. All of this happened very naturally without social workers and doctors to impose their 'knowledge' on us, as was the case at the hospital. We met families from all over the world, some of whom spoke no English, but we communicated anyway.

"One afternoon the Ronald McDonald House director gave me (Dr. Ross's book) *To Live Until We Say Goodbye*. I stayed up until 3:00 A.M. glued to the book, rereading many sections that held particular significance. . . . That evening, I decided that my daughter should experience death at home with me and her nine-year-old sister, Kesso. The following day, I was so excited about the decision, only to find that the director was the only person who shared my excitement; family, friends, and doctors were all opposed to the idea.

"Well, I have never been the sort of person to be swayed easily; so I 'stuck to my guns' by bringing her home when her time was near. . . . I found that 'A Letter to a Child With Cancer' (by Helen Baldwin) answered many questions that the girls had about death, plus it helped me to accept Djenab's inevitable death.

"Djenab and I discussed her pending death extensively; she knew that my parents who died ten years ago would be there too and that she would be in God's hands. We discussed her guardian angels; who would be with her. Her only reservation was her sister Kesso's welfare; Kesso had begged her not to die, indicating that she would not be able to live herself. I tenderly told Djenab that Kesso and I would miss her, but we would adjust. I also assured her that we would be joining her later when our time came.

"The next day, she identified various items as gifts for friends and family members, confided in a ten-year-old neighbor to protect her sister and told me about things we did as a family that didn't particularly excite her, but she didn't want to 'ruin' my enthusiasm. For example, plans for a trip to Bermuda were thwarted by the doctors, and Djenab confided that she wasn't interested in going from the beginning; instead, she wanted to stay in her newly decorated room. . . . We laughed together as she continued to reveal these things to me and I marveled at the sensitivity, maturity, and strength of my little, frail, eleven-year-old.

"Even though I had discussed Djenab's pending death with her, I had not talked with Kesso. . . . You answered my questions and I spoke to Kesso two hours after our conversation. The three of us began to discuss our feelings regarding death. We were open, honest, and emotional, crying a little, and laughing too, but we were preparing ourselves for Djenab's transition.

"During the night before Djenab died, she had diarrhea—I carried her to the bathroom all night, but spent most of the night holding her and stroking her limbs. At 8:30 the next morning, she told me that she 'was not going to make it through the day.' I reassured her that I would be at her side (I had moved into her room when we returned home from New York City), and that everything would be OK because she would have total peace. In the next breath, she asked me to send for two of my friends. By 11:00 both friends had arrived. And she asked me to climb into bed next to her. Then she asked me to prop her up in a sitting position. All of a sudden she called, 'Mommie, Mommie!' bearing an expression of amazement on her face.

"I stroked her arm, saying, 'Djenab, just relax, everything will be all right.' With that statement, she took two breaths and died—flanked by a friend holding her right hand, one standing at the foot of the bed, and me, lying next to her on her left side with my arm around her. Oh Elisabeth, what a beautiful moment! I wept because I knew I would miss her physical presence. I wouldn't have missed being present at the moment of her death for anything in the whole world."

*   *   *

Another mother shares the story of the long illness, suffering, and death of her eleven-month-old baby and how she was able to come to grips with it all:

"Two years ago, we lost our eleven-month-old son Derek. He spent his entire short life in the I.C.U. of two Madison hospitals. He supposedly contracted a strep infection at birth. He was then placed on a respirator [and then he developed pulmonary disease]. Six months down the road, he had cardiac arrest, which subsequently led to a 109° temp, which in turn led to *severe* brain damage. It went on like this until he finally died—twenty days short of his first birthday. It was an ordeal that I wouldn't ever wish on my worst enemy.

"What happened to Derek, had Dennis and me on an emotional rollercoaster. First he was to get out in a week, then by our anniversary, then by Halloween, etc., etc. We would get all excited and then get shot down again. I honestly get tears in my eyes just thinking about it. But, Dr. Ross, we are *not* bitter, for we learned so much from the experience. Derek showed us how strong a person can be; even when they said that he'd be dead soon, he'd make a remarkable comeback. He was an amazing child, who helped us gain religious and marital strength, a greater appreciation for life, and an urge to help other people with dying children. Pretty good accomplishments for an eleven-month-old, huh? And what better reward than Heaven!

"Derek died on a Sunday afternoon. I mention that because we were there when he died. It was unusual for us to come at that time of the day. We usually came in the morning and evening. He wasn't any sicker than usual, so we had no way of knowing. It seemed like *he* had picked the time. Dennis (my husband) was holding him, when Jeremy (Derek's older two-year-old brother) and I came into the room. I happened to look up at the monitors and they all read 'O.' I said, 'Dennis, is he doing all right?'

"Dennis replied, 'He's been doing great, Dix, he really seems to be reacting!' At just that moment, Derek's head fell over. He had finally died peacefully, where and how he wanted. The doctors grabbed Derek out of Dennis' arms and began pounding and resuscitating (although we'd asked for no efforts of this sort). They proceéded to even try cut-downs in both arms as I stood there, screaming at them to finally let him be. It was an unfortunate way to end Derek's peaceful ending. My comfort is in knowing that they were working on the empty cocoon, as you talked about, for the butterfly had finally been set free!

"Now to explain some of our thoughts throughout the year. We went through so many ups and downs! It took us every single day of those eleven months to realize that death was *really* a blessing for Derek. We saw him in agony, struggling for his every breath, or seizuring for twenty-one hours straight—Dr. Ross, he lived in such torment. But we somehow could not realize that dying for Derek would be such a release. Looking back now, I realize just how selfish we really were. Even after his doctors told us that he was surely going to be severely retarded, Dennis kept waiting for a miracle, because throughout the year he had been a miracle and *had* shown up doctors again and again!

"It finally came down to a meeting with his doctors. They told us that there would have to be a decision made regarding his respirator. Dennis hadn't attended this particular meeting. So, that evening I went home and told him about what they had said. For the first time, we agreed it was time to let Derek and God choose what was to become of Derek's life! We decided that on Derek's birthday, May 30, we would have him taken off the respirator and take him outside for the *very first time*. If he wanted to die, in peace in our arms, he had certainly earned that right!

"We felt that we *had* made the right decision. But God in his wisdom and Derek in his love, didn't want us to *have* to make that decision. They waited until we had emotionally accepted Derek's fate and had made our peace with God and ourselves. Derek died May 4. I regret now that it may have been *us* who made Derek hang on and linger through all that suffering. We certainly may have been holding him here. I

only hope and pray that now he is happy and in such peace
that his suffering on earth will be forgotten.

"After hearing your example of the butterfly, I came home
and wrote a poem about it, in relation to our experiences.
Here it is:

The cocoon had been slow to open;
the silken threads of Derek's life had
bound him so very tightly.

He so richly deserved his wings to fly,
but in loving Derek, we often asked
too much of him.

We begged him to stay—when we should have let go.

But God in his wisdom, and Derek in his love, had tried to
make us see that Derek was *not* our possession . . .
but like a butterfly—he was free!

Chapter 12
Funerals

MUCH HAS BEEN WRITTEN about funerals, and we dedicated a
special chapter to this issue in a previous book, *Death, the
Final Stage of Growth*. I will, therefore, add just a few more
additional thoughts and special issues.

It needs to be understood that funerals are for the family.
Although we try to remember the desires and wishes of the
deceased, we need to do what is right for those who are left
behind. Cultural, religious, and local customs need to be respected even if they seem alien to those who ask to help in the
preparation or completion of the ritual.

In times long ago, the dead were buried under an avalanche
of dirt and stones. The saying went that the deeper the person
was buried, the more he was respected and feared, for cen-
turies ago, it was believed the dead might come back and
retaliate. An especially deep burial assured more security from
those who still had an ax to grind. A remnant of this ancient
custom is seen in Jewish cemeteries, where visitors put a peb-
ble on the gravestone "to make it a little heavier," as an old
lady recounted with a chuckle.

Whether we put the ashes of the deceased in the Holy River
Ganges or let them go from an airplane over the Rocky Mountains, whether we put the corpse in a flag and put it out to sea
or seal it in a mausoleum—or simply lower it into a grave and

cover the casket with soil—it is only the shell, the cocoon, the physical body of the person who has left us. It is a ritual, a formal good-bye, a chance for loved ones to be together in a joint farewell to what is left after death has occurred.

It is a chance for those who were not able to participate in a final illness and care to join with those who had this privilege. It also means the arrival of friends and relatives long not seen —to catch up on memories, to know we are not alone in our pain and loss, to reunite with shattered family members, and last but not least, to publicly share the meaning of the life of the person who has left, the meaning it gave to our lives. It is a thank-you, a tribute, a public sharing of grief and pain, of consolation and hope.

It is naturally especially meaningful if the person who left us arranged the funeral ahead of time like my old Eskimo friend, who knew her end was close and prepared her favorite dishes, called all the old friends from faraway villages, and then left her body, after putting on her favorite dress and making little gifts for her friends. Then, the funeral can become a true celebration of life, for all participants know that the deceased was ready for her final journey, and the feast was anticipated and prepared by the departed.

Children, more frequently in recent years, have asked to be able to prepare their own funeral. Adolescents particularly want to know ahead of time what they are going to wear, what music will be played, who is going to speak, and who needs to be especially invited. Needless to say, such preparations demand a cooperating, well-prepared family or friends. It requires an acceptance of the impending death and an openness of communications which is occurring more and more frequently.

We have found that a great number of children who die a sudden, unexpected, often violent death also talk about these matters prior to their death, which would imply an unconscious awareness of the probability of an early death. This has probably always been true, but it is only in the last few years that adults have paid attention and registered such remarks, rather than brushed them away because of their own discomfort or superstition.

As we said earlier, it is of utmost importance to view the body when we have to deal with a sudden death. Mutilated parts can easily be covered, and the relative should be accompanied by a close friend who is unafraid and supportive. Expression of emotions has to be permitted and sedatives should be forbidden, as they only cover up the pain and lead to unnecessary and costly delayed grief reactions and griefwork.

Although it is not possible in many parts of our so-called civilized world to have the deceased at home till the time of the funeral, it has proven to be a therapeutic way of dealing with the death of a loved one, unlike the instant removal of the body into a morgue and the subsequent often extremely painful viewing or identification of the dead child, who is then pulled out of a freezer in a cold and impersonal place which offers little solace or compassion.

Next of kin should at least have the option to wash, dress, and comb the hair of their own child, to rock a baby, to hold a stillborn for a while until they are ready to let go; to carry a dead child into the car of the undertaker or drive their own child to the place of the wake or viewing, if this cannot be done at home. Parents, grandparents, and siblings should have their own private time to express their last good-byes without the curious bystanders and well-meaning neighbors and friends. Siblings should have their own private time, preferably accompanied by a person of their own choice with whom they are comfortable and unashamed to ask questions. Some funeral directors are wonderfully helpful; others are dreadfully uptight about children touching their dead brother or sister, with their questions about artificial makeup, and their curiosity about the need for shoes. It is wise to discuss these matters as early as possible and to express your needs and wishes before it leads to unpleasant dramas that could easily be avoided.

Many young couples and especially unmarried, indigent girls who bear a stillborn ask us in great pain, shame, bewilderment, and anguish about the cost of a funeral for such an infant. They do want to give their baby a "decent funeral," as they put it, but they have barely enough money to survive themselves. We always advise them to talk to the hospital social worker or chaplain, and if they feel they are not helped by the institution where the baby was delivered, the local funeral society, friends, or neighbors have proven to be remarkably helpful and sensitive. Here again we emphasize that it is *not* the baby they bury but its "cocoon," which helps many to get rid of the guilt of not having been able to afford a real funeral.

Divorced and separated parents whose child dies have other problems to deal with, and since the number of single parents increases every year, it may be worthwhile stating a few issues about this special circumstance. Children of divorced parents who alternately lived with father and mother—and stepparents —are usually buried in the place where they felt most at home and had the most friends, where they went to school and had what one father called their "headquarters."

The divorced parent in whose custody the death occurs has the advantage of being there, of being able to view the body, and of having a local support system made up of the minister or rabbi, the schoolteachers and principal, the classmates and playmates of the child, and often, a nurse, an ambulance driver, a local emergency room physician, or a local policeman who can at least verbally share the parent's loss and be a listener. They are the ones who share "moment" memories of last incidents or words spoken, and they become a bridge between the child alive and dead.

The divorced parent who lives out of town is deprived of all these links. This parent's guilt, sorrow, shock, and self-blame are usually more intense, since this parent was deprived of even a last look. It is mandatory that someone in the family take special care of this parent, give support, and provide for viewing the body before it is cremated, donated to a medical school, or buried in a closed casket. Losing this reality of participation in the burial can bring pathological grief, which often occurs after a sudden death (plane crash, drownings) when there is no body or when the body is hidden from view (see Chapter 3, "Sudden Death").

In *Death, the Final Stage of Growth*, we asked a funeral director to share his experience with us when he had used a new and different approach to the removal of a child's body from home, and had allowed the parents to participate in the preparation of the child's body. Although these new ways of helping parents in a sudden death have not yet become the usual way of doing things, there is hope that more and more funeral directors will follow this approach, and thus finally become what they should be: another member of the helping profession.

As though in a return to earlier, simpler days, the parents are encouraged to wash and dress the child's body themselves. One parent, the father usually, is permitted to carry the body of the child to the car and ride with it to the morgue, the funeral home, and the place of the wake. It is then not a body put in a bag and carried away by a stranger, who puts it in an impersonal manner in the back of the black fancy car.

Parents are allowed to brush their girl's hair for the last time, to sing a lullaby to their infant, to hold and rock the dead baby until they are able to let go of it. It is their own private ritual of holding, hugging, crying, singing, and finally releasing the earthly remains to whoever will take care of it for the funeral.

When this happens, parents are better able to go through the often emotionally wringing reunion with arriving relatives and lead them to the casket. Many school children and play-mates have also greatly contributed to the last ritual for their classmates, by arriving at the wake or funeral with drawings made by themselves or other children, by singing a class song together, or by later visiting with the parents as they used to do in the past, when they came to pick up a pal.

* * *

A young man whom I met shortly before his death in Europe had fought valiantly with his cancer. He wrote his own invitation to his funeral, in character with his independent spirit during his lifetime. It read (on the back of his own photograph):

> I have left for my biggest journey:
> Come and say your farewell
> (followed by date and place of funeral)

Others have asked not to have a funeral but a get-together of friends, who will sing their favorite songs and celebrate the short time they had together.

Many parents, especially in rural areas where old customs are fortunately still alive, have been especially touched by friends, grandparents, or neighbors gathering to build a casket together. It gives the friends a chance to actively participate in the healing of pain—their own pain as well as the bereaved family's. A grandfather in his eighties expressed it in his own beautiful way:

> It has been a long time since I did any carpentry work, and my hands have become quite stiff. But when my grandson was taken from us in such an unexpected, cruel way— well, the only way I could do something for him and for me was to build his little casket. Cutting the wood helped me to express the anger—and when I put the final touches on this little casket—well, I was all love for him . . . and for the world. At least I had a grandson for a decade. Others don't even have that . . .

Siblings have a wonderful way of adding a farewell gift by often secretly putting a little toy or love note under the pillow in the casket. We have encouraged little brothers and sisters to pick such little gifts and the choices of these siblings are amazing and very touching. Little Sue chose a puzzle her brother bought shortly before he lost his sight to a brain tumor. Rich was apparently quite upset that he was never able to complete his "masterpiece" as he called it. Sue told me very matter-of-factly that Rich was able to see again and was probably happy to be able to finish it "when he arrives in heaven." Although Sue was only seven years old, she had been allowed to help care for her brother during the final weeks of his life at home and was well prepared for his anticipated death. She had spent hours at his bedside, telling him what was going on in school and on television and reporting even such details as the falling of the first snow, which her brother was unable to see.

It was she—together with an older sister—who was asked to plan for the participation of Rich's classmates at the funeral. With the teachers and a very understanding funeral director (who had lost a young son a few years earlier) they arranged for Rich's funeral, much to the relief and appreciation of Rich's mother, who, as a single parent, was exhausted and relieved when this help was offered.

* * *

Funerals are often a time when a family can share the poems their child had written, offer a philosophy of life that they learned from their dying child, and begin an opening in the awareness of those who participate—a beginning dawn of knowledge that a ship which disappears behind the horizon is not gone, only temporarily out of sight.

Since the consciousness of the people on this planet earth is unfolding at an accelerated rate, it is only a matter of a couple of decades until all people of all creeds, of all cultures, of all places will *know* that this life on earth is just a small, yet the most difficult, part of our long journey from the source we call God, back to our final home of peace, back to God.

A Swiss friend of mine shared with me his understanding of death in life. It correlates so incredibly well with my own understanding of life and death that I asked his permission to include it in its entirety in this book. May it help others to an acceptance and knowledge of the brief span of time we have together to share, to enjoy, to learn, to grow, and, most important, to love each other unconditionally.

This I Believe

On Life:

Live one day at a time—but live each one as though it were your last.

And I pray

> That I may grow a little braver
> To face life's trials and never waver
> From high ideals that I have made,
> To face life squarely, unafraid;
> That I may yet more patient be
> With those who faltering lean on me;
> To profit by mistakes I've made
> And let them from my memory fade;
> That I may always faithful be
> To those who put their trust in me;
> For these dear heavenly Lord I pray
> That I may prove worthwhile today.

On Doing Things:

Never postpone anything because it seems unpleasant. It might not be that way at all; but if it is, you will enjoy a deep satisfaction once it is behind you.

Kind Deeds:

Aspire each day to do just one kind deed toward some fellowman, but with no thought of appreciation.

My Own Affairs:

I always want to keep myself so busy cleaning the temple

of my own soul that I have no time to hear the discords coming from the chimes that ring in my neighbor's temple.

On Tolerance:

It is not enough to be tolerant or broad-minded—we must be open-minded.

On Religions:

To me, religions are like the spokes on a wheel; they all lead to the hub—at-oneness with God.

The Brotherhood of All Men:

The one who evaluates his fellowman based on race, creed, or color exposes his own lacks and incompetence, or is emotionally imbalanced. For the competent and mentally healthy, such distinctions simply have no meaning. After all, by their deeds—and only by their deeds—ye shall know them.

On Friends:

In order to have a friend be a friend.

Smile!

Always try to smile, no matter what. Other people have problems of their own. Let your smile be the window of your soul through which its light may shine and brighten the lives of your fellowmen.

Aspiring to a Higher Consciousness of Life?

Always remain with both feet on solid ground; the too "spiritual" ones are found in insane asylums.

On Death and Immortality:

Many fear death; but we only fear what we don't understand. Man can only be frightened if he is ignorant. The body is just a dwelling place for the soul, which uses it to express itself during the span of time that is allotted to each one of us for this earthly journey—in the light of eternity, always a short one. Therefore, death is only for the physical body; what constitutes the real "You," "I," "We" goes right on living. Dying means only that we discard our body the way we may cast aside an old worn-out coat, or step from one room into another. In Ecclesiastes, 12:7, we read: "Then shall the dust return to the earth as it was; and the spirit shall return unto God who gave it." Jesus said: "I go to prepare a place for you that where I am there you may be also." And to the thief on the cross: "Today thou shalt be with me in paradise."

Victor Hugo, the eminent French literary celebrity, wrote:

"I am a soul. I know well that what I shall render up to the grave is not myself. That which is myself will go elsewhere."

"When I go down to the grave I can say, like many others, 'I have finished my day's work!' But I cannot say, 'I have finished my life.' My day's work will begin again the next morning. The tomb is not a blind alley; it is a thoroughfare. It closes on the twilight, it opens on the dawn." "Let us be just to death, let us not be ungrateful to death. It is not, as has been said, a ruin and a snare; it is an error to think that here, in the darkness of the open grave, all is lost to us. There everything is found again. The grave is a place of restitution. There the soul recovers its plentitude; there it is set free from the body, from want, from its burdens and fatalities. Death is the greatest of liberators, the highest step for those who have lived upon its heights; he who has been no more than virtuous on earth becomes beauteous; he who has been beauteous becomes sublime."

"The eventide brought my own earthly journey to its conclusion and thus my resurrection on a more beautiful plane of life.

"As for you—if you should miss me—I am not really gone, just transformed, freed from the frail cloak, my physical body. 'But I will see you again and your heart shall rejoice' (John, 16:22).

"May our Heavenly Father give you the peace that comes with understanding; bless you, guide you, and protect you, and keep you in His care—until we meet again."

Chapter 13
Spiritual Aspects of the Work with Dying Children

I HAVE BEEN CRITICIZED for "getting involved in spiritual matters," as some people put it, since I was trained in the "science" of medicine. Others, in reacting to a growing spiritual awareness on my part, have dismissed all my work and clearly stated that "Ross has become psychotic; she has seen too many dying children!" I have been called every possible name, from Antichrist to Satan himself; I have been labeled, reviled, and otherwise denounced. Sometimes I think it is almost a compliment, as it obviously indicates that we are working in an area where people have so many fears that their only defense is to attack.

But it is impossible to ignore the thousands of stories that dying patients—children and adults alike—have shared with me. These illuminations cannot be explained in scientific language. Listening to these experiences and sharing many of them myself, it would seem hypocritical and dishonest to me not to mention them in my lectures and workshops. So I have shared all of what I have learned from my patients for the last two decades, and I intend to continue to do so. There have been many medical pioneers who were similarly reviled; in the

1800s, Dr. Semmelweiss pleaded with the Medical Society to listen to him when he begged the midwives, nurses, and doctors to wash their hands with soap before delivering a baby. He was denounced and destroyed, and he died a broken man. Shortly after his death, scientific evidence was found to prove that he was indeed right. But in the meantime, a brilliant man had been destroyed by the ignorance and arrogance of his colleagues. There are many serious investigators who have met the same fate, so at least I know that I am not alone, and I do not intend to abandon my investigations.

Let me share some of my experiences with you. Those who have had similar experiences in their lives surrounding the death of a child may be consoled that they are neither alone nor crazy. In fact, I have studied thousands of patients all around the world who have had out-of-body or near-death experiences similar to the ones described in Raymond Moody's book, *Life After Life*, for which I wrote the foreword.

Many of these people were not ill prior to the life-threatening event. They had sudden, unexpected heart attacks or accidents, so it is not likely that the experiences they shared could have been projections of wishful thinking, as some would like to say. The common denominator of these out-of-body experiences is that these people were totally aware of leaving their physical body. There was a rush of air or wind, and then they found themselves somewhere in the vicinity of where they were originally struck down: the scene of an accident, a hospital emergency room or operating room, at home in their own bed, or even at their place of work. They felt neither pain nor anxiety. They described the scene of the accident in minute detail, including the arrival of people who tried to rescue them from a car or who tried to put out a fire, and the arrival of an ambulance. Yes, they described accurately even the number of blowtorches used to extricate their mangled body from the wrecked car.

They often described the very desperate efforts the medical team made during a resuscitation to bring them back and their own attempts to convey that they were really OK, so the would-be rescuers could cease all efforts. They then began to realize that they could perceive everything, but the others present could not hear or perceive *them*.

The second awareness they shared in these experiences was the fact that they were whole again: amputees had their legs again, those who were in wheelchairs could dance and move around without any effort, and blind people could see. We, naturally, checked these facts out by testing patients who had been blind with no light perception for years. To our amazement, they were able to describe the color and design of clothing and jewelry the people present wore. I am sure no scientist could call this a projection. When asked how they could see, people described it with similar words: "It is like you see when you dream and you have your eyes closed."

The third event they shared was an awareness of the presence of loving beings, who always included next of kin who had preceded them in death. There was always a beloved grandmother waiting for a little girl, or a special uncle who died ten months earlier, or a classmate who was accidentally shot almost two years prior to the critical illness of his friend.

How does a critical and skeptical researcher find out if these perceptions are real? We started to collect data from people who were not aware of the death of a loved one, and who then later shared the presence of that person when they themselves were, as they often call it, at the "gate of no return."

One child who was almost lost during very critical heart surgery shared with her father that she was met by a brother with whom she felt so comfortable; it was as if they had known each other and shared each other's lives. Yet, she had never had a brother. Her father was very moved by his daughter's account and confessed that she did have a brother, but he had died before she was born!

An American Indian woman who was struck by a hit-and-run driver on a highway and died a short time later was comforted by a stranger who stopped his car to help her. He asked her if there was anything he could do for her, not aware that she was so critically injured. She told him that there was nothing he could do for her. But then, on second thought, she asked him for a favor. "If you ever get near the Indian reservation, please tell my mother that I was OK. Not only OK, but very happy because I am already with my dad."

The woman died a few minutes later, before an ambulance arrived. The Good Samaritan was so moved at being at the right place at the right time that he drove far out of his way to the Indian reservation, where the mother of the victim told him that her husband had died of a coronary one hour before the car accident had occurred, seven hundred miles away! Coincidence? I don't think so.

This story gave me an idea of how to proceed with my research rather than just collecting more "near-death experiences," thousands of which are published all over the world.

There are a great number of car accidents in our country in which several people are injured or killed, especially on national holiday weekends like Labor Day, Memorial Day, and the Fourth of July. If several people are injured and/or killed in an accident, the injured children are usually taken to the nearest hospital and, depending on the circumstances and the severity of their injury, later transferred to more specialized centers. Rarely is a child ever informed as to how many members of the family were killed at the site of the accident.

Staff and family usually avoid the sharing of this truth with children, and often truly believe that you can keep such knowledge from the little ones without making them suspicious or more worried. They naturally rationalize that it would upset the children, and that they are too seriously injured to be burdened with such facts (which is often true), or that they are too young to be able to cope with it.

We have spent a great deal of time with such critically injured children. We have never broken our promise not to tell them about other members of the family; since I am "only a visitor," not the primary physician, I have to respect the conditions of the treating physician. Such promises remind me of the early days of my work with dying patients, which I spent in a university hospital where again I had to promise never to tell patients that they were terminally ill. It was easy to keep this promise, since the patients would tell me.

Shortly before children die there is often a very "clear moment," as I call it. Those who have remained in a coma since the accident or after surgery open their eyes and seem very coherent. Those who have had great pain and discomfort are very quiet and at peace. It is in those moments that I asked them if they were willing to share with me what they were experiencing.

"Yes, everything is all right now. Mommy and Peter are already waiting for me," one boy replied. With a content little smile, he slipped back into a coma from which he made the transition we call death.

I was quite aware that his mother had died at the scene of the accident, but Peter had not died. He had been brought to a special burn unit in another hospital severely burnt, because the car had caught fire before he was extricated from the wreck. Since I was only collecting data, I accepted the boy's information and determined to look in on Peter. It was not necessary, however, because as I passed the nursing station there was a call from the other hospital to inform me that Peter had died a few minutes earlier.

In all the years that I have quietly collected data from California to Sydney, Australia; from white and black children, aboriginals, Eskimos, South Americans, and Libyan youngsters, every single child who mentioned that someone was waiting for them mentioned a person who had actually preceded them in death, even if by only a few moments. And yet none of these children had been informed of the recent death of the relatives by us at any time. Coincidence? By now there is no scientist or statistician who could convince me that this occurs, as some colleagues claim, as "a result of oxygen deprivation" or for other "rational and scientific" reasons.

* * *

A few years ago I was asked to speak at a Hospice meeting in Santa Barbara. It was my third lecture in two days, and I was feeling very tired; if it had not been for a very beautiful group of people, I would have declined the invitation. But since I was already on the West Coast and they had just started their efforts to get their hospice going, I accepted the call.

Many participants wanted to hear the experiences which led to my understanding of the actual experience of death. As I stood on the platform I said to myself, "God, if there were only one person in the audience who has had this experience and could tell them first-hand—to give me a break." At that very moment the chairperson gave me an "urgent" note. I called for a break. The note came from a despondent man in Santa Barbara who literally begged to be heard, to speak in public about his near-death experience. He described himself as a "bum," unable to afford the bus fare to the conference. But he informed me in the note of his exact whereabouts and with great confidence wrote that he would wait to be picked up, "to get a chance."

Following my request to go pick up this man, a few minutes later a volunteer brought in a rather well-dressed man who did not fit his own description of a "bum." I knew it was the writer of the note, and since I had proceeded with my lecture, I simply interrupted my speech and asked him to step up on the platform and share what he wanted to share. He seemed stunned at this degree of trust (he did not know he was the answer to my prayer, but I knew he was for real).

His story was probably the most moving I have ever heard in my many years of research, and he was obviously able to move the audience also; he received a standing ovation from a large group of usually skeptical professionals. The content of his story is as follows: He was a hardworking man, the father of five children and happily married. One day his family prepared to go to a big family reunion. His wife and all his children were on the way to pick him up when his wife's car was hit by a gasoline truck, and all went up in flames. The whole family was burned to death.

The man's life changed within these moments. He became unable to work, to think, to function. He lost his job and later his home. He started drinking heavily, tried to sedate himself with every conceivable drug he was able to obtain, and found it quite easy to get as many prescriptions as he wanted, due to his tragic "case history."

He eventually became heavily drugged with cocaine, codeine, and heroin, in addition to consuming a bottle of vodka daily. He tried to commit suicide several times but never seemed to succeed. He was at the bottom, as he called it, when he suddenly saw himself: drugged, drunk on a country road at the edge of a forest, and too sick to move out of the way as a big truck approached. He recalled the paradox that he desperately tried to move his heavy body out of the way of the truck, despite the fact that he regarded himself as always "suicidal."

He watched, half-conscious, as the truck drove over him. He then became aware of drifting out of his body without any pain or anxiety. He floated away and approached a light. Suddenly out of this light came his family: his wife and his children—as happy, healthy, and smiling as he remembered them, and all of them together. "They did not speak, but I was able to understand everything. I suddenly knew that they were well. They had no scars, no burn marks. They were just there to show me that they were all right and together.

"The awareness came to me that I had spent all this time trying to destroy my life because I thought I had lost my whole family, my children. . . ."

At that time he made a commitment that he would not join them yet, that he would willingly come back into his body. He decided he would make up for lost time and would try to find a way to tell as many people as possible what he had experienced. Only then would he be allowed to reunite with his family.

When he saw a poster advertising my lecture, he knew the day had come to keep his promise. He was grateful that I trusted an "unknown bum" to share his story with the many people present, who could not help but be impressed by his deeply moving tale. He was one man who had learned to appreciate the miracle of life after one of the greatest tragedies anyone could possibly survive.

* * *

A mother—L.D.—from Newcastle, Australia, called in to the "Mike Walsh Show," a national talk show, to add an experience with her own child and his reaction to the death of his grandpa.

"In October 1979, my husband and two-year-old son Justin and I were living in Cheshire in the north of England, and were within six weeks of returning to Australia.

"My grandfather, who lived eighteen miles from us in Salford, Manchester, had cancer, and although very ill was not expected to die.

"On October 18 at 9:30 A.M. my son was downstairs playing, when I heard him talking to someone. A minute or two later I heard him cry, 'But I want to, I want to.' He came into the kitchen and got a shopping bag, and put into it his cup, plate, and teddy bear. I asked him if he was leaving home, and this is what he told me: 'Poppa [my grandfather] says he has to go now. He says he is good now. I be a good boy for Mama. I want to go with Poppa, but he won't take me. I got to stay with Mama.'

"At 9:40 A.M. I had a telephone call from my Uncle Bill, who told me that Poppa had died ten minutes before, at 9:30 A.M.

"Justin stuck to his story and repeated it to my husband when he came home from work.

"The following day my next-door neighbor told me she had been coming in to see me about something, but when she realized I had a visitor she went back home. I asked her what made her think I had a visitor; she said she'd heard Justin talking to a man in our hall. She said she had come in about 9:30 A.M.

"When we explained to Justin that Poppa wouldn't be at home, that he had gone to see Grandma, all he said was, 'Yes, he's better now.' "

A Classic "Near-Death" Experience

During the delivery of her child by Cesarean section, Dorothy went into shock on the operating table and for a moment there was doubt that she would "make it." Nobody recognized at that time—twenty-three years ago—that this young mother had a near-death experience. She describes for us here what she had experienced:

"While lying on the operating table waiting for my doctor to perform a Cesarean section on me, I started to feel faint. I told the anesthetist who was there with me. She gave me some oxygen, which did not help me. I remember hearing her yell to the doctor that my blood pressure was falling.

"I then found myself in Heaven. It was so beautiful and peaceful there. I was so at peace there. Jesus started to talk to me. I did not see his face, but I listened to him talk to me. He said, 'Dottie, I am leaving you here [earth] for a purpose. No one will know what you are going through.' He then made known to me all things. I thought as he talked to me, Why did he choose me to reveal all things to? And then I thought that since he did, now that I have had this convincing experience, I can be of help to others. When he finished talking to me, I felt myself floating away from this beautiful place to a dirty and ugly place. This is a comparison of Heaven and Earth. Such a difference!

"I then felt myself back in my body on the operating table. I could feel the doctor putting tape across the bandage on my stomach, but I could not open my eyes. Someone was saying the Lord's Prayer to me. When they said amen, I opened my eyes. I was taken back to my room, and I told my husband and mom that no one will know what I had just gone through: that I had just talked to Jesus.

"That night as I lay on my bed, I tried to remember what he had revealed to me, but I was unable to. Nor have I been able to do so since, but the experience remains as vivid and convincing as when it occurred.

"In the Bible, Paul describes the exact same thing happening to him, in 2 Corinthians, chapter 12, verses 2 to 6. . . ."

When sharing this experience with others, this woman added that a little Psalm card summarized for her what she had learned during her brief but unforgettable experience in one of God's other mansions:

This Is the Day God Hath Made

Look to the day with a challenge!
Lift your eyes to the sun,
not the shade!
Keep your heart filled with song,
as you travel along
For this is the day God hath made!
Look to the day with a purpose
Of fulfilling the plans that you've had.
With a joy in your heart
that will never depart,
For God's made this day to be glad!
Look to the day with a prayer
And a quiet request for His aid,
And be glad all day through
in whatever you do,
For this is the day God hath made!

*"This is the day which the Lord hath made; we will
rejoice and be glad in it."*
Psalm 118:24

* * *

The following is a story handwritten by a young girl. It has traveled with me from workshop to workshop, although I do not remember who gave it to me nor how long before her death the young girl had this mystical experience. All I know is that it is very similar to the experiences I've heard from thousands of people who—prior to their death—were allowed a glimpse of "the other side."

The experiences vary from person to person, but there are certain common denominators: they are always met by people who are familiar to them; they have no fears and only a feeling of calm, peace, and love. Few ever wish to return to their physical existence, but they are often told that they must, as they still have some work to do here. Those who have had these experiences have no fear of death, and when the time of their departing comes, they know where they are going.

If Only

Dazedly I opened my eyes and smelled the clean, fresh, warm air. I'd never seen the sky such a bright and blue color, nor heard birds sing so beautifully.

I found myself lying in a meadow full of soft green grass and flowers, by a forest towering with graceful pines.

Sitting up I saw children laughing and playing with a fawn in the sunlight. Couples and groups of all ages walked or sat talking, and I'd never seen people so vibrantly happy and at peace.

Something was wrong. No one seemed to be watching out for the children. There were no cars and roads, no buildings or power lines. And everyone was wearing long, loose robes. It was too beautiful to be real.

A young man came smiling up to me.

"What's going on? Where am I?"

"Come with me," he said gently, "I'll show you where to go." Puzzled I followed him.

We walked into the cool forest and came to a small waterfall that ran into a pool, cool and shady.

Alone beside it sat a man with long brown hair and a beard, wearing a robe and sandals. He reminded me strongly of someone I knew.

Strangely, I felt no fear at all, but a sensation of contentment. The man had been staring into the dark pool, but as we approached he turned and gazed at me with sad and beautiful brown eyes. He smiled, and his plain face became beautiful and brilliant.

"Thou hath come. Set thyself down by my side." A feeling of wonderment overcame me and in silence I knelt at his feet.

"Child, it is not thy time yet."

I stared at the small pool of water. Sudden realization weighed upon me heavily, but I knew a joy and peace.

I was in heaven.

"Go back? Why? Please let me stay here."

"No," he said gently. "Thou still has time on earth, twelve months."

"Please!" I said, shaking in a powerful emotion I could not identify. "Let me see him just once!"

"Thou came here by error, thou must go back."

I was begging now, "Please let me see him before I go . . ."

The church organ rang in my ears and it began in my daydream world. The reverend began.

"We have come to pay our last respects . . ."

My son . . .

Another bereaved mother wrote of revisiting her daughter in a dream:

A Dream

I was walking past a room. The door to the room was wide open and I glanced inside. Three girls were dancing together in a circle, holding hands. I thought one girl looked like my daughter, Katie. The more I looked, the more I realized she was Katie. "Yes, yes, that's my Katie," I kept saying over and over with such joy, I can't tell you. The other girls seemed to drift from her. My eyes saw only her. Then her eyes—I can't explain what happened—but she was completely, absolutely peaceful and serene. There was no need to speak to each other or touch each other because we instantly knew each other's thoughts. Such peace, love, and happiness I have never felt before. Her eyes seemed to be the only physical part of herself I could focus on. She possessed all knowledge. The feeling of love that glowed from her eyes was indescribable. I can't say how long this "dream" lasted.

When I woke up in the morning, I had to orient myself to my room again. I had no idea where I was but I knew I had not been in the room while I was asleep. If I were asked if all of this was a dream or if I had really been with Katie, the only answer in my mind is, yes, I was with her. It was like nothing I have ever experienced before. The pain I felt in my heart when I realized I was without her again. . . . How I wish I could spend another moment in time like that again with my dear, beloved daughter.

I wish I knew the words to give an accurate description of my dream. I know you can understand the intensity of this peace and love that flowed between Katie and me.

> To be a child is to know the joy of living
> To have a child is to know the beauty of life.

I don't know the author who wrote those words but they are so true for me. I thank God every day for the life I experienced through my daughter's life and through her tragic death.

Thank you for listening—once again.

* * *

It is not the intention of this book to elaborate on near-death experiences and further research on survival. I just wanted to add a few examples of these occurrences in order to help enable others with similar experiences to share what has been revealed to them. I can only say that these encounters come from every corner of the world—from religious and non-religious people, believers and non-believers, from every conceivable cultural and ethnic background—and seem to be a common human experience that has nothing to do with our upbringing. I guess, in death we are finally all brothers and sisters!

The following incident occurred one and a half decades ago, when few if any researchers collected data on near-death experiences. The patient was two years old and obviously unaware of all the research that is going on at the present time. When he returned from his coma he was most excited and told his mother that he had been in the most beautiful place with Mary and with Jesus. Mary told him repeatedly that he had to return, but he tried to ignore her (which is usual with two-year-olds!). She finally took him gently by the hand and told him: "You have to go back, you have to save Mommy from the fire." The toddler told his mother that this was the time he decided to "run all the way back home." This child is alive and well today, and like all people who had such an enlightening personal experience, has no fear of dying.

Several young people who have been critically injured, molested, or raped shared similar experiences but made it very clear that theirs were "only out-of-body experiences," to avoid the pain and anguish of their helpless predicament.

With further research and further publications, more and

more people will know rather than believe that our physical body is truly only the cocoon, the outer shell of the human being. Our inner, true self, the "butterfly," is immortal and indestructible and is freed at the moment we call death.

Our "Dougy Letter" is an attempt to explain to a little dying boy what death is all about (obtainable from Shanti Nilaya, P.O. Box 2396, Escondido, California 92025) and uses the symbolic language of the butterfly and the cocoon.

"Edou"—A Remarkable Life and Death

In the *San Francisco Chronicle* half a decade ago there appeared an article and picture of an incredibly beautiful seven-year-old child who shared with the world his understanding of life and death, a knowledge far beyond that of most grownups. (It is a sign of hope that such nationally known papers are beginning to share good news rather than the usual trash and tragedy which only spread more fear and negativity into this already troubled planet earth.) The article stated that a "precocious seven-year-old Santa Barbara boy terminally ill with leukemia ordered his own medical treatment stopped and died in an unusual case mixing mysticism and personal courage. . . .

" 'He said, "Mother, turn off the oxygen. I don't need it anymore," ' recalled his mother. 'I turned it off. Then he held my hand and a big smile came to his face, and he said, "It is time." Then he left.'

"In his three-year battle against leukemia, he lived both at home with his mother and at the hospital, where he received transfusions of 170 pints of blood as doctors tried to forestall his death."

Details of Edou's death and the child's philosophy came from his mother and from a tape that the mother offered me for sharing in this book. It is a tape that he asked a volunteer worker to make about his views on dying, pain, and reincarnation. Excerpts of this little old wise man's understanding of life and death follow.

VOLUNTEER: You asked me to come up here and bring my tape recorder and ask you some questions that you have been wanting to share with people about your life and how you feel about dying. . . . Edou, you decided about three months ago that you wanted to live until your seventh birthday. Now, how have you decided to do that?

EDOU: Because I prayed to God, I wanted to live until I was seven. . . . After that day or maybe a little later, I could die as I would like to die.

VOLUNTEER: Why have you decided that you want to die?

EDOU: Because I'm so sick. . . . When you are dead, your spirit is in heaven, and you don't have all your aches and pains anymore. Sometimes if you want to, you can come back into a healthy life where you won't have any more aches and pains. . . .

VOLUNTEER: Do you believe in reincarnation?

EDOU: Yes, I do.

VOLUNTEER: Would you like to explain to all of us your feelings about reincarnation?

EDOU: Yes. When I die, I just might come back to a healthy life. I just might not come back in any life at all. Or I might come back in my sick life, just to see what it would be like.

VOLUNTEER: Do you have any idea what you would like to be in your next lifetime?

EDOU: A healthy boy, or maybe what I am now, sick."

VOLUNTEER: Do you think you want to come back and try being sick again?

EDOU: No, I think I do want really to have a healthy life when I come back next time.

VOLUNTEER: Edou, do you have any idea why you chose, in this lifetime, to have an unhealthy life?

EDOU: No, I do not. When you choose your life in heaven, you can come back to earth in a healthy life or no life or in a sick life, but you can't remember what you chose. You might choose to be a healthy life, but it just might not work out that way. You might choose to be a sick life, but it just might not work that way. You might be a healthy life. Do you know what I mean?

VOLUNTEER: I think I do, Edou. Would you explain to all of us how it feels to have so much pain in your body?

EDOU: Yes, I can. It seems like, when you have pain in your body, it feels like someone shocked you very badly—like a streak of lightning or something. And sometimes when you're sick you can have your pain for a long, long time. Sometimes you can even have it for a short time, and then, maybe years after, you have it again—the same thing or maybe something different than you had the first time.

VOLUNTEER: Does it make you afraid?

EDOU: No, it doesn't. It is kind of shocking, if you know what I mean.

VOLUNTEER: Edou, can you tell us what you think heaven looks like? Have you seen it, and do you remember what the other side looks like?

EDOU: No, but I think I can give you an exact example of what it looks like. It's sort of like . . . if you went through another passageway . . . you walked right through a wall to another galaxy or something. It's sort of like walking into your brain. And it's sort of like living on a cloud, and your spirit is there but not your body. You've left your body. It really is like walking through a wall . . . walking into your mind.

VOLUNTEER: Then it is a very easy thing to do. Why do you think people are so afraid of dying?

EDOU: Because sometimes when you die it hurts. You are so afraid of dying because you hurt so much. You would like to hang on to your body and not leave it with your spirit.

VOLUNTEER: Do you think you have any message from your own experience for people who are afraid of dying?

EDOU: Well, sometimes people aren't that afraid of dying, and they just die.

VOLUNTEER: What can you tell the people who are terribly afraid of dying and just do everything to live, no matter how painful it is?

EDOU: Well, if you don't hang on to your body and you just
let yourself ease off, it won't be so painful.

VOLUNTEER: You die and just let go?

EDOU: Yes.

VOLUNTEER: Could you share with us how you feel about leaving your mother?

EDOU: Well, I feel kind of sad to leave my mother, but if she
chooses to die, I can be with her. And sometimes, if you
want to, you can come back down with your spirit and
visit those you love. You know?

VOLUNTEER: Do you think after you die that you will be
coming back in spirit to visit some of us?

EDOU: Yes, I do.

VOLUNTEER: Why do you think a lot of spirits walk around in
the night when it's more frightening for people?

EDOU: Maybe because they want to be with them in the night
and in the daytime too.

VOLUNTEER: Maybe it just seems more scarey at night.

EDOU: Not if you are not afraid. One time in the middle of the
night I heard something going through the house—the spirit
of my grandfather. I think Mom heard it too. . . .

VOLUNTEER: Are you looking forward to seeing your grandfather on the other side?

EDOU: Yes, I am.

VOLUNTEER: Do you think he will be waiting for you?

EDOU: Yes, I do.

VOLUNTEER: It's a nice feeling, isn't it? To go from your
mother who loves you so much to your grandfather who
loves you?

EDOU: Yes, it is.

Edou went on to share his ideas about work in heaven and the
meaning of work while you are in the physical body.

VOLUNTEER: Once you described heaven to me as being like
ancient Egypt or ancient Rome. Do you still think that's the
way it looks?

EDOU: Yes. But I think I have had many lives before my life now, and maybe anybody else who is alive now on earth has had many lives before—maybe 'way back when, like when ancient Egypt was here.

VOLUNTEER: Have you decided how you want to be . . . Do you want to be buried or cremated after you die?

EDOU: Well, when I die I would like to be buried in a garden of flowers.

VOLUNTEER: Why is that?

EDOU: Because I just would like to be buried in a garden of flowers. . . . Yes, I would like a little garden of flowers over me. . . .

When Edou was buried, six months after this interview, each person at the funeral walked past the casket and, according to his native Brazilian custom, dropped a handful of roses. . . .

VOLUNTEER: Do you have any message that you would like to leave people about your life? People will say, 'Oh, it's so sad. He only lived seven years.' Do you think people will cry about it because you are only living seven years and think that's all there is, and it will be the end of you? How do you feel about that?

EDOU: My mother is going to cry about it.

VOLUNTEER: What can you tell people, though, who think this is all the life you're ever going to get? They think you only get one life, and that will be it.

EDOU: They are wrong about that, because I will come back again.

VOLUNTEER: When you come back, will you come back as a person or as an animal or rock, flower, or what?

EDOU: A person.

VOLUNTEER: Do you think you'll be a boy again or a girl?

EDOU: I probably will be a boy.

VOLUNTEER: Do you think you'll come back to this lifetime where you'll know your friends again, or do you think maybe you'll go off to another country?

EDOU: I want to be born who I was before.

VOLUNTEER: In Brazil?

EDOU: Yes.

VOLUNTEER: Is there any reason why you love Brazil so much?

EDOU: Yes, there is—because I have some of my cousins down there, and one of my grandmothers and my aunts.

VOLUNTEER: It's been quite a long time since you've seen them, isn't it?

EDOU: No, it hasn't. I was born down there, and then I came up here when I was two.

VOLUNTEER: How many years have you been sick, Edou?

EDOU: Since I was three years old.

VOLUNTEER: It seems like all of your life, then, doesn't it?

EDOU: Yes.

VOLUNTEER: When you get very cranky with your mother . . . do you do that because you're angry with her, or because you're taking out your frustrations on her?

EDOU: I'm taking out my frustrations on her.

VOLUNTEER: Can you share any feelings about this? Because a lot of people who deal with people like you who are very sick—they don't know what to do. They feel real bad when somebody yells at them.

EDOU: That's the way I feel.

VOLUNTEER: You feel bad when you yell?

EDOU: No, when someone yells at me.

VOLUNTEER: Then how come you yell at your mom so much when you get sick, since you know what it feels like?

EDOU: Well, because sometimes I am so sick. She's not at the bed. Maybe I'm going to have a bone marrow or a spinal tap. She's not over here. And so I yell at her to come over here.

VOLUNTEER: You want her to be with you when you are sick?

EDOU: Yes, I do.

VOLUNTEER: Could you tell me how you feel about the doctors? Have they been pretty good in their treatment of you, do you think?

EDOU: Yes, they have. And they would really like to try to get some medicine or something to cure me of my sickness. But they can't do that.

VOLUNTEER: How would you feel if you decided that you want to die after your birthday and the doctor decided that he wanted to keep you alive?

EDOU: They can't do that because I prayed to God, and they can't stop me from dying.

VOLUNTEER: If you decide to leave your body, the doctor cannot stop you from leaving it?

EDOU: Yes. That is true.

VOLUNTEER: Would you be angry if the doctor tried to stop you from leaving your body?

EDOU: Yes, I would.

VOLUNTEER: Do you think that when a person decides to die the doctor should just say, "All right—go ahead and die. I understand."?

EDOU: Yes, I do feel that way.

VOLUNTEER: Why do you think some doctors can't stand to see their patients die?

EDOU: Well, sometimes they want to save them very badly from their sickness, and so they would not like to let them die. They want to cure them from their sickness or try to.

VOLUNTEER: After your birthday, Edou, if you decide to die and the doctor wants to do more bone marrows or more transfusions, then what will you do about this?

EDOU: Well, maybe by August . . . I might be dead by that time.

VOLUNTEER: You seem to be really looking forward to dying.

EDOU: Yes, I do . . .

VOLUNTEER: What made you decide you would rather die than live?

EDOU: Well, because I don't feel good, and I'm too sick to live on. My sickness that I have comes off and on, and sometimes I'm up running around and then I get weaker and weaker, and I hurt so much that I need a transfusion. . . .

VOLUNTEER: How do you feel about having leukemia?
EDOU: Not very good.
VOLUNTEER: How do you feel about it when you see movies about people who have leukemia? Do you pay very much attention to them?
EDOU: Yes, I do. But really, there aren't that many people with leukemia on television.

A letter I received from Edou's mother reveals how much this little seven-year-old had achieved in his short life. His mother's love and pride shines through; in her own way she is continuing Edou's work.

"Dear Elisabeth,

"In your December newsletter you published a letter on a hospice for children in northern Virginia. There is another one closer to home! Hospice of Santa Barbara, California. It started in June 1978, the year my son died. He is responsible for getting it started.

"In 1977, I told my son that there was not much hope and he might die. He responded that he already knew for some .time, and if I did not mind he wanted to get some sleep. I thought he was protecting me by not talking. It was very hard for me. I asked many friends to come talk to him; all refused, saying they could not bear to. Finally, I found a lady who was head of the PTA at his school. She came to the hospital and talked privately with him to find out his feelings. They talked for an hour, and she told him about Hospice. It was the first time I had heard about it. She was just starting classes.

"After she left, my son was bubbly with the idea. He wanted to be lifted out of bed immediately and put into his wheelchair so he could go throughout the hospital to help other people who were dying. 'If I am not afraid of dying, I can help others. After all, they have lived their lives. I can show them there is nothing to fear, just like I helped grandfather.' I had to stop him, sad to say. I explained that he could not go barging into people's rooms without permission and that the hospital had rules about children. He asked me to get permission. Did I ever step into a hornet's nest trying.

"The doctors were outraged at such an idea and my telling my son he might die. They claimed that children did not understand death. The Hospice people did not believe it was right either; [they believed] that a child could not, at my child's age, understand dying and death. They did not deal with dying children at the time.

"Needless to say, my son was very sad over the whole thing, and no one would talk directly to him about it. He felt that dying children could explain death better and should have an active part in hospice work. 'After all, I just came from God,' he would say. 'I still remember heaven. God and I talk all the time.' He began to convince people that a six-year-old did know about dying, and openly talked to those who would listen.

"Hospice began to consider the special needs of children, and we began talking. I explained that these children and their families needed some organization like Hospice. To deal with it alone was very difficult and ripped families apart—the months and years, the questions and agony with no one to turn to who understood. My son pointed out that most kids die alone because parents and doctors don't or can't talk about it, so the child remains silent. He felt that kids had the right to make decisions about dying just like adults. He did so. He made a will and his funeral arrangements.

"Hospice in Santa Barbara now has a wonderful program for the needs of terminally ill children and their families. . . . Edou's dying produced what he hoped for in part: help for other dying children.

"Love, B.M.C."

Another letter from Edou's mother tells how even though she did discuss things with Edou, it took her quite a while to comprehend all he could teach: the preciousness of life and the significance of unconditional love. I want to thank Edou and his mother for helping us to spread this knowledge!

"Only now am I understanding some of the things he talked about. He would talk to anyone who would listen to him about dying, and they would come away smiling in joy.

"He had an occupational therapist who was very young and terrified because she had never worked with a dying child. They became loving friends. After my son died she and I talked, and she told me of my son's concerns for my well-being and how he watched over me to make sure I got enough rest. How he hoped I would go back to work when he died so I would have something to cling to and keep me going while I grieved. She also told me that my son made her face death, understand it, and how she had become a Hospice care-giver.

"My son and I were alone, just the two of us. His favorite song among many was 'You and Me Against the World.' I felt we were; there was no one I could talk to or turn to who understood. Sometimes I would go off by myself and scream into a pillow or coat and cry, and then come back and hold myself together to fight the battle for my son, who seemed so defenseless.

"I was a terror, and doctors cringed. I do not think I was unreasonable, but some of the stupid things that were done prompted me to stand guard over my child. . . . That is not to say all doctors are bad, most were good and a few were wonderful, but when you are dealing with a life and you're not good at it, then it is very bad for all concerned. It was like waging war, and I resented being treated like 'you're only the mother, therefore stupid or don't count.' I insisted on knowing every procedure and what it was for, and if I could not get answers, I went to the medical library and read up on it.

"I also insisted on everything being explained to my son so he could understand why and deal with it. I tried not to lie to him, but I *never, ever* took hope away from him. Many doctors did not like what I did and did not like my insisting on being present for spinal taps, bone biopsy, etc. Parents have a right to be with their children, and a child has the right to have his parent there. It is much easier to be in the room with your child than outside a door and listen to the screams. . . .

"He was ill on and off for three and a half years. His spine collapsed, and then his long bones started to go. He had to learn to roll over, sit, crawl, and walk all over again three times. He almost never complained, although he did scream with pain often. This was upsetting to everyone as the only pain medication he had was Tylenol and codeine. We turned to hypnosis and, in the end, I got out my dead father's pain medication and, using a diabetic syringe, gave my son shots when he asked for them. I also, with friends, rigged up an oxygen unit to help him breathe. He insisted upon being awake while dying so he could say good-bye and died with a smile.

"I believe that children pick us as parents for our and their souls to grow. For me, it was a privilege to share my son's journey with him and to be chosen as his mother. He taught me so many wonderful things, but most of all how precious life is and the joy of unconditional love.

"Lots of love, B.M.C."

Chapter 14

Resources: Groups and Support Systems

Hospice

A VERY SPECIAL GROUP of different health care professionals and volunteers build a nucleus of a *hospice*, of which we have over five hundred in the United States. All of them should be willing to take on children.

In contrast to a hospital, the hospice emphasis is on (1) pain and symptom control; (2) the patient having control over his/her own life; (3) the patient and family being considered a single unit of care; (4) planning by an interdisciplinary team for each patient individually, and providing active bereavement support. All this combines to place the concentration on life and living, rather than dying, during this final period of life.

Hospices are unfortunately not getting referrals of children, because many health care professionals believe that any child who has parents needs no other help. This is nothing but an avoidance of the real issue; nothing could be further from the truth.

First, there are thousands if not millions of single parents who need to make a living and are incapable of caring alone for a terminally ill child. It is often a long-term care, extremely costly in both emotional and financial terms. No one human being can possibly be available twenty-four hours a day to care for a very ill child without a loving support system.

A hospice can at least offer a few hours for a break, so the parent has some time to go shopping, to switch gears, to read a book, to have some quiet time, or to go to the hairdresser without feeling guilty. All parents need this, single or not.

Hospice volunteers will come in and do housework, cook meals ahead for the family, or just pick and arrange a bouquet of flowers to make the home more cheerful. They allow the mother more time for the sick child and her other children, who are so often ignored and neglected during this time of crisis.

The hospice counselor can become available to the parents who may have difficulties in communicating openly with each other or with the child. A less emotionally involved outsider can function as a marvelous catalyst in times like this and also be available to siblings, who have problems sharing their pain with the already bereaved parents.

The hospice nurse is available twenty-four hours a day for anxious parents, to minister to the medical needs in the home and to answer questions and explain things that the family did not comprehend when they were explained in the formal language of physicians.

San Diego Hospice is the one closest to me; it has never charged a family since coming into existence, and it has grown from nine patients in 1980 to the largest home-care hospice in the United States, with a daily census of over a hundred patients.

The hospice team is also available to act as a close family friend after the child dies when the family has a need to talk, to go over the preceding weeks and the child's illness once more. It can be of much help in bringing to a close the often exhausting, time-consuming end period of a terminal illness, helping to facilitate the active grieving process so that a new family life can be established as soon as possible.

Groups That Care and Help

Some new and not-so-new groups that help our children and their parents in times of trial.

A friend from the East Coast writes:

"Dear Brother/Sister of the Earth,

"Life is a precious gift for us to experience and then to pass on to the next generation. While we are alive we are given the chance to affect the quality of life as it exists during the age we live in. If we are conscious, we recognize what is important and what we can do.

"During the age we live in, the world's governments spend $550 billion a year on weapons while fifty million people die of starvation and starvation-related illness each year!

"During our age, the big challenge is to convert weapons into food. . . .

"It is up to us to solve these problems. To help solve some of these problems, we have created Universal Children's Garden to teach children in all nations to grow food and preserve the environment. The children learn to work and play together, and they learn that children all over the world can be friends."

For information write to Universal Children's Garden, P.O. Box 2698, Grand Central P.O., New York, New York 10017.

* * *

Another totally different, but perhaps even more significant contribution will be made by the *Parents and Teachers Against Violence in Education*, established in Australia in 1978 and with an active volunteer membership in Australia and in the United States. Its aim is to "help speed the progress of education toward a high level, by world standards, of quality and humaneness. A first and obvious step toward this goal

must be the removal of punitive violence from the experience
of school children."

For information, write to PTAVE, 560 South Hartz Avenue, Suite 408, Danville, California 94526.

In their brochure they state the many reasons why physical
punishment is wrong, and I want to add that it is *not* necessary
either in schools or at home!

What children need is firm, consistent discipline at home
and in school, not brutal force and power, but a chance to
grow and learn from mistakes.

* * *

The Lamplighters Leukemia Association in Montreal, Quebec, Canada, serves a similar function. Their address is P.O.B.
1285, Station H, Montreal, Quebec, Canada H3G 2N2.

* * *

Dr. Henry Kempe founded in 1972 the *National Center for
the Prevention and Treatment of Child Abuse and Neglect* in
Denver, Colorado. This organization grew from members of
the Child Protection Team, which originated in 1958 under the
direction of Dr. Kempe, a pediatrician, and Dr. Brandt F.
Steele, a psychiatrist and one of my personal favorite teachers!
A Therapeutic Pre-school has been added for 2½-to 5-year-
olds who have been physically and/or sexually abused. To help
remove the physical and emotional scars of child abuse and
neglect, contact The Friends, 1205 Oneida Street, Denver,
Colorado 80220.

* * *

The Candlelighters Foundation is the organizational, liaison,
and educational arm of an international network of over 155
self-help groups of parents of children with cancer and of the
medical and psychosocial professionals who serve them. It
promotes self-help groups; coordinates communication between groups, parents and professionals; and works to identify

and develop solutions to the problems of living with and treating childhood cancer.

The Candlelighters Foundation: Publications List
Suite 1011, 2025 Eye Street, NW, Washington, D.C. 20006.
(202) 659-5136.

* * *

The Compassionate Friends is a self-help group for bereaved parents and siblings that provides information, empathy, and support at a time when most other people don't know what to say. Father Simon Stephens, an Anglican priest, founded the organization in 1969 after a personal experience he had with two boys who died rather unexpectedly when he worked in hospital ministry in Coventry, England. His book, *When Death Comes Home*, has since been widely read in the United States, and new groups of Compassionate Friends are springing up in every state of our country.

While the national headquarters acts as a clearinghouse, each local chapter acts independently. A monthly newsletter keeps the different groups informed and becomes a link between grieving parents across the country. Members who have stayed on in their local groups years after the death of their child listen sympathetically to the newly bereaved, vividly remembering how important it was to be patient, and offer them a phone number to use when the loneliness becomes unbearable.

National headquarters address:
Compassionate Friends
P.O.B. 1347
Oakbrook, Illinois 60521
(312) 323-5010

Pamphlets available from Compassionate Friends:
"Understanding Grief," "Stillbirth, Miscarriage and Infant Death," "Caring for Surviving Children," "When a Child Dies," "Suggestions for Doctors and Nurses," "Suggestions for Clergy." 50 brochures of a kind for $5.00, 100 brochures of a

kind, $10.00. Make checks payable to "The Compassionate Friends, Inc." A 16mm film is also available for rental ($35.00) or purchase ($200.00).

* * *

Make Today Count is for adult cancer and other terminally ill patients, but the group has helped many older children to receive support, providing a listening ear and sound advice when one of their parents is dying.

Originated by Orville Kelly of Iowa, a cancer patient who is as well-known for his plea on behalf of soldiers exposed to radiation from nuclear testings in the last decades as he is appreciated by the thousands who have learned to *Make Today Count* by sharing their problems with others who live on "borrowed time."

Make Today Count has provided an opportunity for thousands of terminally ill patients, as well as family members, to give and receive from each other, to face their troubled times, knowing that they are not alone and that there are others who go through the same often long and drawn-out crisis. They meet at different places in the hundreds of local groups that have come up all over the country and abroad, and discuss financial concerns, treatment possibilities, child care, and other vital issues.

The list of local chapters is too long to publish here, but information can be received through the National Make Today Count Office, Post Office Box 303, Burlington, Iowa 52601, (319) 753–6521.

* * *

Parents of Murdered Children is the only support organization for survivors of murdered persons. It was begun several years ago by a couple who desperately wanted to share with others in this terribly difficult crisis. Today more and more parents have asked for this kind of special help. At the time of this writing, nearly fifty chapters have been formed, including two in Canada. Families of murdered people meet for mutual support, guidance, and direction.

As it is described in their pamphlet, when a child dies, bereaved families go through intense personal grief. When a child is murdered, the grief process is complicated by intrusions into the parents' grief. Police, lawyers, and other members of the criminal justice system need information, evidence, and testimony. Television and news media focus upon the victim and the grieving family. New pain comes when the suspect is apprehended, tried, and sentenced. Preliminary hearings and postponements force grieving parents to face what often may seem to be a lack of justice. What, they wonder, was my child's life worth?

Parents of Murdered Children are available to newly bereaved parents and other family members in meetings, by letter, and by phone. Needless to say, it is a free service and nondenominational. It has helped endless numbers of families at a time when they thought they could not make it through another day. We hope that any family member who has lost someone through murder will contact the headquarters and help others in need:

Parents of Murdered Children
1739 Bella Vista
Cincinnati, Ohio 45237
(513) 242-8025 or (513) 721-LOVE

* * *

The Ronald McDonald House, often described as "the house that love built," is a home-away-from-home for children with cancer and other serious illnesses. It provides temporary lodging for these children and their families, at minimal cost, near hospitals where the children are being treated. The House provides an emotional haven, an environment where families facing similar situations have the opportunity to lend and receive support, understanding, warmth, and love.

The Ronald McDonald House is a nonprofit organization funded primarily by McDonald's restaurant owners and named after the famous McDonald's clown. Presently, there are forty-three such houses in the United States and abroad.

For more information, contact:

> The Ronald McDonald House
> 419 East 86th Street
> New York, N.Y. 10028
> (212) 876-1590

Bibliography

*Abramson, J. "Facing the Other Fact of Life: Death in Recent Children's Fiction." *School Library Journal*, December 15, 1974.

Adams-Greenly, Margaret. "Children's Perception of Illness and Death." Pediatrics Grand Rounds. September 16, 1982.

Adams-Greenly, Margaret, and Moynihan, Sister Rosemary T. "Helping the Children of Fatally Ill Parents." Dept. of Social Work, Memorial Sloan-Kettering Cancer Center, 1285 York Avenue, New York, N.Y. 10021. October 30, 1982.

Adler, C. S. "The Meaning of Death to Children." *Arizona Medicine*, Vol. 26(3), 1969.

Albany Research Project. A Study in Psychosomatic Pediatrics. *Reducing Emotional Trauma in Hospitalized Children* (A Three-Year Study of 140 Tonsillectomized Children). Albany, N.Y.: Department of Pediatrics and Anesthesiology, Albany Medical College, October 1, 1952.

Albee, Constance Impallaria. "Group Work with Hospitalized Children." *Children* 2:217–221, 1955.

Albertson, Sandy. *Endings and Beginnings.* New York: Random House, 1980.

Alexander, Irving E., and Adlerstein, Arthur M. "Affective Responses to the Concept of Death in a Population of Children

*For children, varying ages.

[239]

and Early Adolescents." *Journal of Genetic Psychology.*
93:167–177, 1958.
Allen, James. *As A Man Thinketh.* Mt. Vernon, N.Y.: The Peter
Pauper Press.
American Academy of Pediatrics. *Care of Children in Hospitals.*
Evanston, Ill.: American Academy of Pediatrics, 1960.
Ames, Louise Bates. "The Development of the Sense of Time in
the Young Child." *Journal of Genetic Psychology.* 68:97–
125, 1946.
Angell, James W. *O Susan!* Indiana: Warner Press, 1973.
Anthony, E. James, and Koupernik, Cyrille, (eds.) *The Child in
His Family. The Impact of Disease and Death.* Yearbook
of the International Association for Child Psychiatry and
Allied Professions, Vol. 2. New York: John Wiley & Sons,
1973.
Anthony, Sylvia. *The Child's Discovery of Death.* New York:
Harcourt Brace, 1940.
Arlen, M. J. "The Air: The Cold Bright Charms of Immortality."
The New Yorker, January 27, 1975.
* Armstrong, William H. *Sounder.* New York: Harper & Row,
1969.
Arthur, Bettie, and Kemme, Mary L. "Bereavement in Childhood."
Journal of Child Psychology and Psychiatry. 5:37–49, June
1964.
* Bach, Alice. *Mollie Make-Believe.* New York: Harper & Row,
1974.
Bach, Susan. *Spontaneous Paintings of Severely Ill Patients.* Printed
in Germany, 1969.
———. "Spontanes Malen Schwerkranker Patienten." *Acta Psy-
chosomatica* 8. Basel, Switzerland: J. R. Geigy, 1966.
Bacon, Francis. *The Works of Francis Bacon.* London: 1874 edition.
Baer, Ruth. "The Sick Child Knows." In *Should the Patient Know
the Truth,* edited by S. Standard and H. Nathan. New York:
Springer, 1955, pp. 100–106.
Baker, Lynn. *You and Leukemia: A Day at a Time.* Rochester,
Minn.: Mayo Comprehensive Cancer Center, 1976.

* For children, varying ages.

Bakwin, Harry. "Pure Maternal Overprotection." *Journal of Pediatrics.* 33, 6:788–794, 1948.
————. "Suicide in Children and Adolescents." *Journal of Pediatrics.* 50, 6:749–769, June 1957.
Bakwin, Ruth M., and Bakwin, Harry. *Psychological Care During Infancy and Childhood.* New York and London: D. Appleton-Century, 1942.
Barnard, M., and Olson, J. "The Abused or Neglected Child." In *Comprehensive Pediatric Nursing,* 2nd edition, edited by G. Scipiens, et al. New York: McGraw-Hill, 1979.
Barry, Herbert, Jr. "Significance of Maternal Bereavement Before Age of Eight in Psychiatric Patients." *Archives of Neurology and Psychiatry.* 62:630–637, 1949.
* Bartoli, Jennifer. *Nonna.* New York: Harvey House, 1975.
Baty, James M., and Tisza, Veronica B. "The Impact of Illness on the Child and His Family." *Child Study* 34, 1:15–19, Winter 1956–1957.
Baudouin, Charles. *Mind of the Child.* London: George Allen and Unwin, 1933.
Bauman, E., and Brint, Armand, et al. *The Holistic Health Handbook.* Compiled by Berkeley Holistic Health Center. Berkeley, Calif.: And/Or Press, 1978.
Bayle, Joe. *The View from the Hearse.* Elgin, Ill.: David Corly Pub.
Beaumont, P. J. V. "Death of First Born—Tenth Plague." *South African Medical Journal.* Vol. 48 (37), 1974.
Beck, J. "Childhood Bereavement and Adult Depression." *Archives of General Psychiatry.* 9:295–302 (Pt. 3), 1963.
Becker, D., et al. "How Surviving Parents Handled Their Young Children's Adaptation to the Crisis of Loss." *American Journal of Orthopsychiatry,* 37:753–757, July 1976.
Becker, E. *The Denial of Death.* New York: Free Press, 1973.
* Beckman, Gunnel. *Admission to the Feast.* New York: Holt, Rinehart, 1979.
Benchley, Nathaniel. *Feldman Fieldmouse: A Fable.* New York: Harper & Row, 1971.

* For children, varying ages.

Bender, David, and Hagen, R. *Death and Dying: Opposing Viewpoints.* St. Paul, Minn.: Greenhaven Press, 1980.

Bender, Lauretta. *Aggression, Hostility, and Anxiety in Children.* Springfield, Ill.: Charles C. Thomas, 1958.

———. *Dynamic Psychopathology of Childhood.* Springfield, Ill.: Charles C. Thomas, 1954.

Bender, Lauretta, and Scholder, Paul. "Suicidal Preoccupations and Attempts in Children." *American Journal of Orthopsychiatry.* 7:225–234, April 1937.

Benedek, Therese. "Adaptation to Reality in Early Infancy." *Psychoanalytic Quarterly.* 7:200–215, 1938.

Bennholdt-Thomsen, C. "Sterben und Tod des Kindes" [Dying and the Death of the Child]. *Deutsche Medizinische Wochenschrift* 84:1437–1442, August 14, 1959.

Berezin, Nancy. *After a Loss in Pregnancy—Help for Families Affected by a Miscarriage, a Stillbirth, or the Loss of a Newborn.* New York: Simon & Schuster, 1982.

Bergman, A. "Sudden Infant Death Syndrome: What Can You Do?" *Medical Times.* Reprint, 1979. (Distributed by the National Sudden Infant Death Syndrome Foundation, Chicago).

Bergman, Abraham, and Schulte, Charles F. A., III, (eds.) "Care of the Child with Cancer." *Pediatrics* 3, Vol. 40, September 1967.

Bergman, Paul, and Escalona, Sibylle K. "Unusual Sensitivities in Very Young Children." *Psychoanalytic Study of the Child.* 3/4:333–352, 1947.

Bergmann, Thesi, in collaboration with Anna Freud. *Children in the Hospital.* New York: International Universities Press, 1965.

Best, Pauline. "An Experience on Interpreting Death to Children." *Pastoral Care.* 1, 2:1948.

Beverly, Bert I. "The Effect of Illness upon Emotional Development." *Journal of Pediatrics.* 8, 5:533–543, May 1936.

Bierman, Howard R. "Parent Participation Program in Pediatric Oncology. A Preliminary Report." *Journal of Chronic Diseases.* 3, 6:632–639, June 1956.

Binger, C. M.; Ablin, A. R.; Fuerstein, R. C.; Kushner, H. H.; Zoger, S.; and Middlesen, D. "Childhood Leukemia: Emotional Impact on Patient and Family." *New England Journal of Medicine*. Vol. 280, 8, February 20, 1969.

Blaine, Graham. "Some Emotional Problems of Adolescents." *Medical Clinics of North America*. 49:387–404, March 1965.

Blake, Florence. *The Child, His Parents and the Nurse*. Philadelphia: Lippincott, 1954.

Bloomfield, Harold. *How to Survive the Loss of Love*.

Bluebond-Langner, Myra. "Awareness and Communication in Terminally Ill Children: Pattern, Process, and Pretense." Doctoral thesis, Champaign-Urbana, Ill.: University of Illinois, 1975.

Bolivar, Jossy A. *With Love from Jo*. San Luis Obispo, Calif.: Padre Productions, 1980.

*Bond, Nancy. *The String in the Harp*. New York: Atheneum, 1976.

Bonine, G. N. "Students' Reactions to Children's Death." *American Journal of Nursing*. 67:1439–1440, July 1967.

*Borack, Barbara. *Someone Small*. New York: Harper, 1969.

Boston Women's Health Book Collective, Inc. *Ourselves and Our Children*. New York: Random House, 1978.

Bowlby, J. "Grief and Mourning in Infancy and Early Childhood." *Psychoanalytic Study of the Child*. Vol. 15, 1960.

Braga, Laurie and Joseph. *Learning and Growing—A Guide to Child Development*. Englewood Cliffs, N.J.: Prentice-Hall, 1975.

Brantamay, H. "Recueil de faits tentative de suicide d'une fillette de 9 ans," *Kinderpsychiatrie*. 2: September 1944.

Bridbord, K. "The Dying Child." Dissertation, University of Chicago, Spring 1969.

Bright, Florence and Frances; France, Sister M. Luciana. "The Nurse and the Terminally Ill Child." *Nursing Outlook*. September 1967.

Briscoe, Karen. "Childhood Leukemia, the Family Disease." Reprinted by the American Cancer Society. No. 0406.

*Brown, Margaret W. *The Dead Bird*. Reading, Mass.: Young Scott Books, 1965.

———. "How to Tell if a Baby Has Cerebral Palsy . . . and What

* For children, varying ages.

to Tell His Parents When He Does." *Nursing 79*, 79:88, May 1979.

Brown, Myra Berry. *First Night away from Home*. New York: Franklin Watts, 1960.

* Buck, Pearl. *The Big Wave*. Scholastic Book Service.

Buckley, Helen. *Grandmother and I*. New York: Lothrop, Lee & Shepard, 1961.

* Burch, Robert. *Simon and the Game of Chance*. New York: Viking, 1970.

Burlingham, D., and Freud, A. *Young Children in Wartime*. London: Allen and Unwin, 1942.

Burrus, W. *The Riddle of Crib Death*. Chicago: National Sudden Infant Death Syndrome Foundation.

Buscaglia, Leo F. *Love*. New York: Fawcett Crest, 1972.

Buswell, Guy Thomas. *How People Look at Pictures*. Chicago: University of Chicago Press, 1935.

Cain, Albert C.; Fast, Irene; and Erickson, Mary E. "Children's Disturbed Reactions to the Death of a Sibling." *American Journal of Orthopsychiatry*. 34:741–752, July 1964.

* Caines, Jeanette Franklin. *Abby*. New York: Harper & Row, 1973.

Calconer, L. "How to Answer the Questions Children Ask About Death." *Parents' Magazine*, November 1962.

Caplan, Gerald. *Emotional Problems of Early Childhood*. New York: Basic Books, 1955.

* Carner, Charles. *Tawny*. New York: Macmillan, 1978.

* Carrick, Carol. *The Accident*. New York: Seabury, 1976.

* Center for Attitudinal Healing: *There Is a Rainbow Behind Every Cloud*. Millbrae, Calif.: Celestial Arts, 1978.

Chandra, R. K. "A Child Dies." *Indian Journal of Pediatrics*. 35:363–364, July 1968.

"Children in Hospitals." *What's New* 217: pp. 2–6, Spring 1960.

"Children in Hospital." *Lancet* 1, XIX: 784–786, May 7, 1949.

* *Children of the World Paint Jerusalem*. Jerusalem: Keter Publishing House, 1978, and New York: Bantam Books, 1978.

Chodoff, Paul, et al. "Stress Defenses and Coping Behavior; Observations in Parents of Children with Malignant Disease."

* For children, varying ages.

American Journal of Psychology 120, No. 8, February 1964.

Christ, Grace, and Adams-Greenly, Margaret. "Therapeutic Strategies at Psychosocial Crisis Points in the Treatment of Childhood Cancer."

* Cleaver, Vera and Bill. *Grover*. Lippincott, 1970.

——. *Where the Lilies Bloom*. Lippincott, 1969.

Cobb, Beatrix. "Psychological Impact of Long Illness and Death of a Child on the Family Circle." *Journal of Pediatrics* 49, 6:746–751, October-December 1956.

* Coburn, John. *Annie and the Sand Dobbies*. New York: Seabury, 1964.

Coffin, Margaret A. "Observation of Behavioral Responses." *Nursing Observations of the Young Patient*. Dubuque, Iowa: Wm. C. Brown Publishers, 1970.

* Cohen, Barbara. *Thank You, Jackie Robinson*. New York: Lothrop, 1974.

* Cole, S. R. "For Young Readers: Introducing Death." *New York Times Book Review*, September 26, 1971.

* Commager, Evan. *Valentine*. New York: Harper & Row, 1961.

Cook, S. *Children and Dying: An Exploration and Selected Bibliographies*. New York: Health Sciences Publishing Corporation, 1974.

* Coutant, Helen. *The First Snow*. New York: Knopf, 1974.

* Cragg, Catherine E. "The Child with Leukemia." *The Canadian Nurse* 30–34, October 1969.

* Cram, Mildred. *Forever*. New York: Knopf, 1979.

* Craven, Margaret. *I Heard the Owl Call My Name*. New York: Doubleday, 1973.

Crawford, Nelson Antrim, and Menninger, Karl A., (eds.) *The Health-Minded Child*. New York: Coward-McCann, 1930.

Danz, Louis. *The Psychologist Looks at Art*. New York: Longmans, Green & Company, 1937.

Dapean, M. *The Current State of SIDS Research*. Presentation to National Sudden Infant Death Syndrome Foundation Board of Trustees. Chicago, 1979.

Darcy-Berube, Françoise. "When Your Child Asks About Death." *New Catholic World*, March 1973.

* For children, varying ages.

Davidson, Ramona P. "Let's Talk About Death—To Give Care in Terminal Illness." *American Journal of Nursing* 66, January 1966.

Davis, J. A. "The Attitude of Parents to the Approaching Death of Their Child." *Developmental Medicine and Child Neurology* 6:286–288, June 1964.

Davoli, G. "The Child's Request to Die at Home." *Pediatrics* 38:925, November 1966.

Dean, D. "Emotional Abuse of Children." *Child Today* 79:18, July–August 1979.

* "Death, Books Concerned with." Harper & Row. Photocopy. 4 pp.

"Death in Childhood." *Canadian Medical Association Journal* 98:967–969, May 18, 1968.

* Dennis, Wesley. *Flip.* New York: Viking, 1941.

* DePaola, Tomie. *Nana Upstairs and Nana Downstairs.* New York: Putnam, 1973.

Deutsch, H. "The Absence of Grief." *The Psychoanalytic Quarterly*, Vol. 6, 1937.

Deutsch, J. M. *The Development of Children's Concepts of Causal Relationships.* Minneapolis: University of Minnesota Press, 1937.

Dimock, Hedley C. *The Child in Hospital.* Toronto, Canada: Macmillan, 1959.

Diskin, Martin, and Guggenheim, Hans. "The Child and Death as Seen in Different Cultures." In *Explaining Death to Children*, edited by E. A. Grollman. Boston: Beacon Press, 1967.

* Dobrin, Arnold. *Scat!* New York: Four Winds Press, 1971.

* Donovan, John. *I'll Get There. It Better Be Worth the Trip.* New York: Harper & Row, 1969.

* ———. *Wild in the World.* New York: Harper & Row, 1971.

Doss, Barbara. "The Meaning of Death to Children." *Baptist Leader*, May 1971.

Downey, Timothy James. "All My Times in the Hospital—A Child Remembers." *American Journal of Nursing*, Vol. 74, No. 12, December 1974, pp. 2196–2198.

* For children, varying ages.

Duda, Deborah. *A Guide to Dying at Home.* Santa Fe, New Mexico: John Muir, 1982.

Dunn, Paul, and Eyre, Richard. *The Birth That We Call Death.* Salt Lake City: Bookcraft Publishers, 1976.

Easson, W. M. "Care of the Young Patient Who Is Dying." *Journal of the American Medical Association* 205:203–207, July 22, 1968.

————. *The Dying Child. The Management of the Child or Adolescent Who Is Dying.* Springfield, Ill.: Charles C. Thomas, 1970.

Edelston, H. "Separation Anxiety in Young Children." *Genetic Psychology Monographs* 28, 1:3–95, June 1942.

Ehrenzweig, Anton. *The Psychoanalysis of Artistic Vision and Hearing.* New York: Julian Press, 1953.

Engle, George L. "Grief and Grieving." *American Journal of Nursing*, Vol. 64, No. 9, September 1964.

Estvan, Frank and Elizabeth. *The Child's World.* New York: Putnam, 1959.

Evans, Audrey E. "If a Child Must Die." *New England Journal of Medicine* 278, 3:138–142, January 18, 1968.

Facts About Sudden Infant Death Syndrome. Chicago: National Sudden Infant Death Syndrome Foundation, 1979.

Fargues, Marie. *Child and the Mystery of Death.* Glen Rock, N.Y.: Paulist Press, 1966.

* Farley, Carol. *The Garden Is Doing Fine.* New York: Atheneum, 1975.

Farrell, Fran L. "Living Until Death: A Case Study of Three Adolescents with Cancer." Master's thesis, Arizona State University, 1977.

* Fassler, Joan. *The Boy with a Problem.* New York: Behavioral Publications, 1971.

* ————. *My Grandpa Died Today.* Gerontology Series. New York: Behavioral Publications, 1971.

* ————. *One Little Girl.* New York: Behavioral Publications, 1969.

* Fassler, J. "Some Special Uses of Children's Literature." Yale University Child Study Center, March 1975. Photocopy. 7 pp.

* For children, varying ages.

Feifel, Herman, Ed. *The Meaning of Death.* New York: McGraw-Hill, 1959.

Fischoff, Jos., and O'Brien, Noreen. *Before and After My Child Dies: A Collection of Parents' Experiences.* Detroit: Emmons-Fairfield, 1981.

Fister, Nelda. "Death in Children." Research Core Seminar. University of Oklahoma, May 1974.

————. *Mothers' Perceptions of Interactions During Their Experiences Surrounding the Terminal Episode of Illness and Death of Their Children.* (Unpublished.)

Folck, Marilyn, and Nie, Phyllis. "Nursing Students Learn to Face Death." *Nursing Outlook* 7, 1959.

Forres, Hildegard. "Emotional Dangers to Children in Hospitals," *Mental Health* 2:58–62, 1953.

Forsyth, David. "Psychological Effects of Bodily Illness in Children." *Lancet* 2:15–18, July 7, 1934.

Frank, Lawrence. "Children in a World of Violence." *Progress of Education* 17:393–399, October 1940.

Frankl, Viktor Emil. *The Doctor and the Soul.* New York: Knopf, 1955.

* Frederick, Regina Wilma. *Charlie's Moment of Truth.* Atlanta: Angel Creations, 1980.

Freud, Anna. *Normality and Pathology in Childhood.* New York: International Universities Press, 1965.

————. "The Role of Bodily Illness in the Mental Life of Children." *Psychoanalytic Study of the Child* 7:69–81, 1952.

Freud, A., and Burlingham, D. *War and Children.* New York: International Universities Press, 1944.

Friedman, Stanford B., et al. "Behavioral Observations on Parents Anticipating the Death of a Child." *Pediatrics*, Vol. 32, October 1963.

Friedman, Stanford B. "Care of the Family of the Child with Cancer." *Pediatrics.* 40, 3:498–507, September 1967.

Frimoth, Lenore Beck. *Little Ones to Him Belong.* Virginia: John Knox Press, 1962.

Furman, E. *A Child's Parent Dies.* New Haven: Yale University Press, 1974.

* For children, varying ages.

Furman, R. "The Child's Reaction to Death in the Family." In *Loss and Grief: Psychological Management in Medical Practice*, edited by B. Schoenberg et al. New York: Columbia University Press, 1970.

Furman, Robert A. "Death and the Young Child: Some Preliminary Considerations." *Psychoanalytic Study of the Child*.

———. "Death of a Six-Year-Old's Mother During His Analysis." *Psychoanalytic Study of the Child*.

Futterman, Ed; Hoffman, Irwin; and Sabshin, Melvin. *Parental Anticipatory Mourning*. Dept. of Psychiatry, University of Illinois College of Medicine, October 7, 1970.

Garfield, Chas. A., ed. *Psychosocial Care of the Dying Patient*. San Francisco Training Conference for Physicians, April 29–May 1, 1976.

Gartley, Wayne, and Bernasconi, Marion. "The Concept of Death in Children." *Journal of Genetic Psychology* 110:71–85, 1967.

Gauthier, Y. "The Mourning Reaction of a Ten-and-a-Half-Year-Old Boy." *Psychoanalytic Study of the Child*. 20:481–494, 1965.

———. "The Mourning Reaction of a Ten-Year-Old Boy," *Canadian Psychiatric Association Journal* 11: Suppl:307–308, 1966.

Gawain, Shakti. *Creative Visualization*. Mill Valley, Calif.: Whatever Publishing, 1978.

Gay, M. J., et al. "The Late Effects of Loss of Parents in Childhood." *British Journal of Psychiatry* 113:753–759, July 1967.

Geis, Dorothy P. "Mothers' Perceptions of Care Given Their Dying Children." *American Journal of Nursing*, Vol. 65, No. 2, February 1965.

* George, Jean C. *Julie of the Wolves*. New York: Harper and Row, 1972.

Gerard, Elisabeth I. "Der Tod als Erlebnis bei Kindern und Jugendlichen" [Death as an Experience in Children and Youth]. *Individual Psychology* 8:551–558, 1930.

Gesell, Arnold; Ilg, Frances; and Ames, Frances. *Youth—the Years from Ten to Sixteen*. New York: Harper Brothers, 1956.

* For children, varying ages.

Gibney, Harriet H. "What Death Means to Children." *Parents'*
    Magazine 65:136–142, March 1965.
Gibran, Kahlil. *The Prophet.* New York: Knopf, 1978.
Gil, D. *Child Abuse and Violence.* New York: AMS Press, 1979.
Giono, Jean. *The Man Who Planted Hope and Grew Happiness.*
    Brooksville, Maine: Friends of Nature, 1981.
Glaser, Kurt. "Attempted Suicide in Children and Adolescents:
    Psychodynamic Observations." *American Journal of Psy-*
    chotherapy 19, 2:220–227, April 1965.
Golden, Susan, et al. *Chemotherapy and You.* DHEW No. (NIH)
    76–1136. Washington, D.C.
Goldfogel, Linda. "Working with the Parent of a Dying Child."
    American Journal of Nursing, Vol. 70, No. 8, August 1970.
Gordon, Audrey, and Klass, Dennis. *Death Crisis at School.* Pre-
    published manuscript, 1980.
Gordon, Joseph, and Zern, Harry. *The Emotional Problems of*
    Children. New York: Crown, 1954.
Gould, Etta M. "A Playroom Helps Children Adjust to a Hos-
    pital." *Nursing World* 129:14–16, December 1955.
Gould, Robert E. "Suicide Problems in Children and Adolescents."
    American Journal of Psychotherapy 19, 2:228–246, April
    1965.
Graham, Victoria. "Sometimes Ricky Accepts Death." *The Boston*
    Globe, November 7, 1974, p. 45.
Grant, Niels, Jr. *Art and the Delinquent.* New York: Exposition
    Press, 1958.
Green, Morris. "Care of the Dying Child." *Pediatrics* 40, 3:492–497,
    September 1967.
Green, Morris; Friedman, Stanford; and Rotherberg, M. B. "Some-
    thing Can Be Done for a Child with Cancer." *Hospital*
    Tribune 1, 27:8, July 3, 1967.
Green, M., and Solnit, A. J. "Reactions to the Threatened Loss of
    a Child: A Vulnerable Child Syndrome; Pediatric Man-
    agement of the Dying Child, Part III." *Pediatrics,* 34, 1:58–66,
    July 1964.
* Greene, Constance. *Beat the Turtle Drum.* New York: Viking,
    1976.

* For children, varying ages.

Greene, Patricia. "The Child with Leukemia in the Classroom." *American Journal of Nursing*, Vol. 75, No. 1, January 1975.

Gregory, I. "Anterospective Data Following Childhood Loss of a Parent." *Archives of General Psychiatry* 13:99–120, 1965.

"Grief and Mourning." Office of Preventive Programs, Kentucky Department of Mental Health, 1973. (Pamphlet.)

Griffiths, Ruth. *A Study of Imagination in Early Childhood.* London: Kegan Paul, 1935.

Grigsby, Olive John. "An Experimental Study of the Development of Concepts of Relationship in Pre-School Children as Evidenced by Their Expressive Ability." *Journal of Experimental Education* 1, 2:144–162, 1932.

* Grimmius, Marie E. *Potatoes.* (Prepublished manuscript.)

Grollman, Earl A., ed. *Concerning Death: A Practical Guide for the Living.* Boston: Beacon Press, 1974.

———. *Explaining Death to Children.* Boston: Beacon Press, 1967.

* ———. *Talking About Death.* Boston: Beacon Press, 1971.

———. *What Helped Me When My Loved One Died.* Boston: Beacon Press, 1981.

* Guest, Judith. *Ordinary People.* New York: Viking, 1976.

Guggenheimer, Richard. *Sight and Insight.* New York: Harper & Brothers, 1945.

Guimond, Joyce. "We Knew Our Child Was Dying." *American Journal of Nursing.* Vol. 74, No. 2, February 1974.

Gunther, J. *Death Be Not Proud.* New York: Harper & Row, 1971.

Gutowski, Frances. " Nursing the Leukemic Child with Central Nervous System Involvement." *American Journal of Nursing* 63:87–89, April 1963.

Hagin, R. A. "Bereaved Children." *Journal of Clinical Child Psychology*, Vol. 3 (2), 1974.

Hailperin, Celia, ed. *Hospital Services for the Child at Home.* Pittsburgh: Mortefiore Hospital Association of Western Pennsylvania, 1968.

Hajal, F. "Post-Suicide Grief Work in Family Therapy." *Journal of Marriage and Family Counseling*, April 1977.

* Hall, Lynn. *Shadows.* Chicago: Follett, 1977.

* For children, varying ages.

Haller, J. Alex, ed. *The Hospitalized Child and His Family.* Baltimore: Johns Hopkins Press, 1967.

Hallet, E. R. "Birth and Grief." *Birth and the Family Journal,* Vol. 1:4, 1974.

Hamovitch, Maurice B. *The Parent and the Fatally Ill Child.* Duarte, Calif.: City of Hope Medical Center, 1964.

Hardgrove, Carol, and Warrick, Louise H. "How Shall We Tell the Children?" *American Journal of Nursing,* Vol. 74, No. 3, March, 1974, pp. 448–450.

* Harris, Audrey. *Why Did He Die?* Minneapolis: Lerner Press, 1970.

Harrison, S. I., et al. "Children's Reactions to Bereavement. Adult Confusions and Misperceptions." *Archives of General Psychiatry* 17:593–597, March 1967.

Hays, Joyce Samhammer. "The Night Neil Died." *Nursing Outlook,* Vol. 19, No. 12, December 1962.

Hazlitt, William. "On the Feeling of Immortality in Youth." In *Complete Works,* edited by P. P. Hose. Vol. XVII. London: J. M. Dent, 1934.

Hedlund, Kent, ed. *They Say We Children Fear the Dark.* Edwardsville: Southern Illinois University, Winter 1974.

Henderson, L. "Crib Deaths: Who Shares the Father's Sorrow?" *Dallas Times Herald,* August 3, 1975. (Reprint.)

Hendricks, C. G., and Wills, R. *The Centering Book: Awareness Activities for Children, Parents and Teachers.* Englewood Cliffs, N.J.: Prentice-Hall, 1975.

Hersh, E. M., et al. "Causes of Death in Acute Leukemia." *Journal of the American Medical Association,* 193, 1965.

Heuscher, J. E. "Death in the Fairy-Tale." *Diseases of the Nervous System* 28:462–468, July 1967.

Hickman, M. W. *Love Speaks Its Voice.* Waco, Tex.: Word, 1976.

Hilgard, Josephine; Newman, Martha F.; and Fisk, Fern. "Strength of Adult Ego Following Childhood Bereavement." *American Journal of Orthopsychiatry* 30:788–798, 1960.

Hillard, A. "Respecting the Child's Culture." *Child Today,* 79:21, January–February, 1979.

* For children, varying ages.

Hinton, J. M. "The Physical and Mental Distress of the Dying." *Quarterly Journal of Medicine* 32, January 1963.

Hoekelma, R. A. "Physicians' Responsibility in Management of Sudden Infant Death Syndrome." *American Journal of Diseases of Children*, Vol. 128 (1), 1974.

Hoffman, Irwin. *Family Adaptation to Total Illness in a Child: An Exploration of Sense-of-Self Under the Impact of Stress.* Chicago: University of Chicago Press, August 1968.

Hoffman, Irwin, and Futterman, E. H. "Coping with Waiting: Psychiatric Intervention and Study in the Waiting Room of a Pediatric Oncology Clinic." *Comprehensive Psychiatry*, Vol. 12, No. 1, January 1971.

Hopkins, Lois Jones. "A Basis for Nursing Care of the Terminally Ill Child and His Family." *Maternal-Child Nursing Journal*, Vol. 2, No. 2, Summer 1973.

Hostler, Phyllis. *The Child's World.* Harmondsworth, Middlesex, England.: Penguin Books, 1959.

Howell, D. A. "A Child Dies." *Hospital Topics* 45:93–96, February 1967.

———. "A Child Dies." *Seminars in Hematology* 3:168–173, April 1966.

Howell, Doris A. "A Child Dies." *Journal of Pediatric Surgery* 1, 1:2–7, February 1966.

———. "Emotional Management of Family Stressed in Care of Dying Child." *Pediatric Currents* 17, 6: June 1968.

* Hunt, Irene. *Up a Road Slowly.* Chicago: Follett, 1966.

Hunt, Leigh. "Deaths of Little Children." In *The Great English Essayists*, edited by W. J. and C. W. Dawson. New York: Harper & Brothers, 1909, pp. 64–69.

Hunter, Edith F. *The Questioning Child and Religion.* Boston: Beacon Press, 1956.

* Hunter, Mollie. *The Sound of Chariots.* New York: Harper & Row, 1972.

Ilg, Frances L., and Ames, Louise Bates. *Child Behavior.* New York: Harper & Bros., 1955.

I Never Saw Another Butterfly . . .: Children's Drawings and Poems

* For children, varying ages.

from Theresienstadt Concentration Camp 1942–1944. New York: McGraw-Hill, 1964.

Jackson, Edgar N. *For the Living.* Des Moines: Meredith, 1964.

———. *Telling a Child About Death.* New York: Channel Press, 1965.

———. "The Theological, Psychological, and Philosophical Dimensions of Death in Protestantism." In *Explaining Death to Children*, edited by Earl A. Grollman. Boston: Beacon Press, 1967.

———. *Understanding Grief.* New York: Abington Press, 1957.

Jackson, Edith. "Treatment of the Young Child in the Hospital." *American Journal of Orthopsychiatry* 12:56–67, 1942.

Jackson, Katherine; Winkley, Ruth; and Faust, Otto. "Problem of Emotional Trauma in Hospital Treatment of Children." *JAMA* 149, 17:1536–1537, 1952.

Jacobs, Tina Claire. "Casework with the Very Young Child in a Hospital." *Social Work.* 3, 2:76–82, April 1958.

Jakab, Irene, ed. *Art Interpretation and Art Therapy.* New York: S. Karger, 1969.

Jean, Sally Lucas. "Mental Windows for Hospitalized Children." *The Child* 13, 1949.

Jensen, Reynold A. "The Hospitalized Child, Round Table." *American Journal of Orthopsychiatry* 25, 2:293–318, April 1955.

Jersild, Arthur T., and Holmes, Frances B. *Children's Fears.* New York: Teachers College, Columbia University, 1935.

Jersild, Arthur; Markey, Frances; and Jersild, Catherine. *Children's Fears, Dreams, Wishes, Daydreams, Likes, Dislikes, Pleasant and Unpleasant Memories.* New York: Teachers College, Columbia University, Bureau of Publications, 1933.

Jetter, Lucille E. "Some Emotional Aspects of Prolonged Illness in Children." *Survey* 84:165, May 1948.

Johnson, Edwin, and Josey, Charles C. "A Note on the Development of the Thought Forms of Children As Described by Piaget." *Journal of Abnormal Social Psychology* 26:338–339, 1931–32.

* Jones, Ron. *The Acorn People.* New York: Bantam Books, 1977.

* For children, varying ages.

* Kantrowitz, Mildred. "When Violet Died." *Parents' Magazine*, April 1973.
* Kaplan, Bess. *The Empty Chair*. New York: Harper, 1978.
Karon, Myron, and Vernick, Joel. "An Approach to the Emotional Support of Fatally Ill Children." *Clinical Pediatrics*, Vol. 7, No. 5, May, 1968, pp. 274–279.
Kastenbaum, R. "The Kingdom Where Nobody Dies." *Saturday Review*, December 23, 1972.
Kastenbaum, R. J., ed. *Omeda Journal of Health and Dying*. Vol. 12, No. 4, 1981–82.
Kastenbaum, Robert. "The Child's Understanding of Death: How Does It Develop?" In *Explaining Death to Children*, edited by E. A. Grollman. Boston, Beacon Press 1967, pp. 89–108.
———. "Time and Death in Adolescence." In *The Meaning of Death*, edited by H. Feifel. New York: McGraw-Hill, 1959, pp. 99–113.
Katz, David and Rosa. *Conversations with Children*. London: Kegan Paul, 1936.
* Keats, Ezra Jack. *Whistle for Willie*. New York: Viking, 1964.
Keyser, Marty. "At Home with Death: A Natural Child-Death." *Pediatrics*, Vol. 90, No. 3,
Klaber, F. W. *When Children Ask About Death*. New York: Society for Ethical Culture, 1950.
Klein, Melanie. *The Psychoanalysis of Children*. London: L. & V. Woolf, 1932.
* Klein, Norma. *Sunshine*. New York: Avon, 1974.
Kliman, G. *Psychological Emergencies of Childhood*. New York: Grune and Stratton, 1968.
Klingberg, Gote. "The Distinction Between Living and Not Living Among 7 to 10-Year-Old Children, with Some Remarks Concerning the So-Called Animism Controversy." *Journal of Genetic Psychology* 90:227–238, 1957.
Klingensmith, S. W. "Child Animism: What the Child Means by 'Alive.'" *Child Development* 24, 1:51–61, March 1953.
Knudson, Alfred G., and Natterson, Joseph M. "Practice of Pediatrics: Participation of Parents in the Hospital Care of

* For children, varying ages.

Fatally Ill Children." *Pediatrics* 26, 3:482–490, September 1960.

Koltnow, Peter. *The Child with Cancer—The Family*. American Cancer Society National Conference on Human Values and Cancer. Atlanta, Georgia, June 23, 1972.

Koocher, G. P. "Conversations with Children About Death—Ethical Considerations in Research." *Journal of Clinical Child Psychology*. Vol. 3 (2), 1974.

———. "Talking with Children about Death." *American Journal of Orthopedics*. Vol. 44 (3), 1974.

———. "Why Isn't the Gerbil Moving Anymore?" *Children Today*, January–February, 1975.

Kris, Ernst. *Psychoanalytic Explorations in Art*. New York: International Universities Press, 1952.

Kübler-Ross, Elisabeth. *Death: The Final Stage of Growth*. Englewood Cliffs, N.J.: Prentice-Hall, 1975.

———. "The Language of Dying," *Journal of Clinical Child Psychology*, 3, 1974.

———. *Letter to a Child with Cancer (The Dougy Book)*.

———. *Living with Death and Dying*. New York: Macmillan, 1981.

———. "Nothing Final." 60-minute video cassette by BBC in 1982 on Dr. E. Kübler-Ross. For rent or purchase from Shanti Nilaya, P.O. Box 2396, Escondido, California 92025.

———. *On Death and Dying*. New York: Macmillan, 1969.

———. *Questions and Answers on Death and Dying*. New York: Macmillan, 1974.

———. *Remember the Secret*. Millbrae, Calif.: Celestial Arts, 1982.

———. "To Die Today." 16mm film from CBC. For rent or purchase from Film Makers Library, Inc., 290 West End Avenue, New York, New York 10023.

———. *To Live Until We Say Goodbye*. Englewood Cliffs, N.J.: Prentice-Hall, 1978.

———. "What Is It Like To Be Dying?" *American Journal of Nursing*, Vol. 71, No. 1, January 1971.

———. *Working It Through*. New York: Macmillan, 1982.

Kutscher and Kutscher. *A Bibliography of Books on Death, Bereavement, Loss and Grief*. New York: Health Science, 1935–1968 (plus update to 1973).

* Kyber, Manfred. *The Three Candles of Little Veronica.* Garden City: Waldorf Press, 1972.

Lamm, Maurice. *Jewish Way of Death.* New York: Jonathan David, 1968.

Langford, William S. "Anxiety in Children." *American Journal of Orthopsychiatry* 7:210–218, April 1937.

———. "The Child in the Pediatric Hospital: Adaptation to Illness and Hospitalization." *American Journal of Orthopsychiatry* 31:667–684, 1961.

———. "Psychologic Aspects of Pediatrics (Physical Illness and Convalescence: Their Meaning to the Child)." *Journal of Pediatrics* 33:242–250, August 1938.

Lasker, Arnold A. "Telling Children the Facts of Death." *National Jewish Monthly*, 1972.

* Lee, Mildred. *Fog.* New York: Seabury, 1972.

* ———. *The Rock and the Willow.* New York: Lothrop, 1963.

* ———. *The Magic Moth.* New York: Seabury, 1972.

Leerhsen, C.; Abramson, P.; and Prout, L. R. "Parents of Slain Children." *Newsweek*, April 12, 1982.

Levine, Stephen. *Lovebeast.* Santa Cruz, Calif.: Orenda-Unity, 1972.

———. *Planet Steward.* Santa Cruz, Calif.: Orenda-Unity, 1974.

———. *Who Dies?* Garden City: Doubleday, 1982.

Levine, Stephen, and Ram Dass. *Grist for the Mill.* Santa Cruz, Calif.: Orenda-Unity, 1977.

Levinson, B. M. "The Pet and the Child's Bereavement." *Mental Hygiene* 51:197–200, April 1967.

Leviton, D. "A Course on Death Education and Suicide Prevention: Implications for Health Education." *J.A.C.H.A.*, Vol. 19, April 1971.

———. "The Need for Education on Death and Suicide." *Journal of School Health*, Vol. 34, No. 4, April 1969.

Leviton, D., et al. "Death Education for Children and Youth." *Journal of Clinical Child Psychology*, Vol. 3 (2), 1974.

Leviton, D., and Forman, E. C. "Death Education for Children and Youth." *Journal of Clinical Child Psychology*, Summer 1974.

* For children, varying ages.

Levy, David. *Maternal Overprotection.* New York: Norton, 1966.

Levy, Edwin. "Children's Behavior Under Stress and Its Relation to Training by Parents to Respond to Stress Situations." *Child Development* 30:301–324, 1959.

Lewis, Melvin. "The Management of Parents of Acutely Ill Children in the Hospital." *American Journal of Orthopsychiatry* 32:60–66, 1962.

Lewis, Nancy. *My Roots Becoming Back.* New York: Bellevue Hospital Touchstone Center for Children, 1973.

Lewis, Nolan, D.C. "The Psychoanalytic Approach to the Problems of Children Under Twelve Years of Age." *Psychoanalytic Review* XIII: 424–443, October 1926.

Lichtenwalner, Muriel E. "Children Ask About Death." *International Journal of Religion* pp. 14–16, June 1964.

Lifton, Robert J. *The Broken Connection.* New York: Simon & Schuster, 1979.

——. "Death Imprints on Youth in Vietnam." *Journal of Clinical Child Psychology.* Vol. 3 (2), 1974.

Lifton, R. J., and Olson, E. *Living and Dying.* New York: Praeger, 1974.

* Lindel, Paul. *The Pigman.* New York: Harper & Row, 1968.

Lindermann, E. "Symptomatology and Management of Acute Grief." *American Journal of Psychiatry.* Vol. 101, 1944.

* Little, Jean. *Home from Far.* Boston: Little, Brown, 1965.

Lonnquist, Jouko. "Suicide in Helsinki." *Monographs of Psychiatria Fennica,* No. 8. Espoo, Finland; 1977.

* Lorenzo, Carol Lee. *Mama's Ghosts.* New York: Harper & Row, 1974.

Lourie, Reginald S. "Panel Discussion: What to Tell the Parents of a Child with Cancer." *Clinical Proceedings of Children's Hospitals* (Wash.) 17, 4:91–99, April 1961.

——. "The Pediatrician and the Handling of Terminal Illness." *Pediatrics* 32, 4, 1:477–479, October 1963.

Lowenberg, June S. "The Coping Behaviors of Fatally Ill Adolescents and Their Parents." *Nursing Forum,* Vol. IX, No. 3, 1970.

* For children, varying ages.

*Lund, Doris. *Eric*. Philadelphia: Lippincott, 1974.

Lundgren, Max. *Matt's Grandfather*. New York: Putnam, 1972.

Lunt, Lida Bell. *Walking Against the Wind*. 1979.

Luzzatti, Luigi, and Dittmann, Barbara. "Group Discussions with Parents of Ill Children." *Pediatrics* 12:269–273, 1954.

MacCarthy, Dermod, and Lindsay, Mary. "Children in Hospital with Mothers." *Lancet* 1:603–608, March 24, 1962.

McAulay, J. D. "What Understandings Do Second Grade Children Have of Time Relationships?" *Journal of Educational Research* 54, 8:312–314, April 1961.

McClelland, Charles. "Relationship of the Physician in Practice to a Children's Cancer Clinic." *Pediatrics*, Suppl Care of the Child with Cancer, 40, 3 (II):537–539, September 1967.

McCulley, Robert S. "Fantasy Productions of Children with a Progressively Crippling and Fatal Illness." *Journal of Genetic Psychology*. 102:203–216, June 1963.

Mace, Nancy L., and Rabins, Peter V., M.D. *The 36-Hour Day: A Family Guide to Caring for Persons with Alzheimer's Disease, Related Dementing Illnesses, and Memory Loss in Later Life*. Baltimore: Johns Hopkins University Press, 1981.

McFarlane, Judith Medlin. "The Child with Sickle Cell Anemia." *Nursing 75*, Vol. 5, No. 5, May 1975, pp. 29–33.

Maclennan, B. W. "Non-Medical Care of Chronically Ill Children in Hospital." *Lancet* 2:209–210, July 30, 1949.

Mahler, Margaret S. "Helping Children to Accept Death." *Child Study* 27. New York: Child Study Association of America, 1950.

Mandino, O. G. *The Greatest Miracle in the World*. New York: Bantam Books, 1975.

*Mann, Peggy. *There Are Two Kinds of Terrible*. New York: Doubleday, 1977.

Markusen, Eric, and Fulton, Robert. "Childhood Bereavement and Behavior Disorders: A Critical Review." *Omega*, Vol. 2, 1971.

Martin, H. L., et al. "The Family of the Fatally Burned Child." *Lancet* 2:628–629, September 14, 1968.

* For children, varying ages.

Martinson, Ida Marie. *Home Care for the Dying Child: Professional and Family Perspectives.* New York: Appleton-Century-Crofts, 1976.

Massanari, Jared and Alice. *Our Life with Caleb.* Philadelphia: Fortress Press, 1976.

* Mathis, Sharon. *The Hundred Penny Box.* New York: Viking, 1975.

Maurer, Adah. "Adolescent Attitudes Toward Death." *Journal of Genetic Psychology.* 105, 1964.

————. "The Child's Knowledge of Non-Existence." *Journal of Existential Psychiatry* 2:193–212, 1961.

Meserve, Harry C. *Let Children Ask.* Monograph. (4th printing.) Boston: Universalist-Unitarian, 1954.

* Miles, Miska. *Annie and the Old One.* Boston: Little, Brown, 1971.

Miller, J. B. M. "Children's Reactions to the Death of a Parent: A Review of the Psychoanalytic Literature." *Journal of the American Psychoanalytic Association,* Vol. 19 (4), October 1971.

Miller, P. G., et al. "Mommy, What Happens When I Die?" *Mental Hygiene.* 57, Spring 1973.

Milner, Marion. "A Suicidal Symptom in a Child of Three." *International Journal of Psychoanalysis.* 25:53–61, 1944.

Mitchell, Marjorie E. *The Child's Attitude to Death.* New York: Schocken Books, 1967.

* Moe, Barbara. *Pickles and Prunes.* New York: McGraw-Hill, 1976.

Moellenhoff, Fritz. "Ideas of Children About Death." *Bulletin of the Menninger Clinic* 3:148–156, 1939.

Moffot, Mary J. *In the Midst of Winter.* New York: Random House, 1982.

Mogar, Mariannina. "Children's Causal Reasoning About Natural Phenomena," *Child Development* 31:59–65, 1960.

Mohr, George J. *When Children Face Crises.* Chicago: Science Research Associates, 1952.

* Mohr, Nicholosa. *Nilda.* New York: Harper & Row, 1973.

Moller, Hella. "Death: Handling the Subject and Affected Students

* For children, varying ages.

in Schools." In *Explaining Death to Children*, edited by Earl A. Grollman. Boston: Beacon Press, 1967.

Morrill, Tom, ed. *Foundlings: The Greatness of Children's Poetry*. Tallahassee: DDB Press.

*Morris Jeannie. *Brian Piccolo: A Short Season*. New York: Random House, 1971.

Morrissey, James R. "Children's Adaptation to Fatal Illness." *Journal of Social Work* 8, 4:81–88, October 1963.

———. "A Note on Interviews with Children Facing Imminent Death." *Social Casework*, XLIV, 6:343–345, June 1963.

Moustakas, Clark, ed. *Existential Child Therapy*. New York: Basic Books, 1966.

Mueller, Mary Louise. "Reducing the Fear of Death in Early Adolescents Through Religious Education." Doctoral dissertation, University of Notre Dame, May 1974.

*Muggeridge, M. *Something Beautiful for God, Mother Teresa of Calcutta*. New York: Image Books, Doubleday, 1971.

Muktananda, Swami. *Does Death Really Exist?* South Fallsburg, N.Y.: SYDA Foundation, 1981.

Mullan, Fitzhugh, M.D. *Vital Signs: A Young Doctor's Struggle with Cancer*. New York: Farrar, Straus & Giroux, 1975, 1982.

Munro, A., et al. "Further Data on Childhood Parent-Loss in Psychiatric Normals." *Acta Psychiatrica Scandinavica* 44, 1968.

Murray, Ruth. "The Terminally Ill Child." *Journal of Practical Nursing*, March 1973.

Murstein, Bernard. "The Effect of Long-Term Illness of Children on the Emotional Adjustment of Parents." *Child Development* 31:157–171, 1960.

Myers, Richard. "Dad, What Is It Like To Die?" *The Director*, September 1971.

Naeye, R. "Sudden Infant Death." *Scientific American* 80:56, April 1980.

Nagera, H. "Children's Reactions to the Death of Important Objects: A Developmental Approach." *Psychoanalytic Study of the Child*, Vol. XXV.

* For children, varying ages.

Nagy, Maria H. "Children's Ideas of the Origin of Illness." *Health Education Journal* 9:6–12, 1951.

———. "The Child's View of Death." In *The Meaning of Death*, edited by H. Feifel. New York: McGraw-Hill, 1959.

———. "The Child's Theories Concerning Death." *Journal of Genetic Psychology* 73, First Half: 3–27, September 1948.

Nass, Martin L. "The Effects of Three Variables on Children's Concepts of Physical Causality." *Journal of Abnormal Social Psychology* 53:191–196, 1956.

Natterson, Joseph M., and Knudson, Alfred G. "Observations Concerning Fear of Death in Fatally Ill Children and Their Mothers." *Psychosomatic Medicine* XXII, 6:456–465, 1960.

*Ness, Evaline. *Sam, Bangs and Moonshine*. New York: Holt, Rinehart & Winston, 1966.

New Light on an Old Problem. DHEW Publication No. (OHDS) 79-31108. Washington, D.C.: Head Start and National Center on Child Abuse and Neglect, 1978.

Northrup, F. C. "Dying Child." *American Journal of Nursing*. Vol. 74 (6), 1974.

"Nursing Care of Patients in the Laminar Air Flow Room." U.S. Department of Health and Welfare (NIH 92–93), 1–16, December 1971.

Opie, Iona and Peter. *The Lore and Language of School and Children*. Oxford: Clarendon Press, 1961.

Orbach, Charles E. "The Multiple Meanings of the Loss of a Child." *American Journal of Psychotherapy* 13, 4:906–915, October 1959.

Orbach, Charles E., et al. "Psychological Impact of Cancer and Its Treatment, III: The Adaptation of Mothers to the Threatened Loss of Their Children Through Leukemia." Part II, *Cancer* 8, 1:20–33, 1955.

*Painter, Nancy K. *The Secret of the Real Billy*, Cranford, N.J.: Allen Printing, 1978.

Parkhurst, Helen. *Exploring the Child's World*. New York: Appleton-Century-Crofts, 1951.

* For children, varying ages.

————. "L'Idea che il bambino ha della morte" [Ideas of the Child on Death]. *Scuola e Citta* (Pescetto) 5:5–16, 1956.

* Parks, Gordon. *The Learning Tree*. New York: Harper, 1973.

Pastan, Linda. *The Five Stages of Grief*. New York: Norton, 1978.

* Paterson, Katherine. *Bridge to Terabithia*. New York: Crowell, 1977.

* Paulus, Trina. *Hope for the Flowers*. New York: Paulist Press, 1972.

Peale, Norman Vincent. "How Much Truth Can a Child Take?" *Family Circle*, p. 31, April 1967.

Peck, Leigh. *Child Psychology*. Boston: D. C. Heath, 1953.

Peck, R. "The Development of the Concept of Death in Selected Male Children." (Ph.D. thesis, No. 66-9468). New York: New York University, 1966.

* Peck, Richard. *Dreamland Lake*. New York: Holt, Rinehart, 1973.

Peniston, D. H. "The Importance of 'Death Education' in Family Life." *Family Coordinator*, Vol. II, January 1962.

Pescetto, Guglielmo. "Rapresentazione della morte nel bambino" [Child's Ideas of Death]. *Rassegna Studi Psichiatrici* 46, 2:165–180, March–April 1957.

Pessin, Joseph. "Self-Destructive Tendencies in Adolescence." *Bulletin of the Menninger Clinic* 5, 1941.

Petrillo, Madeline, and Sanger, Sirgay. *Emotional Care of Hospitalized Children*. Philadelphia: Lippincott, 1972.

Piaget, Jean. *The Child's Conception of Physical Causality*. London: Kegan Paul, 1930.

————. *The Child's Conception of the World*. Paterson, N.J.: Littlefield, Adams, and Company, 1960.

————. *The Construction of Reality in the Child*. New Lork, Basic Books, 1954.

————. *The Language and Thought of the Child*. London: Routledge, 1952.

Pieroni, Antoinette. "Role of the Social Worker in a Children's Cancer Clinic." *Pediatrics* 40, 3:534–536, September 1967.

Pincus, Fily. *Death and the Family*. New York: Pantheon, 1975.

Pitcher, Evelyn Goodenough, and Prelinger, Ernst. *Children Tell*

* For children, varying ages.

Stories. New York: International Universities Press, 1963.
Plank, Emma N. "Death on a Children's Ward." *Medical Times* 92, 7:638–644, July 1964.
Plank, Emma; Caughey, Patricia A.; and Lipson, Martha J. "A General Hospital Child Care Problem to Counteract Hospitalism." *American Journal of Orthopsychiatry* 29, 1:94–101, January 1959.
Plank, E., and Plank, R. "Children and Death: As Seen Through Art and Autobiographies." *Psychoanalytic Study of the Child* 33:593–620, 1978.
Pollock, George H. "Childhood Parent and Sibling Loss in Adult Patients." *Archives of General Psychiatry* 7, 4:295–306, 1962.
Polner, Murray, and Barron, Arthur. *The Questions Children Ask.* New York: Macmillan, 1964.
Postman, Lee, and Bruner, Jerome. "Perception Under Stress." *Psychological Review* 55: 314–323, 1948.
Potts, Willis J. "The Heart of a Child." *JAMA* 161, 6:487–490, June 9, 1956.
Powers, Grover. "Humanizing Hospital Experiences." *American Journal of Diseases of Children* 76, 4:365–379, October 1948.
Pratts, O. R. "Helping the Family Face an Impending Death." *Nursing*, February 1973.
*Preston, Edna Mitchell. *The Temper Tantrum Book.* New York: Viking, 1969.
Prilook, M. E., ed. "The Repeatedly Ill Child: After You Diagnose Fatal Illness." Part 6: *Patient Care* 7, February 1, 1973.
Prugh, Dane G., et al. "A Study of the Emotional Reactions of Children and Families to Hospitalization and Illness." *American Journal of Orthopsychiatry* 23, 1:70–106, January 1953.
Quinlan, Joseph and Julia. *Karen Ann.* Garden City: Doubleday, 1977.
Quint, Jeanne C. "Obstacles to Helping the Dying." *American Journal of Nursing* 66, July 1965.
———. "Teacher Perspectives on Death." *The Nurse and the Dying Patient.* New York: Macmillan, 1967.
*Rabin, Gil. *Changes.* New York: Harper & Row, 1973.
*Rae, D. *Love Until It Hurts: A Tribute to Mother Teresa and the*

* For children, varying ages.

Work of the Men and Women of the Missionaries of Charity. San Francisco: Harper and Row, 1980.

Ram Dass. *Be Here Now.* (Not in print.)

——. *Journey of Awakening.* New York: Bantam, 1978.

——. *Miracle of Love.* New York: Dutton, 1979.

——. *The Only Dance There Is.* Garden City: Doubleday, 1974.

Ramzy, Ishak, and Wallerstein, Robert S. "Pain, Fear, and Anxiety." In *Psychoanalytic Study of the Child.* New York: International Universities Press, 1958.

Rauscher, William V. *The Case Against Suicide.* New York: St. Martin's Press, 1981.

Raven, Clara. "Sudden Infant Death Syndrome: An Epidemiologic Study." *Journal of the American Medical Women's Association,* Vol. 29, 3, March 1974.

Rector, F. L. "Cancer in Childhood." *American Journal of Nursing* 46, 7:449–451, July 1946.

Reed, Elizabeth L. *Helping Children with the Mystery of Death.* New York: Abington Press, 1970.

Religion and Childhood: Religion in the Developing Personality. Proceedings of the Second Academy Symposium, 1958 (Academy of Religion and Mental Health). New York: New York University Press, 1960.

Rheingold, Joseph C. "The Mother, Anxiety, and Death." In *The Catastrophic Death Complex.* Boston: Little, Brown, 1967.

Richards, A. I., and Schmale, A. H. "Psychosocial Conference in Medical Oncology: Role in a Training Program." *Annals of Internal Medicine* 80, 1974.

Rickman, John, ed. *On the Bringing Up of Children.* New York: Robert Brunner, 1952.

Riemer, J. *Jewish Reflections on Death.* New York: Schocken, 1974.

Riley, Thomas Joseph. "Catholic Teaching, the Child, and a Philosophy for Life and Death." In *Explaining Death to Children,* edited by Earl A. Grollman. Boston: Beacon Press, 1967.

* Rinaldo, C. L. *Dark Dreams.* New York: Harper & Row, 1974.

Ring, Kenneth. *Life at Death: A Scientific Investigation of the Near-Death Experience.* New York: Coward, McCann, 1980.

* For children, varying ages.

Robertson, J. "Some Responses of Young Children to Loss of Maternal Care." *Nursing Times*, 49, 1953.

Robertson, James. *Hospitals and Children*. London: Victor Gollancz, 1962.

———. "Some Responses of Young Children to Loss of Maternal Care." *Child-Family Digest* 15:7–22, September–October, 1956.

———. *Young Children in Hospital*. London: Tavistock, 1968.

Robinson, B. "Her Daughter—A Murder Victim. An Ohio Mother Reaches Out to Other Grieving Parents." *People Magazine*, March 16, 1981.

Rochlin, Gregory. "The Dread of Abandonment." *Psychoanalytic Study of the Child* 16:451–470, 1961.

———. "How Younger Children View Death and Themselves." In *Explaining Death to Children*, edited by Earl A. Grollman. Boston: Beacon Press, 1967.

* Rock, Gail. *The Thanksgiving Treasure*. New York: Knopf, 1974.

Rogness, Alvin N. *Appointment with Death*. New York: Thomas Nelson, 1972.

Rosenblatt, B. "A Young Boy's Reaction to the Death of His Sister." *Journal of the American Academy of Child Psychiatry* 8:321–335, April 1969.

Rosenblum, J. *How to Explain Death to a Child*. International Order of the Golden Rule, 1963.

Rosenzweig, Saul. "Sibling Death As a Psychological Experience with Special Reference to Schizophrenia." *Psychoanalytic Review* 30:177–186, April 1943.

Ross, Eulalie Steinmetz. "Children's Books Relating to Death: A Discussion." In *Explaining Death to Children*, edited by Earl A. Grollman. Boston: Beacon Press, 1967.

Ross, Helen. *Fears of Children*. Chicago: Science Research Associates, 1951.

Rotherberg, Michael B. "Reactions of Those Who Treat Children with Cancer." *Pediatrics* 40, 3:507–512, September 1967.

Rubin, T. *The Angry Book*. New York: Macmillan, 1969.

* For children, varying ages.

Rude, Margaret. " 'Play Therapy' Program Helps Child Adjust to Hospital." *Hospital Topics* 37, 1:97–99, January 1959.

Russell, Bertrand. "Your Child and the Fear of Death." *Forum* 81:174–178, 1929.

Russell, D. H. *Children's Thinking*. Boston: Ginn, 1956.

Saint-Exupéry, A. de. *The Little Prince*. New York: Harcourt, Brace, 1934.

Saroyan, William. *The Human Comedy*. New York: Harcourt, Brace, 1944.

Saunders, Cicely. "The Management of Fatal Illness in Childhood." *Proceedings of the Royal Society of Medicine*, Vol. 62, No. 6, June 1969.

Schechter, Marshall D. "The Orthopedically Handicapped Child." *Archives of General Psychiatry* 4:247–253, 1961.

Schiff, Harriet S. *The Bereaved Parent*. New York: Crown, 1977.

Schilder, Paul, and Weschler, D. "The Attitudes of Children Towards Death." *Journal of Genetic Psychology* 45:406–451, December 1934.

Schnell, R. "Helping Parents Cope with Dying Child with a Genetic Disorder." *Journal of Clinical Child Psychology*, Vol. 3 (2), 1974.

Schoenberg, B., et al., eds. "The Child's Reaction to His Own Terminal Illness." *Loss and Grief: Psychological Management in Medical Practice*. New York: Columbia University Press, 1970.

Schwarz, Berthold Eric, and Ruggieri, Bartholomew. *Parent-Child Tensions*. Philadelphia: Lippincott, 1958.

Schwiebert, Pat, and Ramsey, Paul. "Children Only Die When We Forget Them." Slide production. Portland, Oreg.: Rampat Productions.

———. *When Hello Means Goodbye*. Portland: University of Oregon Health Sciences Center, 1981.

Science of Mind Annual: The New Age of Healing. Los Angeles: Science of Mind Pub., October 1979.

* Scoppettone, Sandra. *Trying Hard to Hear You*. New York: Harper & Row, 1974.

* For children, varying ages.

Seller, Genevieve R.; Knapp, Margaret F., and Peterson, Rosalie I. "Children Get Cancer Too." *Public Health Nursing* 42, 12:638–643, December 1950.

Shambaugh, Benjamin. "A Study of Loss Reactions in a Seven-Year-Old." *Psychoanalytic Study of the Child.* 16:510–522, 1961.

Sharkey, F. *A Parting Gift.* New York: St. Martin's Press, 1982.

Sheeran, Sister Patricia. *Nursing Ministry to Parents of Children with Fatal Illness.* Master's thesis, State University of New York at Buffalo, September 1975. (Pre-published form.)

Sherman, Mikie. *Feeding the Sick Child.* DHEW Publication. Washington, D.C.: National Cancer Institute.

———. *The Leukemic Child.* DHEW Publication. Washington, D.C.: National Cancer Institute.

Sichel, J. "Death Fantasies in a Child." *Praxis der Kinderpsychologie* 16:172–175, July 1967.

Silverman, S. M., and Silverman, P. R. *An Aspect of Communication Between Parent and Child in a Widowed Family.* Pre-publication copy.

*Silverstein, Shel. *The Giving Tree.* New York: Harper & Row, 1964.

———. *The Missing Piece.*

———. *Where the Sidewalk Ends.* New York: Harper & Row, 1964.

Smith, A. G., et al. "The Dying Child. Helping the Family Cope with Impending Death." *Clinical Pediatrics* 8:131–134, March 1969.

*Smith, Doris. *A Taste of Blackberries.* New York: Crowell, 1973.

Solnit, Albert J. "The Dying Child." *Developmental Medicine and Child Neurology* 7:693–695, December 1965.

———. "Emotional Management of Familly Stressed in Care of Dying Child." *Pediatric Currents* 17, 8:65, September 1968.

———. "Hospitalization." *American Journal of Diseases of Children* 99:155–163, 1960.

Solnit, Albert J., and Green, Morris. "The Pediatric Management of the Dying Child: Part II. The Child's Reaction to the Fear of Dying." In *Modern Perspectives in Child Development.* New York: International Universities Press, 1963.

* For children, varying ages.

———. "Psychologic Considerations in the Management of Deaths on Pediatric Hospital Services. 1. The Doctor and the Child's Family." *Pediatrics* 24:106–112, 1959.

Solnit, Albert J., and Provence, Sally, eds. *Modern Perspectives in Child Development.* New York: International Universities Press, 1963.

Solnit, Albert J., and Stark, Mary. "Mourning and the Birth of a Defective Child." *Psychoanalytic Study of the Child* 16:523–537, 1961.

Sommerville, R. M. "Death Education As Part of Family Life Education: Using Imaginative Literature for Insights into Family Crises." *The Family Coordinator*, Vol. 20, July 1971.

Sourkes, B. "Siblings of the Pediatric Cancer Patient." In *Psychological Aspects of Childhood Cancer.* Springfield, Ill.: Charles Thomas and Company, 1980.

Spitz, R. A. "Hospitalism." *Psychoanalytic Study of the Child,* I, 1975.

Spitz, R. A., and Wolfe, K. M. "Anaclitic Depression." *Psychoanalytic Study of the Child,* 2, 1946.

Spock, Benjamin. "Telling Your Child About Death." *Ladies Home Journal* 77:14, 1960.

Stacey, Chalmers L., and Reichen, Marie L. "Attitudes Toward Death and Future Life Among Normal and Subnormal Adolescent Girls." *Exceptional Children* 20: 259–262, 1954.

* Stanek, Muriel. *I Won't Go Without a Father.* Chicago: Albert Whitman, 1972.

* Steig, William. *Amos and Boris.* New York: Farrar, Straus & Giroux, 1971, and New York: Penguin Books, 1977.

Stern, Erich. *Kind, Krankheit und Tod* [Child, Disease and Death] Basel, Switzerland: Ernst Reinhardt, 1957.

Stern, William. *Psychologie der Fruher Kindheit* [Psychology of Early Childhood]. New York and London: Holt, 1924.

* Stolz, Mary. *The Edge of Next Year.* New York: Harper & Row, 1974.

Strang, Ruth. "How Children and Adolescents View Their World." *Mental Hygiene* 38:28–33, 1954.

* For children, varying ages.

Strauss, Anselm L., and Glaser, Barney. *Anguish.* Mill Valley, Calif.: Sociology Press, 1970.

Strobel, Elisabeth and Charles S., M.D. *The Kiddie QR: A Choice for Children.* Audio Cassette Program. QR Institute, 1980.

———. *The Quieting Reflex: A Choice for Adolescents.* QR Institute, 1983.

Swain, Jasper. *On the Death of My Son.* Wellingborough, Northamptonshire, England: Turnstone Press, 1974.

Szurek, S. A. "Comments on the Psychopathology of Children with Somatic Illness." *American Journal of Psychiatry* 107:844–849, 1951.

Tallmer, M., et al. "Factors Influencing Children's Concepts of Death." *Journal of Clinical Child Psychology,* Vol. 3 (2), 1974.

Tanner, A. E. *The Child, His Thinking, Feeling, and Doing.* Chicago: Rand, McNally, 1904.

Tanner, I. J. *Healing the Pain of Everyday Loss.* Minneapolis: Winston Press, 1976.

*Taylor, Theodore. *The Cay.* Garden City: Doubleday, 1969.

Temes, Roberta. *Living with an Empty Chair.* New York: Irvington, 1980.

*Thiele, Colin. *Fire in the Store.* New York: Harper & Row, 1969.

Timmins, Noreen. *Our Gift.* (Pre-published form.)

Tisza, Veronica B. "Management of the Parents of the Chronically Ill Child." *American Journal of Orthopsychiatry,* 1962.

———. "Management of the Parent in Pediatric Practice." Workshop—1960. *American Journal of Orthopsychiatry,* 1960.

Tisza, Veronica B., and Angoff, Kristine. "A Play Program and Its Function in a Pediatric Hospital." *Pediatrics* 19:293–302, 1957.

———. "A Play Program for Hospitalized Children: The Role of the Playroom Teacher." *Pediatrics* 28:841–845, 1961.

*Tobias, Tobi. *Petey.* New York: Putnam, 1978.

Tobin, T. E. *Mother! The Child You Lost Is a Saint.* Ligouri, Mo.: Liguorian Pamphlets, 1958.

* For children, varying ages.

Toch, Rudolph. "Management of the Child with a Fatal Disease." *Clinical Pediatrics* 3, 7:418–427, July 1964.
Tonyan, Angela. "Role of the Nurse in a Children's Cancer Clinic." *Pediatrics* 40, 3:532–534, September 1967.
Tripp, Tony, and Mayhew, Kathy. *Loss and Its Impact: Getting Through Grief.* Pre-published manuscript, 1979.
* Vavra, Robert. *The Lion and Blue.* New York: Reynal, 1974.
Vernick, Joel J. Selected Bibliography on Death and Dying. DHEW Publication. Bethesda, Md.: National Institute of Child Health and Human Development.
Vernick, Joel, and Karon, Myron. "Who's Afraid of Death on a Leukemia Ward?" *American Journal of Diseases of Children* 109:393–397, May 1965.
Vernick, Joel, and Lunceford, Janet. "Milieu Design for Adolescents with Leukemia." *American Journal of Nursing* 67, 3, March 1967.
*Viorst, Judith. *The Tenth Good Thing About Barney.* New York: Atheneum, 1971.
Volavkova, Hana. *Children's Drawings and Poems from Terezin Concentration Camp, 1942–1944.* New York: Schocken, 1978.
Von Hug-Hellmuth, H. "The Child's Concept of Death." *Psychoanalytic Quarterly* 34:499–516, October 1965.
Vore, D. A. "Child's View of Death." *Southern Medical Journal,* Vol. 67 (4), 1974.
* Waber, Bernard. *Irs Sleeps Over.* Boston: Houghton Mifflin, 1972.
Waechter, Eugenia H. "Children's Awareness of Fatal Illness." *American Journal of Nursing,* Vol. 71, No. 6, June, 1971, pp. 1168–1172.
———. "Death Anxiety in Children with Fatal Illness." Doctoral dissertation, Stanford University. Ann Arbor, Mich.: University Microfilms, No. 69-310, 1968.
Wagner, Bernice. "Teaching Students to Work with the Dying." *American Journal of Nursing* 64, November 1964.
Wallace, M., and Feinauer, V. "Understanding a Sick Child's Behavior." *American Journal of Nursing,* 48:517–522, 1948.
Walton, M. "A Hospital School." *American Journal of Nursing* 51:23–24, 1951.

* For children, varying ages.

* Warburg, Sandol Stoddard. *Growing Time.* Boston: Houghton Mifflin, 1969.
Washburn, Ruth Wendell. *Children Have Their Reasons.* New York and London: Appleton-Century, 1942.
Watt, A. S. "Helping Children to Mourn," *Medical Insight,* July 1971.
Weir, Robert F. *Ethical Issues in Death and Dying.* New York: Columbia University Press, 1977.
Wessel, Morris A. "A Child Faces Death of a Loved One." *Physician's World.*
————. "What to Tell Children About Death," November 1974.
West, K. L. *Crystallizing Children's Dreams.* Lake Oswego, Oreg.: Amata Graphics, 1978.
Weston, D., and Irwin, R. C. "Preschool Child's Response to Death of Infant Sibling." *American Journal of Diseases of Children* 106, 6:564–567, 1963.
Whisman, Sandra. "Turn the Respirator Off and Let Danny Die." *RN Magazine,* Vol. 38, No. 4, April, 1975, pp. 34–35.
* White, E. B. *Charlotte's Web.* New York: Harper & Row, 1952.
* Whitehead, Ruth. *The Mother Tree.* New York: Seabury, 1971.
Whitehouse, D. "Johnny, The Little Boy Who Never Smiled." *American Journal of Nusing* 55, 9:1110, September 1955.
Whittaker, James K., and Trieschman, Albert E., eds. *Children Away from Home.* New York: Aldine-Atherton, 1972.
* Wilder, Thornton. *Our Town.* New York: Harper & Row, 1960.
Williams, H. "On a Teaching Hospital's Responsibility to Counsel Parents Concerning Their Child's Death." *Medical Journal of Australia* 2, 16:633–645, October 1963.
Williams, Margery. *The Velveteen Rabbit.* Garden City: Doubleday, 1975.
* Windsor, Patricia. *The Summer Before.* New York: Harper & Row, 1973.
* Winthrop, Elizabeth. *Walking Away.* New York: Harper & Row, 1973.
Wise, Doreen J. "Learning About Dying." *Nursing Outlook,* Vol. 22:1, January 1974.

* For children, varying ages.

Wojciechowska, Maia. *Hey, What's Wrong with This One?* New York: Harper & Row, 1969.

Wolf, Anna W. M. *Helping Your Child to Understand Death.* Rev. ed. Washington: Child Study Press, 1973.

Wolfelt, Alan D. *Children and Death: A Discussion Manual and Resource Guide.* Springfield, Illinois: OGR Service Corporation, 1980.

Wolfenstein, M. "How Is Mourning Possible?" *Psychoanalytic Study of the Child* 21: 93–123, 1966.

Wolfenstein, M. "Loss, Rage, and Repetition." *Psychoanalytic Study of the Child* 24:432–460, 1969.

Wolfenstein, Martha, and Kliman, Gilbert, eds. *Children and the Death of a President.* Garden City: Doubleday, 1965.

Wolff, Sula. "The Dying Child and His Family." *Modern Medicine* (London), Vol. 19, 1974.

Work, H. "Making Hospitalization Easier for Children." *Children* 3, 3:83–88, 1956.

Wright, L. "Emotional Support Program for Parents of Dying Children." *Journal of Clinical Child Psychology,* Vol. 3 (2), 1974.

Yudkin, S. "Children and Death." *Lancet* 1:37–41, January 7, 1967.

Zeligs, R. "Children's Attitudes Toward Death." *Mental Hygiene,* Vol. 51:393–396, July 1967.

Zeligs, Rose. "Death Casts Its Shadow on a Child." *Mental Hygiene,* Vol. 51, No. 1, January 1967.

* Zolotow, Charlotte. *A Father Like That.* New York: Harper & Row, 1971.

———. *My Grandson Lew.* New York: Harper & Row, 1974.

———. "Process of Mourning." *International Journal of Psychoanalysis* 42.

* For children, varying ages.

From the Shanti Nilaya Library*

FIRST PERSON ACCOUNTS OF DYING

Carman, George D. *My Mark*. A first-person account of a forty-six-year-old man's experience of his terminal illness, from bitterness to cosmic awareness, stated in poetry and joy. 160 pages.

Dunton, Sharon. *Dying*. A young woman's experience with cancer and her subsequent accelerated growth and gratitude for life. 20 pages.

Fraleigh, Lynn. *Privileged*. A middle-aged woman's experience of breast cancer that metastasizes to the liver. A mention of other-worldly voices that were her source of strength and joy. A booklet, not intended for publication, but for advice to her family and young relatives. Spirited and precious advice.

Pfanner, Hans. *A Tiny Touch of Cancer*. An extremely joyous twenty-five-year-old man's experience with two bouts of cancer, both of which he won. A personal testimony of "laughing death in the face." Honest, poignant, and entirely different from all other accounts. Great! 174 pages.

Smith, Joann Kelly. *The Freefall*. A Christian woman's faith and expected behavior shaken by her terminal cancer, and how she copes.

Smith, Rita. *I'm Sorry You Have Cancer and Will Die . . .* A young

* Shanti Nilaya, P.O. Box 2396, Escondido, California 92025

mother of four children expresses in diary form her accelerated growth—psychological, spiritual, emotional—during her four-year "foe to friendship" cancer. Includes facing her unloving husband and deciding to divorce him. 3 copies.

Vogel, Arthur, M.D. *Letters.* Actual copies of letters written by Dr. Vogel during his terminal illness; drawings and doodles. Bright and radiant with insight.

Warder, Fred and Anne. *As I Lie Hoping.* A man's experience with cancer, his death, and his wife's separate story, mostly of the hospitalization.

NON-FICTIONAL ACCOUNTS OF RELATIVES' DEATHS

Conn, Maggy. *Maggy: The Working Days.* An autobiography. 174 pages.

Field, Reshad. *To Know We Are Loved.* Love story and spiritual awareness/union of all souls. 254 pages.

Goldwag, Elliot. *Inner Balance, the Power of Holistic Healing.* Epilogue by Elisabeth Kübler-Ross. An anthology of issues relating to holistic healing.

Grady, F. Patrick. *Deathwatch: Three Brief Profiles.* Case histories of the author as counselor with three terminally ill persons.

Halo, Karilee, R.N., M.S., Ph.D. *Emerging from the White Cocoon: Nursing, Healing, and the Feminine Principle.* Intimate confessions of nurses who want to change themselves and the cold, unloving, medical/technological system. Included are suggestions to change it from big business back to a healing art.

Justice, Louise. *A Strange Woman with ESP.* An autobiographical account of extrasensory perceptions.

Kushner, Harold S., Rabbi. *When Bad Things Happen to Good People.* A rabbi and father's account of his son's life aı.d death at age fourteen. The father's religious torment and the theme of unfairness. The author never rises above his dilemma of good/bad.

Langone, John. *Vital Signs: The Way We Die in America.* An informational account, stressing vital signs. Interviews include a 1974 interview with Elisabeth Kübler-Ross.

Lefco, Stanley. *Till Death Do Us Part.* A husband's beloved wife dies. 200 pages.

Miller, Mary Ann. *Longtime Bemidji Resident Dies.* An account of a daughter's feelings and experiences surrounding her eighty-year-old father's death. Journal style.

Oppenheimer, J. Robert. *An End of a Beginning: Being One Man's Search for the Foot of the Mountain.* Generally a novel about spiritual search and development with intergalactic themes, as well as ancient historical themes. 192 pages.

Rodman, Robert F., M.D. *Not Dying.* A psychiatrist and husband's confrontation with his thirty-seven-year-old wife's terminal illness, which was characterized by denial.

Sheehy, Patrick F., M.D. *Dying with Dignity.* Different aspects of special significance for cancer patients explained in understandable lay language to help provide the patients with a sense of control over their own body and greater understanding. 228 pages.

Small, Lynne. *Journal.* A lay person's experience of counseling in the field of thanatology. 66 pages.

Snow, Lois Wheeler. *When the Chinese Came.* A wife's experience during her husband's carcinoma of the pancreas. Special material concerning the husband's numerous influential Chinese friends who changed the attitudes of patient and family.

Van, Eeden. *Paul's Awakening.* A father's biographical account of his twenty-four-year-old son's life and death.

Wade, Grace. *How She Died.* A novel, unknown if fiction or non-fiction. 196 pages.

RESEARCH PAPERS

Ananthu, T. S. "Integrating the Social and Physical Sciences: Birth of a New Paradigm." A research paper linking mysticism, Elisabeth Kübler-Ross's work, and modern physics and psychologist Robert Ornstein's work. Printed by the Gandhi Peace Foundation, New Delhi, India. 32 pages.

Audette, John R. "Proximity to Death and Physician's Attitudinal Disposition Toward Patients and Their Families." A master's thesis in sociology. Academic.

Berman, Jeffrey. "The Death and Dying of Ivan Ilych." An essay comparing Tolstoy's great classic novel with Elisabeth Kübler-Ross's *On Death and Dying*.

Burton, Arthur. "The Mentoring Dynamic in the Therapeutic Transformation.'" A 30-page treatise.

Josephs, Roselee B. "Dealing with Death." A 38-page paper on death education, helping the terminally ill, and the importance of mourning.

Kinsbury, Katherine. *I Want to Die at Home—A Study of Alternative Models of Care for the Frail, Aged, the Handicapped, and the Dying*. A "how-to" booklet providing descriptions of hospices throughout Europe and Canada . . . as well as instructions on how to secure an adult diaper. Excellent resource material.

Rydberg, Wayne. "The Role of Religious Belief in the Suicidal Crisis." A dissertation submitted to the Chicago Theological Seminary for Bachelor of Divinity. A sensitive hypothesis derived from Frankl, Bultmann, and Bonhoeffer about (1) perspective—or point of view of life, (2) worth—man's uniqueness and singularity, and (3) depth—man's profoundness of being, whether a passion for being exists or not. This study found that if the worth and depth became diseased—but the perspective remained clear—suicide was not an option. If all three scattered, then suicide became an option. Incomplete in the author's opinion; much more research is needed.

BOOKS FOR YOUNG PEOPLE ON DEATH AND DYING
(PUBLISHED BY LIPPINCOTT)

Cleaver, Vera and Bill. *Grover*. (Grade level 4–6)
———. *Where the Lilies Bloom*. (Grade level 5–9)
Eyerly, Jeannette. *The Girl Inside*. (Grade level 5–9)
Forbes, Tom H. *Quincy's Harvest*. (Grade level 5–9)
Holland, Isabelle. *Of Love and Death and Other Journeys*. (Grade level 7–10)
Lund, Doris. *Eric*. (Grade level young adult)
Slote, Al. *Hang Tough, Paul Mather*. (Grade level 4–6)

CHILDREN'S STORIES FOR CHILDREN (MANUSCRIPTS)

Denham, Suzanne. Untitled 3-page narrative by her two- or three-year-old. How it feels when your dog and your Grampa die.

Grimmius, Marie E. *Potatoes*. A 24-page manuscript for children.

Harriet, Richie. *Leaf*. A 4-page children's story about the death of a leaf.

Hughes, Phyllis Rash. *Dying Is Different*. Illustrated children's book for ages three and up.

Jeffrey, Shirley H., and Jeffrey, David (illustrator, age seven). *Allen Anderson McFuddell*. A short story about preexistence and birth into this earth plane.

Palzere, Jane. *Grampa's House*. A short story about Jimmy and his Grampa's death.

PARENTS' FIRST-PERSON ACCOUNTS OF THE LOSS OF THEIR CHILD (MANUSCRIPTS)

Lund, Doris. *Eric*. A manuscript of a mother's account of the life and death of her college-age son.

Timmins, Noreen. *Our Gift*. A mother's account in diary form of the life and death of her seven-year-old son.

INSTRUCTIONAL MATERIAL ON CHILDREN AND DEATH (MANUSCRIPTS)

Albertson, Sandy. *A Book*. Part 1 is the personal account of this young wife's relationship with her dying husband. Part 2 relates her enriched philosophy, which resulted from her experiences with very practical suggested quasi-legal forms, and practical information to assist professionals and family. A chapter on children and death. 259 pages.

Tripp, Tony, and Mayhew, Kathy. *Loss and Its Impact: Getting Through Grief*. A "how-to" and "what-to-expect" information booklet of 68 pages, with a chapter on children and death.

INSTRUCTIONAL MATERIAL ON CHILD DEVELOPMENT
(MANUSCRIPTS)

Braga, Joseph and Laurie. *Growing with Children*. Authors are professors at the University of Illinois. A thorough anthology drawing from noted authorities in the field of human development (from birth to six years).

RESEARCH ON CHILDREN AND DEATH (MANUSCRIPTS)

Gaines, Ronford G. *Death, Denial, and Religious Commitment*. An excerpt from the manuscript on death denial and the mother-child relationship.

"Parental Adaptation to Leukemia in a Child." Title of Chapter III. Excerpt from a presently *unknown* research paper. Scholarly research and statistics on the specific title.